The Book of Elf Names:

5,600 ELVEN NAMES TO USE FOR MAGIC, GAME PLAYING, INSPIRATION, NAMING ONE'S SELF AND ONE'S CHILD, AND AS WORDS IN THE ELVEN LANGUAGE OF THE SILVER ELVES

BY THE SILVER ELVES

DEDICATION

This book is dedicated to all the elves whose names are contained within and to Silver Flame who insisted we publish them.

"ELVEN NAMES ARE A MAGIC THAT GROWS

GREATER WITH USE,

THE MORE THEY ARE SPOKEN THE MORE FAERIE'S LOOSED,

TO SPREAD THROUGH THE WORLD AND THUS IT TO SWAY,

THE HEARTS THAT DO HUNGER FOR THE BRIGHT

ELVEN WAY."

—THE SILVER ELVES

TABLE OF CONTENTS

INTRODUCTION

In the Beginning

Zardoa Silverstar has been giving out names for ages. He began giving elf names before he entirely realized he was an elf. The first ones he gave were in English. Thus he gave such names as Debbie Moondust, Morning Moonstar, Silver Flame and names of this kind. In time, he began to give names with a more direct elven tone such as Kartakor and Kendor. In the 1990's when he began creating our elven language Arvyndase or Silverspeech (see our book *Arvyndase (silverspeech): a short course in the magical language of the Silver Elves*) and with the advent of the internet, he began giving out Arvyndase names, which are the 5,600 names you will find within this volume.

Requests for Elf Names

We created a place on our website (http://silverelves.angelfire.com) where elves can request a magical name and we give instructions there on the information that we need to do so. Over years, besides elves, we also have received a few requests from dwarves (see if you can figure out which are the dwarven names) and otherkin of numerous sorts. We also have gotten requests from writers wanting elf names for stories they were creating and from gamers desiring names for their characters. We have obliged as best we have been able, although we encouraged the writers to create their own names. We elves always encourage creativity.

Picking an Elf Name

Every elf name is unique. It may be a variation of another name, as in English there is Sue, Susan, Suzette, Suzanne, etc. and this is the case in Arvyndase, as well. However, unlike most other languages we don't repeat names. We don't have hundreds of Johns, Michaels and Tiffanys and Deborahs.

Alas, while we have given out over 5,600 names (we still receive requests), the vast majority of those who receive names never use them. It is not wrong to use a name from this book that is not being used, but it is considered highly rude by the elven to use a name that someone else is using and no elf would want to do that. And perhaps even worse, it is considered uncreative to do so. So before using any name in this book please do an Internet search to see if it is currently in use.

Far better, from an elven point of view is to request a name from these elves at the site listed above, or through Facebook. Or perhaps even better still, to use this book as an example of the names that are out there and to create a variation of a name that you like. For instance, we currently have Våvardor and Våvardorn but there is not, as yet, a Våvarthor, or Våvardorys, or Våvardoryn, etc. Remember, however, we are still giving out names, so even when creating a variation, you may wish to do an Internet search. No elf would want a name that another is using; although using a name that has been cast into someone's magical mystical trash-bin is ever fair game.

Of course, one might ask, if creativity is so important to the elves, why give elf names at all? And that fact is that most of the names we give are gifted to those who have just discovered their elven nature and need a bit of encouragement. Giving them an elf name is giving them a bit of elf magic and power. When we gift each name, we also indicate how the name may be pronounced but it is up to each elf to put emphasis where it feels best to them or alter the name to suit one's own s'elf. How it sounds, how it vibrates in one's ear, soul and imagination is most important.

Names of Power

As we stated, each elf name is unique. It is a magical tool, like a wand or chalice or ring of power that increases one's magical potency. There are traditions that say that if someone knows your true name they will gain power over you, and we have kin who were concerned about us publishing their name in this book. So let us speak to this concern.

First, as we pointed out in *The Book of Elven Magick, 1 and 2,* your true name is the vibrational sound your being makes. To know a person's true name is to understand them psychologically, and yes, if you know a person's true name, that is if you truly understand them, you will have great power to influence them. But Arvyndase names, as we indicate when we gift them, are not true names but are a sort of magical nickname that helps one gain entry into Faerie.

Second, in the tradition of true names and the idea that one gains power over another by knowing their true name, such names are often kept secret and only revealed to other members of one's inner circle. In fact, we have such names given to us by the Elf Queen's Daughters, which we will not reveal here. Elf names on the other hand gain power by being used. To receive an elf name and then to keep it secret or never use it is just throwing away power. The more the name is used, the more it is known, the greater its power becomes.

Arvyndase Words

Every Arvyndase elf name has a meaning, which is also unique, although some convey similar ideas. These names can also be used as words when writing or speaking Arvyndase. These names, however, usually represent phrases. Thus the name Esarathel means "serves the cause" and could be used to say, "He esarathel," that is He serves the cause, or "They esarathel," thus "They serve the cause."

Or take the name Pèladåryn that means, "I was more than I was lead to believe." One could simply say, "*Pèladåryn," the asterisk indicating that is being used as a word rather than a name, or one could say, "I, Stephen, pèladåryn," meaning, "I, Stephen, was more than I was lead to believe." Or "Jack pèladåryn," meaning "Jack was more than he was lead to believe." Excuse us for using English names here, but to do otherwise might prove confusing at this point. Note that except in the very start of the sentence a elven name is Capitalized and when used as a word will be uncapitalized.

Similarly the name Tåleåre means "wise beyond their years," and could be used to say, "Tiffany tåleåre", or, "Tiffany is wise beyond her years." Or if you wrote it *Tåleåre Tiffany, you'd be saying, "Wise beyond her years is Tiffany."

In another example, the name Våvardorn means "strange connection", therefore one could use it to say, "I have a våvardorn to Faerie," for instance. On the other hand if we said, "Pėladåryn has a våvardorn to Elfin," we'd be saying, since there is no asterisk before Pėladåryn, that the individual named Pėladåryn has a strange connection to Elfin." We trust you will find power and inspiration in these elven names.

HOW DO WE FIND AN ELF'S TRUE NAME?

H OW DO WE FIND AN ELF'S TRUE NAME?
WHO'S BEEN SO LOST

AND CANNOT REGAIN

THE MEMORIES SHE FEELS

DEEP IN HER SOUL

THE HUNGER HE HAS

TO ONCE MORE BE WHOLE

THINKING WON'T DO IT

NEITHER WILL FORCE

RETURN ALL THE MAGIC

FROM HER SOUL DIVORCED

HOW DO WE HELP HIM?

WHAT VISION HAVE WE?

BUT THAT OF THE ELVEN

TO BE EVER FREE

AND FREELY TO GIVE

AND IN GIVING RECEIVE

ALL THAT WE HAVE

SO NO LIES CAN DECEIVE

AND SINCE WE SEE TRULY

THE TRUTH WE DO KNOW

AND FROM THIS CLEAR SIGHT

OUR MAGIC DOES GROW

SO FAR IN THE FUTURE

AND DEEP IN THE PAST

WE VIEW ALL THAT IS

THAT NEVER DID LAST

AND FIND THERE THE NAME

THEIR SOUL YEARNS TO HEAR

AND IN HEARING IT RINGS

LIKE A BELL SOUNDED CLEAR.

A GROUP OF FISH IS CALLED A SHOAL. A GROUP OF CROWS IS CALLED A MURDER. WHAT DO YOU CALL A GROUP OF ELVES? WHY A PARTY! THE NEXT TIME YOU'RE IN A RESTAURANT AND HEAR SOMETHING LIKE "LOVE: PARTY OF SEVEN", LOOK FOR THE POINTED EARS.

WE ELVES SAY IT IS NOT THE NAME THAT
MAKES THE ELF BUT THE ELF THAT MAKES
THE NAME.
—OLD ELVEN SAYING

AN ELVEN NAME IS A GIFT OF MAGICAL
POWER. THOSE WHO ARE NOT READY FOR
THAT POWER, CAST AWAY THEIR NAME AND
SELDOM, IF EVER, USE IT AND OFTEN SOON
FORGET IT.
—ELVEN WISDOM

ELF NAMES

A.

Elven Name and Meaning	Pronunciation			

Elven Name and Meaning				
Aånåfar brings changes	a - ah	-	nah	-	fair
åbarådyn open to all magic	ah - bare	-	rah	–	den
åbareyn senses the difference	ah - bare	-	re	–	in
åbėloryn searches the ancient scrolls	ah - bell	-	lore	–	ren
åborea have battled many and won	ah - boar	-	re	-	ah
åboreäl of the trees	ah - boar	-	re	-	al
åboreyl dryad wisdom	ah - boar	-	re	-	L
åbreån would like to know for sure	ah -		bree	-	ahn
abreåna magic with horses	a -	bree	-	ah	-	nah
åbrenålyn senses the pain	ah -	bree	-	nah	-	lynn
abynar obsessed with the forest	a -		ben	-	nair
åbynoryl always happy	ah -	ben	-	nor	-	rill

ådålynya	ah	-	dah	-	lynn	–	yah

awakens love

ådånåle	ah	-	dah	-	nah	-	lee

thanks and blessings

ådånda	ah	-	dahn	-	dah

strive for harmony

adändyryn	a	-	dan	-	der	–	ren

possibility hidden in the formless

adansa	a	-	dane	-	sah

beneath the bright blue sky

ådaråthyn	ah	-	dare	-	rah	–	thin

follows the trail

adarorgyn	a	-	dare	-	roar	–	gen

stirring the fire

ådaru	ah	-	dare	-	rue

my love is free for those who will it to be in their lives

adåvynėl	a	-	dah	-	vin	-	nell

open to whatever spirits might be around

adelyn	a	-	dee	-	lynn

sensual mystery

åderådyn	ah	-	deer	-	rah	–	den

listening to the sounds of the forest

ådere	ah	-	deer	-	ree

en-souled

åderna	ah	-	deer	-	nah

always looking for good in the world

ådoråde	ah	-	door	-	rah	–	dee

relearning what was once known

ådorea	ah	-	door	-	re	-	ah

great cycle of the universe

ådorena	ah	-	door	-	re	-	nah

little dark

ådoreyl	ah	-	door	-	re	-	L

merging the elements

14   The Silver Elves

adoryn beauty maker	ah	-	door	-	ren	
ådoryn invisible guides	ah	-	door	-	ren	
ådorys yearns for adventure	ah	-	door	-	riss	
ådrågoryn weaves the good	ah	-drah	-	gore	–	ren
ådreåna now I know who I am	ah	-	dree	-	ah	- nah
ådureyn all the best things in life	ah	-	due	-	re	- in
åduryn mysterious and calming aura	ah	-	due	-	ren	
adynala true sight	a	-	den	-	nah	- lah
ådynåle true spirit	ah	-	den	-	ah	- lee
åelola on the beach	ah	-	e	-	low	- lah
afiala loved by the magic	a	-	fie	-	a	- lah
äfmoryn power of the small	aff	-	more	-	ren	
afryndor hovers near	a	-	frin	-	door	
åfyndreyl faerie connection	ah	-	fin	-	dree	- L
åhåndryn even as a child	ah	-	hahn	-	drin	
åhåvynår elfin light	ah	-	hah	-	vyn	-nar
ahyrn what do you mean	a	-			hern	

The Book of Elf Names   15

aile	a	-	eye	-	lee
forever soul friends					
ajalys	a	-	jay	-	liss
sparkles in the dark					
åjånåda	ah	- jah -	nah	-	dah
gathers friends					
åjånådur	ah	- jah -	nah	dur (as in endure)	
white mane					
åjånådurys	ah	- jah -	nah	- dur	– riss
the sight returns					
åjånda	ah	-	jahn	-	dah
nature's perfume					
åjåndåle	ah	-	jahn	-dah	- lee
meant to be something more					
ajanu	a	-	jay	-	new
seeks to help the world					
åjeryn	ah	-	jeer	-	ren
wandered into Elfin					
åjile	ah	-	jie	-	lee
I belong					
åjuryn	ah	-	jour	-	ren
staring at the leaves and branches					
ajuryndur	a	-	jour	- ren	- dur
walks with the deer					
åkanar	ah	-	kay	-	nair
rising fire					
åkyndra	ah	-	ken	-	drah
things always listen					
ålådar	ah	-	lah	-	dare
one who shows the way					
alådare	a	-	lah	- dare	- ree
courtly grace					
alaleyl	a	-	lay	- lee	- L
dreams coming true					

The Silver Elves

älålyndor tree's shadow	al	-	lah	-	lynn	-	door
ålålyndys chronicles our history	ah	-lah	-	lynn	-	diss
ålåndor hauntingly sweet fragrance	ah	-	lahn	-	door
ålåndrea loves life even when it's hard	ah	-	lahn	-	dree	-	ah
alånzåle conscious of other's feelings	a	-	lah	-	zah	-	lee
ålåtaron home in the wild	ah	-	lah	-	tear	rone
älåvåndryn butterfy faerie	al	-	lah	-	vahn	-	drinn
ålåvarfyn songs from the wood	ah	-	lah	-	vair	-	fin
aldadelån dawn of the trees	ale	-	day	-	dee	-	lahn
aldåneda helped me get through it all	ale	-	dah	-	knee	-	dah
aldanys tree like	ale	-	dane	-	niss
aldareyn facing the sun	ale	-	dare	-	ree	-	in
aldaryn at the foot of the tree	ale	-	dare	-	ren
aldåvyn among the roots	ale	-	dah	-	vin
åleåla Elfin true	ah	-	lee	-	ah	-	lah
åleåle no mere mortal	ah	-	lee	-	ah	-lee
åleånor dreaming of the light	ah	-	lee	-	ah	-	nor

The Book of Elf Names   17

alfare of long past	ale	-	fair	-	ree
alfynda one who is in a good place	ale	-	fin		dah
ålidyn all the strays seem to know where I am	ah	-	lie	-	den
almåsa on the air	ale	mah		-	sah
alolyn great spirits from the past	ale	-	low	-	lynn
ålolyndyn like a whirlwind	ah	-	low	-	lynn	-	den
ålonådål a little forest	ah	-	low	-	nah	-	dahl
ålorfyn related to the water faeries	ah	-	low	-	nah	-	dahl
äloronvår wolf kin of the dawn	al	-	lore	-	roan	-	var
aloryndor through the dark reaching	ale	-	lore	-	ren	-	door
alvadar glides on leaves	ale	-	vay	-	dare
ålynde guardian of her people	ah	-	lynn	-	dee
åmareyn gift of glamour	ah	-	mare	-	ree	-	in
åmerafyn delight of the sea	ah	-	mere	-	ray	-	fin
åmerys rushing with the stream	ah	-	mere	-	riss
åmidor wisdom of dragons	ah	-	my	-	door
åmirys the next step	ah	-	my	-	riss

The Silver Elves

åmoryn	ah	-	more	-	ren			
steady rain fall								
ånådriėl	ah	-	nah	-	dry	-	L	
wanders afar								
ånåfålyn	ah	-	nah	-	fah	-	lynn	
hearth and home								
ånåfyn	ah	-	nah	-	fin			
sweet rainbow								
anålanu	ah	-	nah	-	lay	-	new	
truth seerer								
ånåndrea	ah	-	nahn	-	dree	-	ah	
chance encounter								
ånåndyryn	ah	-	nahn	-	der	-	ren	
open and lyrical								
ånaråke	ah	-	nair	-	rah	-	key	
to make things right								
ånaråle	ah	-	nair	-	rah	-	lee	
comely delights								
ånårasta	ah	-	nah	-	ray	-	stah	
joy bringer								
anardyn	a	-	nair	-	den			
as old as the trees								
anarfana	a	-	nair	-	fay	-	nah	
tree by the sea								
anarfyn	air	-	nair	-	fin			
beneath the glowing lights								
ånarkyn	ah	-	nair	-	ken			
among the dwarves								
anata	a	-	nay	-	tah			
please remind me								
åndåle	ahn	-	dah	-	lee			
loved by the trees								
andaniyl	ane	(as	in	sane)	-	day	nigh	-	L
the dreamer awakens								

The Book of Elf Names   19

ändaråfyn	ann	-	dare	-	rah	-	fin
deep affinity							

andarfia	ane	-	dare	-	fie	-	ah
knows full well							

ändårynda	ann	-	dah	-	ren	-	dah
vacations with gnomes							

åndraca	ahn	-	dray	-	cah
trying to reach the far mountains					

åndradyn	ahn	-	dray	-	den
inherited from previous lives					

åndrågor	ahn	-	drah	-	gore
knows a secret					

åndrågoryn	ahn	-	drah	-	gore	-	in
memories of elsewhere							

åndrasa	ahn	-	dray	-	sah
immediately began considering that					

åndrathyn	ahn	-	dray	-	thin
lives for art					

andreoryn	ane (as in sane)	-	dree	-	or	ren
finds the way						

åndreorys	ahn	-	dree	-	or	-	riss
seeks deeper meaning							

åndrogore	ahn - dro (rhymes with grow) - gore - ree
for the people	

andureyl	ane	-	dur	-	ree	-	L
one of the merry band							

anewae	a	-	knee	-	way
lady of the golden wood					

ångreoryn	ahn	-	gree	-	or	-	in
ever faithful							

ånia	ahn	-	nigh	-	ah
star song					

åniale	ahn	-	nigh	-	a	-	L
because I like							

20   The Silver Elves

aniaryn born an animal	a	-	nigh	-	air	-	ren
ånieyl could you help me?	ahn	-	nigh	-	e	-	L
anila wild bird	a	-	nigh	-	lah
aniyådor asks the good faeries for guidance	a	-	nigh	-	yah	-	door
aniyn loves to draw fantasy figures	a	-	nigh	-	in
åniyo fell in love	ahn	-	nigh	-	yo
ånjånådoryl watches from perch	ahn rill	-	jahn	-	nah	-	door	-
anorådre feels the pull	a	-	nor	-	rah	-	dree
anordårys nascent awareness	a	-	nor	-	dah	-	riss
ånordre always been	ahn	-	nor	-	dree
ånthorea leaves of gold	ahn	-	thor	-	ree	-	ah
aodnåna eye on everything	a	-	ode	-	nah	-	nah
aolyndåfa shield of healing	a	-	o	-	lynn	-	dah	-	fah
apånåtål reflects the s'elf	a	-	pahn	-	nah	-	tall
arådaryn dances on water	a	-	rah	-	dare	-	ren
arådnathyn flys across the field on horseback	a	-	rad	-	nay	-	thin
arådreym born of star dust	a	-	rah	-	dree	-	M

arådyn	a	-	rah	-	den			
treads the red road								
arafari	a	-	ray	-	fair	-	rye	
eye to friendship								
aråfyn	a	-	rah	-	fin			
moonlight glow upon the skin								
aråfyndra	a	-	rah	-	fin	-	drah	
soothing light of the moon								
aralyn	a	-	ray	-	lynn			
peeks through the leaves								
aralyndėl	a	-	ray	-	lynn	-	dell	
true seer								
arålyndyn	a	-	rah	-	lynn	-	den	
faery guide								
arana	a	-	ray	-	nah			
shifting light								
arånälda	a	-	rahn	-	nal	-	dah	
eyes of the forest								
åråndae	ah	-	rahn	-	day			
descended from a higher realm								
årånduryn	ah	-	rahn	-	dur	-	ren	
can't figure them out								
aråtår	a	-	rah	-	tar			
keen eye								
åråtarea	ah	-	rah	-	tay	-	ree	- a
takes after the ancestors								
aråtruryn	a	-	rah	-	true	-	ren	
healing vortex								
aråtruvyn	a	-	rah	-	true	-	vin	
clear sighted								
aråvynda	a	-	rah	-	vin	-	dah	
watches the earth								
aråvyndra	a	-	rah	-	vin	-	drah	
eye for trouble								

aråvyndre heart of a child	a	-	rah	-	vin	-	dree
aråvyndryl glowing wings	a	-	rah	-	vin	-	drill
årdåndyn shimmer of moonlight	ah	-	dahn	-	den		
årdåneyl opens the way	ah	-	dahn	-	knee	-	L
ardruna since as far back as memory serves	air	-	drew	-	nah		
ardyn knows without knowing why	air		-		den		
åreanån one who sees the direct course	ah	-	ree	-	ah	-	non
årear strong family ties	ah		-		re	-	air
arelomeyl it would all seem so real	air	-	ree	-	low	-	me	-	L
areolyn eye of a hawk	air	-	ree	-	oh	-	lynn
åreorlyn light shining through water	ah	-	ree	-	or	-	lynn
areoryl sees the magic	air	-	re	-	or	-	rill
areoryn peering ahead	air	-	ree	-	or	-	ren
arevådre at peace with the world	air	-	ree	-	vah	-	dree
arevyndre flower of the sea	air	-	ree	-	vin	-	dree
areylyn moves with ease	air	-	ree	-	L	-	lynn
argonath eye of steel	air		-		go	-	nayth

The Book of Elf Names   23

åriådel more than a tad	ah	-	-	rye	-	ah	-	dell
ariåfyn living on the edge of the arroyos	air	-	rye	-	ah	-	fin
aricordryn dragon green	air	-	rye	-	core	-	drinn
aridea dances among the flowers	air	-	rye	-	dee	-	ah
aridyn that which I really am	air	-	rye	-	den
arlånra inspires peace	air	-	lahn	-	rah
årlea eye for the beautiful	R	-	lee	-	ah
arodea considered to be ambrosia	air	-	row	-	dee	-	ah
arofar another who cares	air	-	row	-	fair
arondel one who provides	air	-	roan	-	dell
årondreyl secret meaning of all things	ah	-	roan	-	dree	-	L
arturyn feathered pen	air	-	too	-	ren
åruna it was scary how correct it was	ah	-	rue	-	nah
arushyn only a few know of my powers	air	-	rue	-	shin
arvyndea silver glow	air	-	vin	-	dee	-	ah
arvynfela born of the sacred flame	air	-	vin	-	fee	-	lah
arwynbar large among the littles	air	-	win	-	bare

arydeyn first in battle	air	-	rid	-	dee	-	in
arynal way of life	air	-	ren		-		nail
arynda explorer of dreams	air	-	ren		-		dah
aryndåla cat's eye	air	-	ren	-	dah	-	lah
aryndara glides softly	air	-	ren	-	dare	-	rah
aryndarys senses the spirits	air	-	ren	-	dare	-	riss
aryndèl elegant and intelligent	air	-	ren	-	dree	-	L
åryndreyl sense of magic	ah	-	ren	-	dree	-	L
åryndryl the earth has always spoken to me	ah	-		ren	-		drill
aryndyn have always known of other things	air	-		ren	-		den
arynsa helped me realize how to use my power	air	-		ren	-		sah
arynshondra shapes situations with her mind	air	-	ren	-	shown	-	drah

arynthe   air - ren - thee   (rhymes with fee)
began young

arysyn dares to go deeper	air	-		riss	-		sin
arythonièl summons the air	air	-	rith	-	thon	-	nye	-	L
åsålayth ponders the possibilities	ah	-		sah	-		lay	-ith
asarynda with the dawn	a	-	sair	-	ren	-	dah

The Book of Elf Names   25

åshana star singer	ah	-	shay	-	nah			
åshåndreyl for the longest time I could not figure out why	ah	-	shahn	-	dree	-	L	
åshårånda shadow leaf	ah	-	shah	-	ron	-	dah	
åstriel born of stars	ah	-	stry	-	eel			
atearasa named by the glows	a -	te -	air -	ray -	sah			
åthånådel slipping into dreams	ah	-	thahn	-	nah	-	dell	
åthårondel in the lead	ah	-	thah	-	roan	-	dell	
åvådaru from the far peaks	ah	-	vah	-	dare	-	rue	
åvådryn appeared in my mind	ah	-	vah	-	drinn			
åvådylan destined for great things	ah	-	vah	-	dill	-	lane	
åvålådreyn alone but never lonely	ah	-	vah	-	lah	-	dree	- in
åvålae ancient among us	ah	-	vah	-	lay			
åvålelyn part of the past	ah	-	vah	-	lee	-	lynn	
åvålynsa at the bottom of the garden	ah	-	vah	-	lynn	-	sah	
åvånån talks to gnomes	ah	-	vah	-	non			
åvåndare searching for a helping hand	ah	-	vahn	-	dare	-	ree	
åvåndåryn at peace with the Eternal	ah	-	vahn	-	dah	-	ren	

åvåndåver	ah	-	vahn	-	dah	-	veer
concerned for the future							
åvåndrea	ah	-	vahn	-	dree	-	ah
mysteries of the stars							
åvåndreån	ah	-	vahn	-	dree	-	ahn
star riddles							
åvåndrèl	ah	-	vahn	-	drill		l
ooks at life anew							
åvåndreyl	ah	-	vahn	-	dree	-	L
sings often for what we once were							
åvåndreyn	ah	-	vahn	-	dree	-	in
close to the spirit							
avåndryl	a	-	vahn	-	drill		
has the right spirit							
avanor	a	-	vay	-	nor		
born of a dream							
åvånore	ah	-	vahn	-	nor	-	ree
senses the reality							
åvåråndår	ah	-	var	-	ron	-	dar
leaf in the breeze							
avårdyna	a	-	vahr	-	den	-	nah
seeking the sacred							
åvåreånda	ah	-	vah	-	ree	-	ahn	-	dah
cares for the injured							
åvåredareyn	ah	-	vah	-	ree	-	dare	-	ree -
not like everyone else	in						

åvareyn	ah	-	vair	-	ree	-	in
in his eyes the look of the other world							

åvåronda	ah	-	vah	-	roan	-	dah
settles within							
åvåronder	ah	-	vah	-	roan	-	deer
justly worthy							
åvåronsar	ah	-	vah	-	roan	-	sair
observes from the shadows							

avarshadyn writes in ancient script	a	-	vair	-	shay	-	den
åvarthyn gathers elves	ah	-	vair	-	thin		
åvaru fell in love with a beautiful stranger	ah	-	vair	-	rue		
avårůdal childlike innocence	a	-	vah	-	rude	-	dale
åvåryncore willow wood	ah	-	vah	-	ren	-	core	-	ree
avarynko senses life all about	a	-	vair	-	ren	-	co
åvaryntel ache for the loss of kindness and love	ah	-	vair	-	ren	-	teal
åvarynzål follows his nose	ah	-	vair	-	ren	-	zall
åvearys gets it done	ah	-	vee	-	air	-	riss
avimeryn pixie cat	a	-	vie	-	mere	-	ren
åvondarsa approaching the shimmer	ah	-	vone	-	dare	-	sah
åvondere healing effect	ah	-	vone	-	deer	-	ree
avondyryn unusual, unique and beautiful	a	-	vone	-	der	-	ren
åvoråzån follows the birds home	ah	-	vour	-	rah	-	zahn
åvoreyn every moment on earth is precious	ah	-	vour	-	ree	-	in
avoronder tends to the fire	a	-	vour	-	roan	-	deer
avoryn enlightened by mythic beings	a	-	vour	-	ren

28   The Silver Elves

åvoryndyn	ah	-	vour	-	ren	-	den
realized who I am							
avyladeyn	a	-	vill	-	lay	-	dee	-	in
honored among us							
åvylådon	ah	-	vill	-	lah	-	doan
unusual and unique							
åvyladys	ah	-	vill	-	lay	-	diss
started behaving differently							
avyleyn	a	-	vill	-	lee	-	in
sees beyond the ordinary							
åvyndålyn	ah	-	vin	-	dah	-	lynn
touching lives							
åvyndår	ah	-	vin	-	dar
escapes the world							
åvyndare	ah	-	vin	-	dare	-	ree
deep rumbling echoes							
åvyndarys	ah	-	vin	-	dare	-	riss
voice of the garden							
åvyndėl	ah	-	vin	-	dell
shines in the shadows							
åvyndor	ah	-	vin	-	door
tree sparkle							
åvyndråla	ah	-	vin	-	drah	-	lah
strives to know more							
åvyndrås	ah	-	vin	-	drahss
touched by the fae							
åvyndre	ah	-	vin	-	dree
restraining power							
åvyndrea	ah	-	vin	-	dree	-	ah
restrained power							
avyndrean	a	-	vin	-	dree	-	ane
affects subtle changes							
åvyndyre	ah	-	vin	-	der	-	ree
everything will sort itself out in its own time							

ayndåvea yearning of the spirit	a	-	in	-	dah	-	vee	-	ah
åzåle stone wyzard	ah	-	zah	-	lee
åzålea shifting into faerie	ah	-	zah	-	lee	-	ah
azånådål surrounded by magic	a	-	zahn	-	nah	-	dahl
azåndare five petaled yellow flower	a	-	zahn	-	dare	-	ree
åzåndårėl old beyond years	ah	-	zahn	-	dah	-	rell
åzåndore marvels at Elfin	ah	-	zahn	-	door	-	ree
åzåndoryn beacon of light and love	ah	-	zahn	-	door	-	ren
åzåndurėl dream like reality	ah	-	zahn	-	dur	-	rell
azareyn sounds of the earth	a	-	zair	-	ree	-	in
åzaru never grows up	ah	-	zair	-	rue
azeryn friend of the wind	a	-	zeer	-	ren
åzora yearns to know	ah	-	zoar	-	rah
åzzoryn power of touch	oz	-zoar	-	ren

ℬ

Elven Name and Meaning

Pronunciation

Elven Name and Meaning						
baåthyn by the lake	bay	-	ah	-	thin	
bådåner for anyone who believes	bah	-	dahn	-	near	
bådeåle my senses grow ever keener	bah	-	dee	-	ah	- lee
båhålynda loved by elves	bah	-	hah	-	lynn	- dah
bäladea creating magic for people around me	baa	-	lay	-	dee	- ah
bälea always intrigues me	baa	-	lee	-	ah	
båledåntha blessed by the forest	bah	-	lee	-	dahn	- than
bålela seeks peace	bah	-	lee	-	lah	
bålerynfador there when needed	bah	-	lee	- ren	- fay	- door
balodryn wide of girth (sexually)	bay	-	low	-	drinn	
bäloryn someone watching over me	baa	-	lore	-	ren	
bålyndår offers the sacred branch	bah	-	lynn	-	dar	
bälyndaryn bears the sacred branch	baa	-	lynn	- dare	- ren	
båmeryn inner voice telling me to accept who I am	bah	-	mere	-	ren	

båmerys	bah	-	mere	-	riss
big romantic					
baorändel	bay	- or - ran	-	deal
runs with the clan					
barådånthor	bare	- rah - dahn	-	thor
strong in the magic					
baradasa	bare	- ray - day	-	sah
create shade					
baråkynor	bare	- rah - ken		-nor
healed by the trees					
båraleon	bar	- ray - lee	-	ohn
elf logic					
baråndea	bare	- ron - dee	-	ah
silver wind					
barasar	bare	- ray	-	sair
leaps with glee					
barasyndra	bare	- ray - sin	-	drah
one of us					
baråthel	bare	- rah	-	theel
until I found my love					
baråthelyn	bare	- rah - thee	-	lynn
angelic muse					
baråzåyl	bare	- rah zah	-	L
sprouting wings					
baresol	bare	- ree	-	soul
born of earth					
baryncharys	bare	- ren - char	-	riss
unseen magic					
barynda	bare	- ren	-	dah
sings of magic					
baryndår	bare	- ren	-	dar
dragon's song					
baryndara	bare	- ren - dare	-	rah
intense deep wisdom					

The Silver Elves

baryndor independently minded	bare	-	ren	-	door
baryndyn looks from beneath the water	bare	-	ren	-	den
baryngyl dragon unseen	bare	-	ren	-	gill
barynzål memory from the soul	bare	-	ren	-	zahl
barynzor noble dragon	bare	-	ren	-	zoar
båshålen prances about	bah	-	shah	-	lean
båverva light and airy	bah	-	veer	-	vah
baynala rising through the mist	bay	-	in	-	nay	-	lah

bearåfyn because it feels right	bee	-	air	-	rah	-	fin
bearåle accepting fate with peace and tranquility	bee	-	air	-	rah	-	lee
bearålyn optimist of the upmost degree	bee	-	air	-	rah	-	lynn
bearathyl becomes aware	bee	-	air	-	ray	-	thill
beareyn waves from the hill	bee	-	air	-	ree	-	in
bearsyn hid among the trees	bee	-	air	-	sin

bélådyryn black wings	bell	-	lah	-	der	-	ren
béländåfyn feels a new power within	bell	-	lan	-	dah	-	fin
bélåndea works with the elementals	bell	-	lahn	-	dee	-	ah

The Book of Elf Names   33

bėliålyn related to wyzards	bell	-	lie	-	ah	-	lynn	
bėlnasareyn hear them speaking in one voice	bell	-	nay	-	sair	-	ree	- in
bėlynåda always believed they were there	bell	-	lynn	-	nah	-	dah	
bėlyndor quest goes ever onward	bell	-	lynn	-	door			
bėlyndraa place I could belong	bell	-	lynn	-	dray	-	ah	
belyndrys attaining control	bee	-	lynn	driss				
bėlynre very good shot	bell	-	lynn	-	ree			
belynsarys it all started with dreams	bee	-	lynn	-	sair	-	riss	
bemåryn schooled in magic	bee	-	mar	-	ren			
benarsa fair of face	bee	-	nair	-	sah			
benaryn magic happens	bee	-	nair	-	ren			
benerys hidden self	bee	-	near	-	riss			
beryndår of this I am sure	bee	-	ren	-	dar			
berynvara slender white tree	bee	-	ren	-	vair	-	rah	
beynarys unheard music	bee	-	in	-	nair	-	riss	
beyntara searches the earth	bee	-	in	-	tay	-	rah	
biåndreys only gets stronger	bi	-	ahn	-	dree	-	S	

biasa bubbling stream	bi	-	a	-	sah		
bidåndåthor a violent strom swept in	bi	-	dahn	-	dah	-	thor
biderea favorite time of year	bi	-	deer	-	ree	-	ah
bilåndor affectionate gestures of everyday life	bi	-	lahn	-	door		
bilelyn will devote my entire life	bi	-	lee	-	lynn		
biloralyn late one night	bi	-	lore	-	a	-	lynn
biyndalyn my only goal is to be happy	bi	-	in	-	day	-	lynn
biynduryn feel I can make it in an unknown sea	bi	-	in	-	dur	-	ren
bobynba second breakfast	bo	-	bin	-	bah		
boladryn mighty arm	bo	-	lay	-	drinn		
bolyndrae remembers beyond the veil	bo	-	lynn	-	dray		
bonarfa happy willow	bo	-	nair	-	fah		
bonarlo hears chants on the wind	bo	-	nair	-	low		
bonsari inches closer	bone	-	sair	-	rye		
borådea hearing what others did not	bo	-	rah	-	dee	-	ah
boradryn touching spirits	bo	-	ray	-	drinn		
boradyn kernel of truth	bo	-	ray	-	den		

boradyna word seed	bo	-	ray	-	den	-	nah
borålidas nurtured by the trees	bo	-	rah	-	lie	-	dace
boraliyn comes to play	bo	-	ray	-	lie	-	in
boranėl wed of light and dark	bo	-		ray	-		nell
borantha faery crossed	bo	-		rahn	-		than
boratha connected at first sight	bo	-		ray	-		thah
boreåfyn sun dabble	bo	-	ree	-	ah	-	fin
boreala feel so at home	bo	-	ree	-	a	-	lah
boreåndre love of all things fair	bo	-	ree	-	ahn	-	dree
boreyl language of the earth	bo	-		ree	-		L
boreyna sacred connection	bo	-	ree	-	in	-	nah
boriånėl always returns	bo	-	rye	-	ah	-	nell
borledryn always there to help	boar	-		lee	-		drinn
bormadyn reflects others moods	boar	-		may	-		den
bornandaru prepared to take the next step	boar	-	nane	-	day	-	rue
bornazar dreams the future	boar	-		nay	-		zair
bornidyn everyone around me is affected	boar	-		nigh	-		den

borodyn misty voice	boar	-	row	-	den		
borsålys doesn't hold back	boar	-	sah	-	liss		
borudyn I know it with every ounce of my being	boar	-	rue	-	den		
borunyn importance of logic	boar	-	rue	-	nin		
borynål knows their way in the water	boar	-	ren	-	nall		
borynår flips over	boar	-	ren	-	nar		
boryndamer yearns for adventure	boar	-	ren	-	day	-	mere
boryndåzar lends a helping hand	boar	-	ren	-	dah	-	zair
boryndiyl star upon their neck	boar	-	ren	-	dye	-	L
boryndryl love of travel	boar	-	ren	-	drill		
boryndyl nameless craving	boar	-	ren	-	dill		
borynėl knows their way around	boar	-	ren	-	nell		
borynvar dragon laughing	boar	-	ren	-	vair		
borynzor wandering wyzard	boar	-	ren	-	zoar		
borynzyna adopted by elves	boar	-	ren	-	zen	-	nah
bosareyn much more than is apparent on the surface	bo	-	sair	-	ree	-	in
braålyn stars are my guide	bray	-	ah	-	lynn		

The Book of Elf Names

brador turns hate to love	bray		-		door
bråmådèl just a feeling	bra	-	mah	-	dell
branadyn runs along the ridge	bray	-	nay	-	den
branåthfyn catches a glimpse	bray	-	nahth	-	fin
brånvornyn woods safe	brahn	-	vour	-	nin
breåbryn gives pretty things	bree	-	ah	-	brinn
breådalyn special magics	bree	-	ah	-	day	-	lynn
breåfyryn dangerously good aim	bree	-	ah	-	fer	-	ren
brealborn they speak to me in dreams	bree	-	ale	-	born
brealfyn understands the way	bree	-	ale	-	fin
brealyn flower care faerie	bree	-	a	-	lynn
breålyna voice of silver	bree	-	ah	-	lynn	-	nah
brealynsa among the flower faeries	bree	-	ale	-	lynn	-	sah
breåndåle taught by the trees	bree	-	ahn	-	dah	-	lee
breånder rides the wild water	bree	-	ahn	-	deer
breåndre wholistic approach	bree	-	ahn	-	dree
breåndreyn sense of wholeness	bree	-	ahn	-	dree	-	in

breåndryn whispering wind	brcc	-	ahn	-	drinn
breåndrys feeling deep down	bree	-	ahn	-	driss

breåndyre my heart feels more akin to them then any other	bree	-	ahn	-	der	-	ree

breantha enchanted whispers	bree	-	ain	-	thah
brearfyn moonlight night	bree	-	air	-	fin
brearvyn I feel it in the sacred places	bree	-	air	-	vin
bredonra awakens with the spring	bree	-	doan	-	rah
bredynsa of the blood	bree	-	den	-	sah
breniar protected by the fair	bree	-	nigh	-	air
breonda making the dream real	bree	-	own	-	dah

breondaryn words cannot begin to express how I feel	bree	-	own	-	dare	-	ren

brevara white winged	bree	-	vair	-	rah
breylyn quiet sigh	bree	-	L	-	lynn

breyndondoryl dreams of a place I have never been	bree	-	in	-	doan	-	door	-	rill

breynjårsa lady of edendale	bree	-	in	-	jar	-	sah
breynre ways of healing	bree	-	in	-	ree

brialaryn speaks the ancient way	bry (rhymes with cry)	-	a	-	lair	-	ren

brialdre old, loamy forest	bry	-	ale	-			dree
briamoryn makes her own spells	bry	-	a	-	more	-	ren
briåmorys discovering deeper sides to my existence	bry	-	ah	-	more	-	riss
brieryn a whisper that floats on a rose petal	bry		-	ear	-		ren
brimorådyn near the edge	bry	-	more	-	rah	-	den
brimorlyn ever aware	bry	-	more		-		lynn
brinålys crimson aura	bry	-	nah		-		liss
brioryn one with the trees	bry	-	or		-		ren
briqwynsa awakens the child	bry-		quinn		-		sah
bromereyl never felt quite right in my family	bro	-	mere	-	ree	-	L
bromiyl soft hearted	bro	-	my		-		L
bromordyn thick as a tree	bro	-	more		-		den
bromoryn touched by the Goddess	bro	-	more		-		ren
bronarsyn paint everywhere	bro	-	nair		-		sin
bronaryn reaches for the dream	bro	-	nair		-		ren
brovoyl part of the sea	bro	-	voe		-		L
browynda piper's breath upon her ear	bro	-	win		-		dah

40   The Silver Elves

| bruådryn | brew | - | ah | - | drinn |
shares the world's sadness

| bruereyn | brew | - | ear | - | ree | - | in |
new, exciting and simultaneous calming

| bruradea | brew | - | ray | - | dee | - | ah |
lots of things fit

| bruvordyn | brew | - | vour | - | den |
they aren't just stories

| brynåfyn | brin | - | nah | - | fin |
soothes quarrels

| bryndoryn | brin | - | door | - | ren |
loves the sparkling

| brynlovyn | brin | - | lore | - | vin |
dream birther

| bularle | bew | - | lair | - | lee |
talks with the spirits of the dead

| bydyndae | bid | - | den | - | dae |
if that's okay?

| bylynsår | bill | - | lynn | - | sar |
builds new worlds

bynaryn bin - nair - ren for love of elves

| byndånåfar | bin | - | dahn | - | nah | - | fair |
shaper of treehomes

| byndårea | bin | - | dar | - | ree | - | ah |
when I walked alone

| byndåver | bin | - | dah | - | veer |
code of honor

| byndonefål | bin | - | doe | - | knee | - | fahl |
sees the path

| byrndålyn | burn | - | dah | - | lynn |
opens her heart

| byrnvåle | burn | - | vah | - | lee |
has long felt

The Book of Elf Names   41

byryndea	ber	-	ren	-	dee	-	ah
from then on, I know							
bythanél	bit	-	thane	-			nell
rides the waves							

WE ARE NOT OUR NAMES NOR ARE OUR NAMES US, BUT LIKE CLOTHES OUR ELVEN NAMES CAN EXPRESS OUR NATURES.

C

Elven Name and Meaning	Pronunciation			
cabryni makes a stand	cah	- brinn	- nigh	
cadanafa keeps coming back	cah	- dane	- nay	- fah
cadånåfyn wanders the endless mountain ranges	cah	- dahn	- nah	- fin
cadånyna flys into moonlight	cah	- dahn	- in	- nah
cadenadyn longs for true love	cah	- dee	- nay	- den
cafadra laughter on the wind	cah	- fay	- drah	
cafålodryn multifaceted	cah	- fah	- low	- drinn
cafåndaa rain falling from the eaves	cah	- fahn	- day	- ah
cafelaryn sweet and helpful	cah	- fee	- lair	- ren
caladarys river tree	cah	- lay	- dare	- riss
caladoryn tree of shining	cah	- lay	- door	- ren
cälådraa sound of bells	cal	- lah	- dray	- ah
calådyn elf sure	cah	- lah	- den	
calålea licks her paws	cah	- lah	- lee	- ah

calåledyn something is about to happen	cah	-	lah	-	lee	-	den
calålidea wee bit of powers	cah	-	lah	-	lie	-	dee - ah
calålyndre knows by touch	cah	-	lah	-	lynn	-	dree
calåvar ponders the way	cah	-	lah			-	vair
caldrynån seeks shelter	cal	-	drinn			-	non
caleålyn natural peace	cal	-	lee	-	ah	-	lynn
calearyn piskie sister	cal	-	lee	-	air	-	ren
calelea really understands how they feel	cal	-	lee	-	lee	-	ah
calesaryn finding some answers	cal	-	lee	-	sair	-	ren
calevaryn believe me or not	cal	-	lee	-	vair	-	ren
caleyndryn nurses wounded animals	cal	-	lee	-	in	-	drinn
calfarna morning dancer	cal	-	fair			-	nah
calfeladryn living the life	cal	-	fee	-	lay	-	drinn
califryn a better understanding	cal	-	lie			-	frinn
calilasyn water faerie	cal	-	lie	-	lay	-	sin
caliyn voice of the rain	cal	-	lie			-	in
calorvyn feels the resonance	cal	-	lore			-	vin

The Silver Elves

calule	cal	-	lou	-	lee

blessed with gifts used everyday

calvaryn	cal	-	vair	-	ren

feels the way

calyndaryn	cal	-	lynn	-	dare	-	ren

along the border

camålys	cam	-	mal	-	lyss

extremely laid back

camèleyn	cam	-	mell	-	lee	-	in

sunshine returns

canådar	can	-	nah	-	dare

subconscious connection with nature

canadre	can	-	nay	-	dree

without any action on my part

canåvarwe	can	-	nah	-	vair	-	we

I feel their ways

candåladra	can	-	dah	-	lay	-	drah

sunlit lace

candålarea	can	-	dah	-	lair	-	ree	-	ah

tan that not many can match

candarasys	can	-	dare	-	rah	-	sis

likes to travel

candarea	can	-	dare	-	ree	-	ah

intricate lacing

candaryn	can	-	dare	-	ren

starts to remember

candoryn	can	-	door	-	ren

dreams of Faerie

carårevåsa	car	-	rah	-	ree	-	vah	-	sah

out to play

carasièn	car	-	ray	-	sigh	-	in

rooted to the earth

carèladån	car	-	rell	-	lay	-	dahn

white feathers tied in hair

The Book of Elf Names   45

carèlor seeking roots	car	-	rell	-	lore		
careorys finds their s'elf	car	-	ree	-	or	-	riss
caretås soothing fluidity of motion	car	-	ree	-	tahs		
cariålyndos light on the leaf	car	-	rye	-	ah	-	lynn	-	dose
carndrasa wants to return	carn	-	dray	-	sah		
carynda with the archers	car	-	ren	-	dah		
caryndås born knowing	car	-	ren	-	dahs		
caryndor secretly determined to find out	car	-	ren	-	door		
caryndorèl close to the trees	car	-	ren	-	door	-	rell
carynszorsa embraces the night	car	-	rince	-	zoar	-	sah
catånya defender and guide	cat	-	tah-n	-	yah		
cavalasa glimmer of realization	cav	-	vay	-	lay	-	sah
cavålea wolf wind	cav	-	vah	-	lee	-	ah
cavanadyl wanders the woods in solitude	cav	-	vay	-	nay	-	dill
cavändor of the spirit	cav	-	van	-	door		
cavara following an impulse	cav	-	vay	-	rah		
cavarea relives the past	cav	-	vay	-	ree	-	ah

46   The Silver Elves

cavryndryn	cav	-	ren	-	drinn				

cavryndryn   cav   -   ren   -   drinn
stands in awe of the trees

cavyndi   cav   -   vin   -   die
free dancer

cavyndryl   cav   -   vin   -   drill
keeps the peace

cazånådur   caz   -   zahn   -   nah   -   dur
large little

cazanayl   caz   -   zay   -   nay   -   L
warm, comforting feeling

cazazyndra   caz   -   zay   -   zen   -   drah
so much more than most of us see

cazyndareyl   caz   -   zen   -   dare   -   ree   -   L
wind's serenade

cazyndaryn   caz   -   zen   -   dare   -   ren
into much

cazyndre   caz   -   zen   -   dree
listening to the source within

cazyndryn   caz   -   zen   -   drinn
stars are here to guide me

cazyndura   caz   -   zen   -   dur   -   rah
their heartbeat is mine

celador   sell   -   lay   -   door
something vibrates deeply within

celadoryn   sell   -   lay   -   door   -   ren
everything a person should want to be

celadrea   sell   -   lay   -   dree   -   ah
heals the mind

celidea   sell   -   lie   -   dee   -   ah
sorry to lay that on you

celyndara   sell   -   lynn   -   dare   -   rah
called to the ancient lands

cenådaryn   sin   -   nah   -   dare   -   ren
sees from a different angle

cenådra drawn to the party	sin	-	nah	-	drah		
cerarea wants to know	ser	-	a	-	ree	-	ah
chålålyndrys shadow on the sun	chahl	-	lah	-	lynn	-	driss
chåndåle asked for them	chahn	-	dah	-	lee		
chåndara something is trying to tell me something	chahn	-	dare	-	rah		
chandor watcher	chain	-	door				
chandoryn hears the bells	chain	-	door	-	ren		
chandra yearning for the light	chain	-	drah				
chåndura moment of truth	chan	-	dur	-	rah		
chariyndryl intuitive grasp of reality	chair	-	rye	-	in	-	drill
cheändal guardian of mystery	chee	-	ann	-	dale		
cheåndåle energy of the sea is flooding into me	chee	-	ann	-	dale	-	lee
cheandra spreading magic throughout the earth	chee	-	ane	-	drah		
cheardåle yearns to open the door	che	-	air	-	dah	-	lee
chelarys goes unnoticed	chee	-	lair	-	riss		
chelordys feel deep down	chee	-	lore	-	dis		
chévaryn born to be elegant	chev	-	vair	-	ren		

cheyndryl   chee - in - drill
ancestry of sailors

chiandar   chi   (rhymes   with   high)   ane - dare
only recently

chiandre   chi - ane - dree
decides for their s'elf

chiaryn   chi - air - ren
talent for silence

chidarys   chi - dare - riss
drawn to everything to do with them

chiladryn   chi - lay - drinn
anticipate things that are going to happen

chilidra   chi - lie - drah
magic child of dreams

chilire   chi - lie - ree
I know it's funny

chilorys   chi - lore - riss
it is never enough

chinaryn   chi - nair - ren
leaves gifts for the fae

chivaryn   chi - vair - ren
art maker

chiyndryn   chi - in - drinn
long before I can remember

choloreyn   cho - lore - ree - in
embraced by the people

chorynsa   cho - ren - sah
nurses the ill

chynåru   chin - nah - rue
my great passion

chyndåru   chin - dar - rue
faith in s'elf

chynmaryn   chin - mare - ren
drawn to Fairy

The Book of Elf Names   49

cilyndros   sill   -   lynn   -   dross
realize I've held these views all along

cleåndra   clee   -   ahn   -   drah   how
others respond to me

cloledar   clo   -   lee   -   dare
beneath the brambles

clolyndyn   clo   -   lynn   -   den
intense lover

colådryn   coal   -   lah   -   drinn
we understand each other

colådynėl   coal   -   lah   -   den   -   nell
wants to know all the possibilities

colåndryn   coal   -   lahn   -   drinn
accepted into the magical world

coleålyn   coal   -   lee   -   ah   -   lynn
taking time to lay in the grass

colendra   coal   -   lean   -   drah
spirit that lives in the world forever

colidryn   coal   -   lie   -   drinn
be yours'elf

colidrys   coal   -   lie   -   driss
too busy reading to notice at first

colisyn   coal   -   lie   -   sin
finds the one

colthyndor   coal   -   thin   -   door
fair destiny

colyndåle   coal   -   lynn   -   dah   -   lee
awakened by memories

colysån   coal   -   liss   -   sahn
mother's elf

comålyn   com   -   mah   -   lynn
appreciates the great

comåndreyn   com   -   mahn   -   dree   -   in
never doubted their existence

comaryn elfin beautiful	com	-	mare	-	ren		
comerys friend to all animals	com	-	mere	-	riss	frim	
comondrys found it fit me	com	-	moan	-	driss		
conådrea of the ancient earth	con	-	nah	-	dree	-	ah
conaryn wishfully thinking of past lives	con	-	nair	-	ren		
condadryn standing up for those who cannot stand up for themselves	con	-	day	-	drinn		
condånafår creates the circle	con	-	dah	-	nay	-	far
condiala draws from the trees	con	-	die	-	ale	-	lah
coniallyn first in the fray	con	-	nigh	-	ale	-	lynn
convorys sharp eyes	con	-	vour	-	riss		
cordynvåla serendipitous imagination	cor	-	den	-	vah	-	lah
cordynvårys called to the other	cor	-	den	-	var	-	riss
coriyla watches in silence	cor	-	rye	-	L	-	lah
corvåndyryn shares the power	cor	-	vahn	-	der	-	ren
corvyndryn raven kin	cor	-	vin	-	drinn		
corvyndrys raven spirit	cor	-	vin	-	driss		
coryndarėl up to tricks	cor	-	ren	-	dare	-	rell

corynder	cor	-	ren	-	deer		
craves the ocean							
crysalyn	cris	-	say	-	lynn		
blade that glitters							
culåndor	coo	-	lahn	-	door		
truth be told							
culåndreyn	coo	-	lahn	-	dree	-	in
embodies life to its fullest							
culdalys	coo	-	day	-	lyss		
sees what the cat sees							
culedyn	coo	-	lee	-	den		
not certain							
culelu	coo	-	lee	-	lou		
silver lining in every cloud							
culeynla	coo	-	lee	-	in	-	lah
just interested							
culiåna	coo	-	lie	-	ah	-	nah
dream tender							
culidyn	coo	-	lie	-	den		
evokes strong feelings							
culiryn	coo	-	lie	-	ren		
soft pale moonlight							
cunarys	coo	-	nair	-	riss		
eternally grateful to mother moon							

"AN ELVEN NAME IS LIKE A PASSWORD THAT
UNLOCKS A SECRET WORLD OF MAGIC AND
MYSTERY."
—OLD ELVEN KNOWLEDGE

𝒟

Elven Name and Meaning | Pronunciation

Elven Name and Meaning	Pronunciation					
daåndra that is what truly makes me happy	day	-	ahn	-	drah	
daaryni among the shadows	day	-	air	-	ren	-	nigh
daforvålyn one who can be counted on	day	-	for	-	vah	-	lynn
dafyndra rhythyms of neverending life	day	-	fin	-	drah	
dågaryn sound advice	dah	-	gair	-	ren	
dågarys since then our life has changed	dah	-	gair	-	riss	
dagonarèl near to devotion	day	-	go	-	nair	-	rell
dåjånårae sheltered by the magic	dah	-	jah	-	nah	-	ray
dåjänare sweet to caress	dah	-	jan	-	nair	-	ree
dåjånrys more than words can say	dah	-	jahn	-	riss	
dajordyn has waited long	day	-	jour	-	den	
dalareyn dallys with the elfin	day	-	lair	-	ree	-	in
dålea took awhile	dah	-	lee	-	ah	
dåleåla show joy to those who cannot see it	dah	-	lee	-	ah	-	lah

dåleålyn secret hopes come true	dah	-	lee	-	ah	-	lynn
dåleåshon shown births a flame	dah	-		lee	-		ah
dåleda stones glinting	dah	-		lee	-		dah
dåledyn deep down I know	dah	-		lee	-		den
dålefyn beginning the journey	dah	-		lee	-		fin
dålela power of the dark moon	dah	-		lee	-		lah
dålelea the moon sings to me in my dreams	dah	-	lee	-	lee	-	ah
dålelys moonlight in the soul	dah	-		lee	-		liss
dåleshuryn wolf light	dah	-	lee	-	sure	-	ren
daliåvyn slips out of reality	day	-	lie	-	ah	-	vin
dålorthyn ears in my eyes	dah	-		lore	-	thin	t
dålos secret seeker	dah			-			lowce
dålovyn green magic	dah	-		low	-		vin
dalyndyn passing through	day	-		lynn	-		den
dalyshon lives in the dance	day	-		lyss	-		shown
dålzår action sage	dahl			-			czar
dåmåndea actualizing dreams	dah	-	mahn	-	dee	-	ah

54   The Silver Elves

dåmåndryn out of the mist	dah	-	mahn	-	drinn
damarna would fulfill my dreams	day	-	mare	-	nah
damondas wyzard worker	day	-	moan	-	dace
dänaboryn wanders in dreamland	dan	-	nay	-	boar	-	ren
dånådadrea cheeky little pixie	dah	-	nah	-	day	-	dree	-	ah
dånadyn something extremely powerful within	dah	-	nay	-	den
dånålor one of use to us	dah	-	nah	-	lore
danåsålor in the circle of the s'elf	day	-	nah	-	sah	-	lore
dåndålea delicate undulations of billowing clouds	dahn	-	dah	-	lee	-	ah
dåndåleon sympathy for the lost	dahn	-	dah	-	lee	-	ohn
dåndålor I am deeply moved	dahn	-	dah	-	lore
dåndalyn plays music deep in the forest	dahn	-	day	-	lynn
dåndälys staring at the stars	dahn	-	dal	-	liss
dändåmer spirit of the stream	dan	-	dah	-	mere
dåndaryn power of the mind	dahn	-	dare	-	ren
dandåthor destined hero	dane	-	dah	-	thor
dåndåthor soothed by water	dahn	-	dah	-	thor

The Book of Elf Names

dåndordyn	dahn	-	door	-	den				
knowledge of things that are hard to explain									
dandoreyl	dane	-	door	-	ree	-	L		
quick mind									
dåndyl	dahn	-			dill				
late for lunch									
danfineyn	dane	-	fie	-	knee	-	in		
butterfly logic									
danica	dane	-	nigh	-	cah				
vale of mist									
dånjånåfėl	dahn	-	jahn	-	nah	-	fell		
whispers with the wind									
danuryn	dane	-	new	-	ren				
daughter of the goddess									
dånzåla	dahn	-	zah	-	lah				
spirit seeker									
dånzålyn	dahn	-	zah	-	lynn				
elven warlock									
daokynda	day	-	oh	-	ken	-	dah		
of the old land									
daråreasa	dare	-	rah	-	ree	-	a	-	sah
drawn ever closer									
daråreda	dare	-	rah	-	ree	-	dah		
face that glows									
darårynåra	dare	-	rah	-	ren	-	nah	-	rah
takes a chance									
darasandryn	dare	-	ray	-	sane	-	drinn		
communes with the animals									
daråsha	dare	-	rah	-	shah				
if such a thing is possible									
daråthea	dare	-	rah	-	thee	-	ah		
quiet surroundings									
daråtheyl	dare	-	rah	-	thee	-	L		
pattern seerer									

darathyn across the river	dare	-	ray	-	thin		
daråvyndre draws power to her	dare	-	rah	-	vin	-	dree
dardynar from the wild	dare	-	den	-	nair		
dårdynthe path of beauty	dar	-	den	-	thee		
daredyn drawn to explore	dare	-	ree	-	den		
dariarél deep in shadows	dare	-	rye	-	air	-	rell
darlynel from elsewhere	dare	-	lynn	-	neil		
darmia feather glow	dare	-	my	-	ah		
darogaryn many colors	dare	-	row	-	gay	-	ren
darsafelea dark nightingale	dare	-	say	-	fee	-	lee - ah
darshåna meaning of small occurences	dare	-	shah	-	nah		
darsharyn part of each	dare	-	shay	-	ren		
darshåyl peeks over the waves	dare	-	shah	-	L		
dårval magic link	dar	-	vale				
dårylard remembers Faerie	dar	-	rill	-	laird		
daryndarkor midnite fire	dare	-	ren	-	dare	-	core
daryndys green healer	dare	-	ren	-	diss		

The Book of Elf Names

dårynfar finds the connection	dar	-	ren	-	far
dåryngaryl drawn to the music	dar	-	ren	-	gay	-	rill
darynlor aspires to wonder	dare	-	ren	-	lore
darynsir shadow's shade	dare	-	ren	-	sire
darynsorsa ring of reckoning	dare	-	ren	-	soar	-	sah
dasåkafar shadow protector	day	-	sah	kay	-	fair
dasålyndėl dreams the ancient tongue	day	-	sah	-	lynn	-	dell
dasareyl shadow warrior	day	-	sair	-	ree	-	L
dasaryn walks at night	day	-	sair	-	ren
dasaryndor shares from the shadows	day	-	sair	-	ren	-	door
dasdoryn one with the metals	dayse	-	door	-	ren
daseůs charming one	day	-	see	-	you-ss
dåshandor sits on tombstones	dah	-	shane	-	door
dåshånėl mastering the magic within	dah	-	shah	-	nell
dåshorsyn defending the trees	dah	-	shore	-	sin
dåshoryn secret conversations	dah	-	show	-	ren
dåshyndyra whispers to the animals	dah	-	shin	-	der	-	rah

58   The Silver Elves

dasyndar soothes the animals	day	-	sin	-	dare
dåthänyn prowls with cats	dah	-	thah	-	nin
dåtharyn sings in the trees	dah	-	thay	-	ren
dåvåndea feels their inner pain	dah	-	vahn	-	dee	-	ah
dåvårdyn little princess	dah	-	var	-	den
davareon in the breeze	day	-	vair	-	ree	-	ohn
dåvaryn warrior of the light	dah	-	vair	-	ren
dåvyndåva silver light running through the hair	dah-	vin	-	dah	-	vah
dåvynsoryl watches the trees dance	dah	-	vin	-	soar	-	rill
daynda ready to begin	day	-	in	-	dah
dåzyndåra accepted by the pack	dah	-	zen	-	dah	-	rah
deådålor helps the less fortunate	dee	-	ah	-	dah	-	lore
deådaryn quiet but strong	dee	-	ah	-	dare	-	ren
deåderyn lifeforce of the trees	dee	-	ah	-	deer	-	ren
deåndaru fast rider	dee	-	ahn	-	dare	-	rue
deåndåthån far out thoughts	dee	-	ahn	-	dah	-	thahn
deändre guided by the universe	dee	-	ann	-	dree

The Book of Elf Names   59

dearådyn many enchanting experiences	dee	-	air	-	rah	-	den
deardryn joy of discovering so many kindred souls	dee	-	air	-	drinn		
deåvryn come home	dee	-	ah	-	vrinn		
dėladea strong heart	dell	-	lay	-	dee	-	ah
delåndra gentle nudge	dee	lahn	-	drah			
delandre finally I just couldn't take it	dee	-	lane	-	dree		
dėlfynål followed by the children	dell	-	fin	-	nall		
dėlfynasa by the lagoon	dell	-	fin	-	nay	-	sah
dėlfynwe nectar of the trees	dell	-	fin	-	we		
dėlronårae listens to the tree's whisper	dell	-	roan	-	nah	-	ray
dėlyndor driven by honor	dell	-	lynn	-	door		
dėlyndre small, blond and mischevious	dell	-	lynn	-	dree		
dėlyndreyl except for a few	dell	-	lynn	-	dree	-	L
dėlynėl other light	dell	-	lynn	-	nell		
delyneyl prone to day dreaming	dee	-	lynn	-	knee	-	L
dėlynlor well of inspiration	dell	-	lynn	-	lore		
denådyn makes little sense to me	dee	-	nah	-	den		

denathas leads the dance	dee	- nay	- thace	(rhymes with face)	
derawyndėl dream flyer	deer	- ray	- win	dell	
derlyndos power to see	deer	- lynn	-	dose	
dersarel dares to discover	deer	- say	-	reel	
dervasha hates to be a bother	deer	– vay	-	shah	
derynde mystic diviner	deer	- ren	-	dee	
derynthor provider of safe haven	deer	- ren	-	thor	
derynvar things become clearer	deer	- ren	-	vair	
derynyl soul bell song	deer	- ren	-	nil	
derzlagor soul of the bear	deers	- lay	-	gore	
devänåde just beyond the stars	dee	- van	- nah	- dee	
devåndåvor survived dark things	dee	- vahn	- dah	- vour	
devåndor with nature's music to soothe me	dee	- vahn	-	door	
devändrea filled with the light of life	dee	- van	- dree	- ah	
devina where love and peace rules	dee	- vie	-	nah	
devyndryn surprisingly proper	dee	- vin	-	drinn	
diådåndon voice made of crystal	dye	- ah	- dahn	- doan	

diådavyn on a different level	dye	-	ah	-	day	-	vin
diådayn more than most can see	dye	-	ah	-	day	-	in
diadea reads emotions	dye	-	a	-	dee	-	ah
diadeda the willow has taught me to laugh no matter what	dye	-	a	-	dee	-	dah
diador dead give away	dye	-	a	-	door		
diålea behind the veil	dye	-	ah	-	lee	-	ah
diålofyn free to show who I truly am	dye	-	ah	-	low	-	fin
diålosyn they remained in my mind	dye	-	ah	-	low	-	sin
diåndor leaps from on high	dye	-	ahn	-	door		
diåndorys elementals of the sky	dye	-	ahn	-	door	-	riss
diåntha starts from the beginning	dye	-	ah	-	thah		
dilaryn born out of time	dye	-	lair	-	ren		
dilathys wandering in the early hours of the morning	dye	-	lay	-	thyss		
dileådyn magic deeply ingrained	dye	-	lee	-	ah	-	den
dilerys ever changing song of the rivers	dye	-	leer	-	riss		
dilodån slides by	dye	-	low	-	dahn		
dilyndre a brush with the fae world	dye	-	lynn	-	dree		

dilyndyn	dye	-	lynn	-	den				
content with my surroundings									
dimaryn	dye	-	mare	-	ren				
ever graceful									
dimordys	dye	-	more	-	diss				
that's why I came here									
dinarèl	dye	-	nair	-	rell				
just be									
divays	dye	-	vay	-	iss				
from many comes									
divoreyn	dye	-	vour	-	ree	-	in	l
eaves offerings									
divoryn	dye	-	vour	-	ren				
music flows through fingers									
diynara	dye	-	in	-	nay	-	rah	
found their wings									
diynde	dye	-	in	-	dee				
before I even knew what they meant									
diyndra	dye	-	in	-	drah				
unanny relation to elven life									
dofäleyn	doe	-	fowl	-	lee	-	in	
I live in Elfin									
dofynda	doe	-	fin	-	dah				
gazes toward the stars									
dolådea	doe	-	lah	-	dee	-	ah	
before my very eyes									
dolasyn	doe	-	lay	-	sin				
beyond the obvious									
dolealyn	doe	-	lee	-	a	-	lynn	
reaching out for something more									
dolefa	doe	-	lee	-	fah				
touches the stars									
dolynara	doe	-	lynn	-	nair	-	rah	
looks to the moon for guidance									

dolyndre hidden from society	doe	-	lynn	-	dree		
dolyndrea problems from other lifetimes	doe	-	lynn	-	dree	-	ah
donådea which I really admire	doe	-	nah	-	dee	-	ah
donådornyn righter of wrongs	doe	-	nah	-	door	-	nin
donådyn need to search for more	doe	-	nah	-	den		
donåwyn searcher for understanding	doe	-	nah	-	win		
dŏndåfėl like a leaf	don	-	dah	-	fell		
dondarea bright sunny day	doan	-	dare	-	ree	-	ah
dondorålyn crystal blue eyes	doan	-	dorr	-	rah	-	lynn
dondoryn still learning	doan	-	door	-	ren		
donetha rainy morning	doan	-	knee	-	thah		
donnaiyl hanging in the trees	doan	-	nay	-	eye	-	L
doradyn runs in the family	doe	-	ray	-	den		
dorakna one who intercedes	doe	-	rake	-	nah		
dorangar brother of stone	doe	-	rain	-	gair		
doreyl something magic within	doe	-	ree	-	L	feeling	
dorgåndryl without being sure why	door	-	gahn	-	drill		

dorgaryn	door	-	gair	-		ren
a being in hiding						
doriama	door	-	rye	-	a -	mah
eyes of fire						
dorieél	door	-	rye	-	e -	L
there for you						
dorlånåver	door	-	rye	-	ah - nah -	veer
responsibility of love						
dorlåndre	door	-	lahn		-	dree
old connections deep in my blood and soul						
dorlånvar	door	-	lahn		-	vair
emerging star						
dorloråle	door	-	lore	-	rah -	lee
heightened sense of who I am						
dornasyl	door	-	nay		-	sill
hides in the open						
dorsånalu	door	-	sah	-	nay -	lou
near to perfection						
dorthåndari	door	-	thahn	-	dare -	rye
at home in the forest						
dorthena	door	-	thee		-	nah
none will ever know						
dorvara	door	-	vair		-	rah
for the greater good						
dorvaråshyn	door	-	vair	-	rah -	shin
steps unseen						
dorvaryn	door	-	vair		-	ren
rides the clouds						
dorvashyn	door	-	vay		-	shin
I really don't know						
dorwynar	door	-	win		-	nair
in sacred places						
doryndågår	door	-	ren	-	dah -	gair
makes an entrance to music						

The Book of Elf Names   65

doryndålyn	door	-	ren	-	dah	-	lynn
feels it in the blood							
doryndåryn	door	-	ren	-	dah	-	ren
in tune with the magic sight							
doryndyn	door	-	ren	-	den		
guided by dreams							
dorynsata	door	-	ren	-	say	-	tah
song source							
dorynthel	door	-	ren	-	theal		
great satisfaction from helping others							
dorynve	door	-	ren	-	vee		
even if they don't know							
dozyndar	doe	-	zen	-	dare		
awaits the time							
draaryn	dray	-	air	-	ren		
little dragon							
draåthryn	dray	-	ah	-	thrin		
most wonderful semi precious stones							
draca	dray	-	cah				
dragon dreamer							
dracala	dray	-	cah	-	lah		
dragon princess							
dracana	dray	-	can	-	nah		
recovered memories							
dradånthånor	dray	-	dahn	-	thahn	-	nor
dragon spirit							
drådoryn	drah	-	door	-	ren		
won through							
dradym	dray	-	dim				
demon lover							
draėlåner	dray	-	L	-	lah	-	near
of dragon's born							
drafynias	dray	-	fin	-	nigh	-	ace
frolics in the forest							

drafynru plays in dreams	dray	-	fin	-	rue		
dragåndoryn accompanied by spirits	dray	-	gahn	-	door	-	ren
dragoran fierce in defense	dray	-	gore	-	rain		
dragoryn hangs with dragons	dray	-	gore	-	ren		
dralokyn whirl of sand	dray	-	low	-	kin		
drandor dwarf shield	drain		-		door		
drasålyn moon tides	dray	-	sah	-	lynn		
drasålys face in the sea	dray	-	sah	-	liss		
drasorvarna kin of the sky	dray	-	soar	-	vair	-	nah
drathel calls the elementals	dray		-		theal		
drava dwarf friend	dray		-		vah		
dravanvaru created from his own imagination	dray	-	vain	-	vair	-	rue
dravyn summoned by dragons	dray		-		vin		
dravyndar summoned to the quest	dray	-	vin	-	dare		
dråvyndor shifts into the dreamtime	drah	-	vin	-	door		
drayndra from the trees	dray	-	in	-	drah		
dreådne came to me in dreams	dree	-	odd	-	knee		

The Book of Elf Names

dreadorèl enters the sacred	dree	-	a	-	door	-	rell
dreådyn gives everything for the people	dree	-		ah	-		den
dreånda dream flying	dree	-		ahn	-		dah
dreåndåre flying in dreams to distant lands	dree	-	ahn	-	dah	-	ree
dreandora wings of blue	dree	-	ane	-	door	-	rah
dreåndra spinning with joy	dree	-		ahn	-		drah
dreåndrana voice of the ocean	dree	-	ahn	-	dray	-	nah
dreåndre rings true	dree	-		ahn	-		dree

dreånthyl   dree - ahn - thyl (rhymes with fill)
I feel it is my duty to utilize this gift

dreånvyl finding family	dree	-		ahn	-		ville
dreardynae have always been able to	dree	-	air	-	den	-	nay
dredålys extreme love	dree	-		dah	-		liss
dredarys wonder of a child	dree	-		dare	-		riss
drefynra stirring magics	dree	-		fin	-		rah
drelåndre on the road	dree	-		lahn	-		dree
dreonsyl welcomed back	dree	-		ohn	-		sill
drevåna as if I met an old friend	dree	-		vah	-		nah

The Silver Elves

drevaråshån not quite up	dree	-	vair	-	rah	-	shan
drevasa entering the light	dree	-		vay	-	sah	
dreynara wandering artist	dree	-	in	-	nair	-	rah
dreyndara away from the sorrow of the world	dree	-	in	-	dare	-	rah
dreyndreyl voice from the other world	dree	-	in	-	dree	-	L
dreynvare mystical power of music	dree	-	in	-	vair	-	ree
driadea tree sheltered	dry	-	a	-	dee	-	ah
driåndre vivid dream	dry	-		ahn	-	dree	
drocåndor artic wolf	dro	-		cahn	-	door	
drocatorae dragon tamer	dro	cah	-	tour	-	ray	
drodasha hedge witch	dro	-		day	-	shah	
drodynėl eye in the leaves	dro	-		den	-	nell	
drogora dark dragon	dro	-		gore	-	rah	
drolorys on mountain crag	dro	-		lore	-	riss	
dromeyl riend to many	dro	-		me	-	L	f
dromiyl began to realize	dro	-		my	-	L	
drondådėl from the heights	dro	-		dah	-	dell	

The Book of Elf Names 69

drosånalån	dro	-	sah	-	nay	-	lahn
one who does the ritual of the raven						
drothynda	dro	-	thin	-	dah	
appears calm						
drovändor	dro	-	van	-	door	
sun soul						
drovardyn	dro	-	vair	-	den	
on mountain high						
drovashu	dro	-	vay	-	shoe	
bringer of flowers						
droyndar	dro	-	in	-	dare	
iron hammer						
druåntraa	drew	-	ahn	-	tray	-	ah
speaks the language of the fathers						
druvanvaru	drew	-	vane	-	vair	-	rue
endless possibilities						
dryndåle	drin	-	dah	-	lee	
free spirit on the loose						
dryndor	drin	-	door			
works with dragons						
dryndora	drin	-	door	-	rah	
reflection of moonlight on a puddle						
drynfardor	drin	-	fair	-	door	
greatly complex						
duåndor	due	-	ahn	-	door	
true personality						
dudoryn	due	-	door	-	ren	
secrets of the trees						
dudynde	due	-	den	-	dee	
nevers asks for help in return						
dulela	due	-	-lee	-	lah	
on a higher plane						
dunåda	dune	-	nah	-	dah	
ancient sacred connection						

dunhereon	dune	-	hear	-	ree	-	ohn

dunhereon   dune   -   hear   -   ree   -   ohn
blessed with luck all their life

duondra   due   -   ohn   -   drah
sparkles as she walks

duondre   due   -   ohn   -   dree
sacred space

duråndådor   due   -   rahn   -   dah   -   door
at home in the wild

duråndyn   due   -   rahn   -   den
these people feel like home to me

duresa   due   -   ree   -   sah
said something that triggered it

duridrea   due   -   rye   -   dree   -   ah
my sense of s'elf has never been stronger

duriel   due   -   rye   -   eel
feather touch

durwyndor   dur   -   win   -   door
needs no key

durynåzel   dur   -   ren   -   nah   -   zeal
wants to have real adventures

durynåzora   dur   -   ren   -   han   -   zoar   -   rah
away with the pixies

duryndår   dur   -   ren   -   dar
different then anyone they've met before

duryndåvyl   dur   -   ren   -   dah   -   ville
faery dragon

duryndur   dur   -   ren   -   dur
entirely unique

dwarynor   dware   -   ren   -   nor
dwarf speaker

dylåndor   dill   -   lahn   -   door
the power of nature rules our lives

dyndare   den   -   dare   -   ree
develops her healing powers

The Book of Elf Names   71

dyndasa	den	-	day	-	sah		
always thought and felt							
dyndorėl	den	-	door	-	rell		
of two tribes							
dynfylfarea	den	-	fill	-	fair	-	ree - ah
takes the unknown path							
dynrändyryn	den	-	ran	-	der	-	ren
called by the wanderlust							
dynzåle	den	-	zah	-	lee		
in the shade of the trees							
dynzara	den	-	zair	-	rah		
finally know what I am							
dynzåra	den	-	zah	-	rah		
excellent judge of character							
dynzaryn	den	-	zair	-	ren		
whispers to the wind							
dynzarys	den	-	zair	-	riss		
ever healing							
dynzreyl	dens	-	ree	-	L		
ready to listen							
dyrkondås	der	-	cone	-	dahs		
dark dagger							
dyrlalyn	der	-	lay	-	lynn		
beyond the here and now							
dyrshavon	der	-	shay	-	vone		
shifting tones							
dysdåndyn	diss	-	don	-	den		
little wise one							

Æ

Elven Name and Meaning	Pronunciation						
eåduryn senses magic in the air	e	-	ah	-	dur	-	ren
eåfyndra longs for Elfin	e	-	ah	-	fin	-	drah
ealidyn found my true home	e	-	a	-	lie	-	den
eara elfin eyes	e	-	air			-	rah
earea so I went to my books	e	-	air	-	ree	-	ah
eareyl reverence for beauty	e	-	air	-	ree	-	L
eareyn it all seemed right	e	-	air	-	ree	-	in
eareys from books beautiful	e	-	air	-	ree	-	S
eboreyn time to come home	e	-	boar	-	ree	-	in
eboryn passion for the dance	e	-	boar			-	ren
ebynda it's something I work at	e	-	ben			-	dah
echene awakens others to their true calling	e	-	chee			-	knee
edålvyn unusual one	e	-	dahl			-	vin
edålyn swimming under a full moon	e	-	dah			-	lynn

The Book of Elf Names

edana quiet forest	e	-	day	-	nah
edånåfyn knows how to help	e	-	dah	-	nah	-	fin
edåndåle where I am most at home	e	-	dahn	-	dah	-	lee
edåniyl here for a special purpose	e	-	dahn	-	nigh	-	L
edånya steps into Elfin	e	-	dahn	-	yah
edarea a dove flew over	e	-	dare	-	ree	-	ah
edareyn hair flying loose	e	-	dare	-	ree	-	in
edavea the forest holds something for me	e	-	day	-	vee	-	ah
edéleyn I insist that I am not	e	-	dell	-	lee	-	in
edere all of nature should be respected	e	-	dear	-	ree
ederfyn dark dreams waking	e	-	dear	-	fin
ederlyn makes great changes	e	-	dear	-	lynn
edervyn weathered the storm	e	-	dear	-	vin
ederyn own special category	e	-	dear	-	ren
ediadyn in tune with inner s'elf	e	-	dye	-	a	-	den
ediåfyn do so regularly	e	-	dye	-	ah	-	fin
edivan it wasn't until she had her own child that she realized	e	-	dye	-	vane

edonåde paths of the stars	e	-	doe	-	nah	-	dee
edonadel wind of fire	e	-	doe	-	nay	-	dell
edonådre avidly curious	e	-	doe	-	nah	-	dree
edonådyl at home in the ocean	e	-	doe	-	nah	-	dill
edonavayn hears the bard's harp	e	-	doe	-	nay	-	vay	-	in
edronådan hears elfin whispers	e	-	drone	-	nah	-	dane
edurea haven't been able to step thinking about all this	e	-	dur	-	ree	-	ah
edwyndel listens to the stars	eed	-	win	-	dell
edynadel love of all things mystical	e	-	den	-	nay	-	dell
edyndra fights for justice	e	-	den	-	drah
eereyn without knowing it	e	-	ear	-	ree	-	in
efadryn finally realized the truth	e	-	fay	-	drinn
efålån many talents	e	-	fah	-	lahn
efånåde longs for the sea	e	-	fah	-	nah	-	dee
efåndara sees the way	e	-	fahn	-	dare	-	rah
efändare visionary dreams	e	-	fan	-	dare	-	ree
efändåryl visions from the past	e	-	fan	-	dah	-	rill

The Book of Elf Names   75

efändarys manifesting harmony	e	-	fan	-	dare	-	riss
efåndryn things balance	e	-	fan	-	drinn		
efåndrys orange sunset	e	-	fahn	-	driss		
efarea smell of fresh air	e	-	fair	-	ree	-	ah
efareån enhances the wonder of the audience	e	-	fair	-	ree	-	ahn
efareys loves unicorns	e	-	fair	-ree	-	iss	
efarnåde totally carefree	e	-	fair	-	nah	-	dee
efelea always felt luck and blessed	e	-	feel	-	lee	-	ah
efoleara beneath the branches	e	-	foe	-	lee	-	air	-	rah
efondyryn sometimes I don't feel that way though	e	-	phone	-	der	-	ren
efyldrys power of the wilds	e	-	fill	-	driss		
efylidyn elf witch	e	-	fill	-	lie	-	den
efyndra calms the soul	e	-	fin	-	drah		
efyndre walks along the shore	e	-	fin	-	dree		
efyndros could walk in the countryside forever	e	-	fin	-	drowce		
efyndryl this has been going on since I was little	e	-	fin	-	drill		
efyndrys what the wind reveals	e	-	fin	-	driss		

efyngryn special gift	e	-	fin	-	grin		
efynle watching from afar	e	-	fin	-	lee		
efynzèl love child	e	-	fin	-	zell		
egyleyn withdrawals from the ungrateful	e	-	gill	-	lee	-	in
ekåda sorceress whispers	e	-	kah	-	dah		
èlådon at peace with life	L	-	lah	-	doan		
elådrea creates visions	e	-	lah	-	dree	-	ah
èlådryn delights in laughter	L	-	lah	-	drinn		
èlale figures it out	L	-	lay	-	lee		
elålea a little shy	e	-	lah	-	lee	-	ah
elålulyn very cool experience	e	-	lah	-	lou	-	lynn
èlalyn most fair	L	-	lay	-	lynn		
elanara crying for no apparent reason	e	-	lay	-	nair	-	rah
elånarsa star shimmers	e	-	lahn	-	nair	-	sah
elåndara moon reflected in smoke	e	-	lahn	-	dare	-	rah
elåndare touched by moonbeams	e		-lahn	-	dare		-ree
elarea heals the spirit	e	-	lay	-	ree	-	ah

The Book of Elf Names

èlavyn subtle shadows	L	-	lay	-	vin			
èlcador finds treasures	L	-	cah	-	door			
èldånada smiles amid the stars	L	-	dahn	-	nay	-	dah	
eldanar ove of all things elven	eel	-	dane	-	nair	l		
eldralyn I of magic	eel	-	dray	-	lynn			
èldrynia called to the trees	L	-	drinn	-	nigh	-	ah	
eldynala cares for the elfin	eel	-	den	-	nay	-	lah	
eldynår soulstar	eel	-	den	-	nar			
eleåla tranquility of the bush	e	-	lee	-	ah	-	lah	
èleålyn ways of the people	L	-	lee	-	ah	-	lynn	
èlefarea protects the people	L	-	lee	-	fair	-	ree	-	an
èlefyn inner thought	L	-	lee	-	fin			
èlelyn crystal wind	L	-	lee	-	lynn			
èleyn starfire	L	-	lee	-	in			
eliale one of the many names	e	-	lie	-	a	-	lee	
èlidåle devote my life to that	L	-	lie	-	dah	-	lee	
èlidar it makes no difference	L	-	lie	-	dare			

elidreyl enchanted awakening	e	-	lie	-	drec	-	L	
elidrys looks to the future not the past	e	-	lie	-	driss			
elinea feeling of hate for uncaring cruelty	e	-	lie	-	knee	-	ah	
eliylyn loves the silly	e	-	lie	-	L	-	lynn	
èlmere lightening like energy	L	-	mere	-	ree			
èlnaniyl sun shimmering on hair	L	-	nay	-	nigh	-	L	
elodån true joy	e	-	low	-	don			
elodea spells of protection	e	-	low	-	dee	-	ah	
elodryn deep in reflection	e	-	low	-	drinn			
elodyn as though they were my very own	e	-	low	-	den			
elofyn wild hair	e	-	low	-	fin			
elordyn when strange things are going to happen	e	-	lore	-	den			
eloreylys huge hug for them all	e	-	lore	-	ree	-	L	-	liss
eloreys elf healer	e	-	lore	-	ree	-	iss	
èlovyn inciter of merry making	L	-	-	low	-	vin		
èlowyn wind rider	L	-	low	-	win			
èlperi eager to help	L	-	peer	-	rye			

élratha assists in the healing	L	-	rayth	-	thah
elrathyn art in shadow	eel	-	ray	-	thin
elrondor defender of elfin	eel	-	roan	-	door
eluna contact with guides	e	-	lou	-	nah
eluniyl people keep telling me	e	-	lou	-	nigh	-	L
elurea never forgot it	e	-	lure	-	ree	-	ah
elvåna returns to the heart	eel	-	vah	-	nah
élvynda selfless beauty	L	-	vin	-	dah
elyndre in the back of my mind	e	-	lynn	-	dree
elyndryl has the gift	e	-	lynn	-	drill
elynél grew to be beautiful	e	-	lynn	-	nell
élynleyn family heritage	L	-	lynn	-	lee	-	in
elynsia song of the brook	e	-	lynn	-	sigh	-	ah
élynthea standing in the light of the moon	L	-	lynn	-	thee	-	ah
élyntra close to the faeries	L	-	lynn	-	trah
elyntrea softly whispers	e	-	lynn	-	tree	-	ah
élynuel weather powers	L	-	lynn	-	new	-	eel

emarådil	e	-	mare	-	rah	-	dial
extraordinary dancer							
emaråsyn	e	-	mare	-	rah	-	sin
sudden awakening							
emerådyn	e	-	mere	-	rah	-	den
makes a choice							
emeråfyn	e	-	mere	-	rah	-	fin
filled with light							
emerthyn	e		mere	-			thin
drawn to the archer							
emordrys	e	-	more	-			driss
that's all I know							
enadara	e	-	nay	-	dare	-	rah
sky blue hood							
enålea	e	-	nah	-	lee	-	ah
unseen forces							
enålyn	e	-	nah	-			lynn
on the true path							
enålyna	e	-	nah	-	lynn	-	nah
making things right							
enånådre	e	-	non	-	nah	-	dree
crowned by starlight							
enaradyn	e	-	nair	-	rah	-	den
sensual side of magic							
enardi	e	-	nair	-			dye
cool wind							
enare	e	-	nair	-			ree
setting forth							
enåri	e	-	nar	-			rye
sunbeams falling							
enarthyn	e	-	nair	-			thin
surrounds us, fills us and guides us							
enasa	e	-	nay	-			sah
speaks with trees							

The Book of Elf Names   81

enathea happy in Faerie	e	-	nay	-	thee	-	ah
enåvea it started from there	e	-	nah	-	vee	-	ah
endarån at first I laughed	in	-	dare	-		-	ron
endaråthe perfumed beauty	in	-	dare	-	rah	-	thee
endaråthyn walks with grace	in	-	dare	-	rah	-	thin
endare doing all I can	in	-	dare	-		-	ree
endareon singing to the moon	een	-	dare	-	ree	-	ohn
endareyn living in alternate realities	in	-	dare	-	ree	-	in
endarys recognizes the light	een	-	dare	-		-	riss
enderea living responsibly	een	-	deer	-	ree	-	ah
endereyl breath of the forest	in	-	deer	-	ree	-	L
enfaryn ecret haven	in	-	fair	-		ren	s
enida child of the fae	e	-	nigh	-		-	dah
enorålyn humble child of Faerie	e	-	nor	-	rah	-	lynn
ensålar poet-ian	in	-	sah	-		-	lair
eoryn calms skittish horses	e	-	or	-		-	ren
eponia an affinity with horses	e	-	poe	-	nigh	-	ah

eqarea eternal ways of nature	e	-	qway	-	ree	-	ah
ėradasa speaks to the heart	err	-	ray	-	day	-	sah
eradea shadow bearer	ear	-	ray	-	dee	-	ah
eradeyn sometimes I feel like flying	e	-	ray	-	dee	-	in
erador after years of questioning and denial	e	-	ray	-	door
erädre for as long as I can remember	e	-	rad	-	dree
eradu ever smiling	e	-	ray	-	due
ėrådyn as an eagle	err	-	rah	-	den	free
eradyna can see the spaces between	e	-	ray	-	den	-	nah
erålesa always remembered	e	-	rah	-	lee	-	sah
erånådyn knows the way	e	-	rah	-	nah	-	den
erånåfyn mist rolling in from the river	e	-	rah	-nah	-	fin
erånåthyn part of the stars	e	-	rah	-	nah	-	thin
eråndås sit back and analyse the situation	e	-	rahn	-	dahss
eråndoryn a different calling	e	-	rahn	-	door	-	ren
eråthyn psychic inklings	e	-	rah	-	thin
erau consoled by romance	e	-	ray	-	you

eråvyn	e	-	rah	-	vin		
untangles the web							
erealys	ear	-	ree	-	ale	-	liss
well mixed							
eriadyn	e	-	rye	-	a	-	den
instinctive grasp of magic							
eriavyn	e	-	rye	-	a	-	vyn
amicable presence							
erondas	e	-	roan	-	dace		
part of the tree							
erondèl	e	-	roan	-	dell		
seeks guidance and counsel							
erondil	e	-	roan	-	dial		
struggles for freedom							
erondryn	e	-	roan	-	drinn		
of the Other							
eronduryn	e	-	roan	-	dur	-	ren
plays in Faerie							
eronva	e	-	roan	-	vah		
glimpse of a vision							
erulyn	ear	-	rue	-	lynn		
wanted so badly to know							
ervandrys	ear	-	vane	-	driss		
lights the beacon							
eryleyn	e	-	rill	-	lee	-	in
swims like a fish							
erynda	e	-	ren	-	dah		
shift of light							
eryndåla	e	-	ren	-	dah	-	lah
longs for the simple life							
eryndåle	e	-	ren	-	dah	-	lee
longs to connect							
eryndatha	e	-	ren	-	day	-	thah
fantasy of flight							

erynde travels the realms	e	-	ren	-	dee		
eryndi calls to the wind	e	-	ren	-	dye		
eryndothsa wind in the trees	e	-	ren	-	dough-th	-	sah
erynsa flashes of another life	e	-	ren	-	sah		
erynsel allays suffering	e	-	ren	-	seal		
erynthe loving for love's sake	e	-	ren	-	thee		
eryseyn ageless soul	e	-	riss	-	see	-	in
esåndara it would be nice to share tea	e	sahn	-	dare	-	rah	
esåndre today I am much the same	e	-	sahn	-	dree		
esarålyn just waiting to burst out	e	-	say	-	rah	-	lynn
esarathel serves the cause	e	-	say	-	ray	-	theal
esareyl therefore I will embrace it with all my being	e	-	say	-	ree	-	L
esaryn born with the sight	e	-	say	-	ren		
esråsyn dragon flying	eess	-	rah	-	sin	fire	
etarea that's how you fix it	e	-	tayr	-	ree	-	ah
etereyl very big deal	e	-	tear (as in cry)	-	ree	-	L
etereyn I don't live like other people	e	-	tear	-	ree	-	in

etereys behind the scenes	e	-	tear	-	ree	-	iss
etherea soul dreamer	e	-	thee	-	ree	-	ah
ethereylys passing on the knowledge	e	-	thee	-	ree	- L -	liss
ethereyn	e	-	thee	-	ree	-	in

smelled the scent of many things that were not visible to mortal eye

etyryn so good	e	-	ter	-	in	smells
euråde very gifted healer	e	-	you	-	rah	- dee
eurdyn feels the loss	e	-	your	-	den	
eusa be they god, fae or spirits	e	-	you	-	sah	
evådar uncanny ability to find the way	e	-	vah	-	dare	
evålådyn feels the pain of the trees	e	-	vahl	-	lah - den	
evålea would like to know more	e	-	vah	-	lee - ah	
evåles blessed by the water	e	-	vah	-	lease	
evåleyn see how to	e	-	vah	-	lee - in	
evånågryn stone fairy alive	e	-	vah	-	nah - grin	
evånayl friendly shoulder	e	-	vah	-	nay - L	
evåndare something I'm forgetting	e	-	vahn	-	dare - ree	
evåndåre tangible reality of Elfin	e	-	vahn	-	dar - ree	

The Silver Elves

evåndåryn dreaming the future	e	-	vahn	-	dah	-	ren
evändåryn awakens in Faery	e	-	van	-	dah	-	ren
evåndåthel believing one's s'elf	e	-	vahn	-	dah	-	theal
evåndor in search of others like me	e	-	vahn	-	door
evåndra can read a person from the first meeting	e	-	vahn	-	drah
evåndråfyn star knower	e	-	vahn	-	drah	-	fin
evåndre scholar's life	e	-	vahn	-	dree
evåndrea letting things happen	e	-	vahn	-	dree	-	ah
evåndreyl allowing it to happen naturally	e	-	vahn	-	dree	-	L
evändreyl nobody else around me does	e	-	van	-	dree	-	L
evåndreyn stroking bees	e	-	vahn	-	dree	-	in
evånle waits on the edge	e	-	vahn	-	lee
evånsån sees the true world	e	-	vahn	-	sahn
evåntha ever loyal	e	-	vahn	-	thah
evånthel moving beyond	e	-	vahn	-	theal
evarådre knows but won't tell	e	-	vair	-	rah	-	dree
evarådyn dark wood	e	-	vair	-	rah	-	den

evaråfe magic comes naturally	e	-	vair	-	rah	-	fee
evarålyn rises in battle	e	-	vair	-	rah	-	lynn
evaråthyn refines one's powers	e	-	vair	-	rah	-	thin
evarethyn transcends gender	e	-	vair	-	ree	-	thin
evareyl softly singing	e	-	vair	-	ree	-	L
evarita hair so soft	e	-	vair	-	rye	-	tah
evarsa ever searching	e	-	vair	-	sah		
evarshåryn feels the rain coming	e	-	vair	-	shah	-	ren
evaryn moon raven	e	-	vair	-	ren		
evarynsa pixie lover	e	-	vair	-	ren	-	sah
evarysyn faerie dreamer	e	-	vair	-	riss	-	sin
evasa moon dreamer	e	-	vay	-	sah		
evåsare healing and protective powers	e	-	vah	-	say	-	ree
evedre charms the world	e	-	vee	-	dree		
everålyn stares in amazement	e	-	veer	-	rah	-	lynn
everåsyn feel as though I belong with them	e	-	vee	-	rah	-	sin
evereyn writes of nature	e	-	veer	-	ree	-	in

eviadryn	e	-	vie	-	a	-	drinn

it was like the whole world opened up completely

| eviåfyn | e | - | vie | - | ah | - | fin |

flowing magic

| eviale | e | - | vie | - | ale | - | lee |

foxgloves on my fingers

| evidor | e | - | vie | - | door |

so much to learn

| evidra | e | - | vie | - | drah |

dressed in black

| eviu | e | - | vie | - | you |

desire for purity

| evodora | e | - | voe | - | door | - | rah |

of long ago

| evondrys | e | - | vaughn | - | driss |

voices in the wind

| evondure | e | - | vaughn | - | dur | - | ree |

power of love

| evonleyl | e | - | vaughn | - | lee | – | L |

born in Elflight

| evorådyn | e | - | vour | - | rah | - | den |

absolute obsession

| evorårasyn | e | - | vour | - | rah | - | ray | - | sin |

in the corner of your eye

| evoråre | e | - | vour | - | rah | - | ree |

bright one

| evorasyl | e | - | vour | -ray | - | sill |

protects the village

| evorniyn | e | - | vour | - | nigh | - | in |

from the mist emerging

| evoroshån | e | - | vour | - | row | - | shahn |

unnatural grace

| evynålys | e | - | vin | - | nah | - | liss |

looking for certainty

The Book of Elf Names   89

| évyndålas | ev | - | vin | - | dah | - | lace |
| sways to the song of Faerie | | | | | | | |

| evyndel | e | - | vin | - | deal |
| beginning to see | | | | | |

| evyndil | e | - | vin | - | dial |
| many powers | | | | | |

| evyndre | e | - | vin | - | dree |
| nothing in between | | | | | |

| evyndreyl | e | - | vin | - | dree | - | L |
| new worlds are opening to me daily | | | | | | | |

| evyndrys | e | - | vin | - | driss |
| has a way with the spiders | | | | | |

| evynsol | e | - | vin | - | soul |
| shimmering twilight | | | | | |

| evynsyl | e | - | - | vin | - | sill |
| ranger pure | | | | | | |

| evynthel | e | - | vin | - | theal |
| completely oblivious | | | | | |

| ewynda | e | - | win | - | dah |
| flash of daggers | | | | | |

| ewyndrasa | e | - | win | - | dray | - | sah |
| always up one tree or another | | | | | | | |

| ewyndrea | e | - | win | - | dree | - | ah |
| flys in dreamland | | | | | | | |

| eyånda | e | - | yahn | - | dah |
| faery touched | | | | | |

| eyåndåle | e | - | yahn | - | dah | - | lee |
| floating above my head | | | | | | | |

| eynåla | e | - | N | - | nah | - | lah |
| thinks it over | | | | | | | |

| eyndåle | e | - | N | - | dah | - | lee |
| infatuate with the stars | | | | | | | |

F

Elven Name and Meaning

Pronunciation

faådedryn good instincts	fay - ah - dee - drinn		
faåfyn rich with fantasy	fay - ah - fin		
faarådyn lady sea urchin	fay - air - rah - den		
fabaryn soundless calling	fay - bare - ren		
fåboreyn seems to have been preparation	fah - boar - ree - in it		
fådåndor unusual agility	fah - don - door		
fådåntor mighty bear	fah - don - tour		
fadorys recommended places to learn	fay - door - riss		
faere stars running in my veins	fay - ear - ree		
faerydyn to once again see dragon's fly	fay - ear - rid - den		
faeryn want to understand	fay - ear - ren		
fafara faerie fond	fay - fair - rah		
falådara sensor	fay - lah - dare - rah		
fåladra the path which I walk led me here	fah - lay - drah		

fålålasa new sound	fah	-	lah	-	lay	-	sah
fålandar fire dancer	fah	-			lane	-	dare
faleåla interested in all forms of wisdom	fay	-	lee	-	ah	-	lah
fåleålyn wind spinner	fah	-	lee	-	ah	-	lynn
fåleja seeking utopia	fah	-			lee	-	jah
fålela gone to the sacred well	fah	-			lee	-	lah
faleon petal dance	fay	-			lee	-	ohn
faliwyndra shimmering feather wings	fay	-	lie	-	win	-	drah
fålodyn senses the change	fah	-			low	-	den
fålonis on the moss	fah	-			low	-	niss
falsåjor swooping down	fay	-			sah	-	jour
fälyndarys still looking for answers	fah	-	lynn	-	dare	-	riss
fålynde magic in the air	fah	-	lynn	-			dee
fålyndor swift and graceful	fah	-	lynn	-			door
fålyndre graceful wanderer	fah	-	lynn	-			dree
falynthae her heart's blood	fay	-	lynn	-			thay
fåmara fierce love	fah	-	mare	-			rah

92   The Silver Elves

fåmaråvyn night travels	fah	-	mare	-	rah	-	vin
fåmareyn until the wee hours of the morning	fah	-	mare	-	ree	-	in
fåmareys enchanting visage	fah	-	mare	-	ree	-	iss
fåmarys returns in company	fah		-mare		-		riss
fanaålyn face aglow	fay	-	nay	-	ah	-	lynn
fånålea started looking up	fah	-	nah	-	lee	-	ah
fånarfeyl message was given me	fah	-	nair	-	fee	-	L
fånarfyn memories arising	fah	-	nair	-	fin
fånarthyn return to sanctity	fah	-	nair	-	thin
fåndålala trys to remember	fahn	-	dah	-	lay	-	lah
fåndålåsa of ancient ways	fahn	-	dah	-	lah	-	sah
fändälea keeper of the key	fahn	-	dowl	-	lee	-	ah
fåndara sounds of color	fahn	-	dare	-	rah

fåndaråfyn fahn - dare - rah - fin
this is the only thing that ever makes sense to me

fåndarea fahn - dare - ree - ah
where everything shines brighter

fändareyl fahn - dare - ree - L
feeling the universal force

fändareyn fahn - dare - ree - in
shining white robes

The Book of Elf Names   93

fåndarfyn natural healing	fahn	-	dare	-	fin
fåndåryl full of spunk	fahn	-	dar	-	rill
fåndoryn strong tie to the old stories	fahn	-	door	-	ren
fanjåla one with the wilderness	fane	-	jah	-	lah
fanjylosåvån born among the trees of old	fane	- jill -	low	- sah	vahn
fånoryn provides rest	fah	-	nor	-	ren
fåntåfa bright beauty	fahn	-	tah	-	fah
fäntåsa dreams of becoming	fahn	-	tah	-	sah
farådånsa embraces Elfin	fair	- rah -	dahn	-	sah
faradarėl truth was hidden	fair	- ray -	dare	-	rell
faråde shy fox	fair	-	rah	-	dee
farådre seeks asylum	fair	-	rah	-	dree
farådreyl heals the psyche	fair	- rah -	dree	-	L
farådyn weaving the patterns	fair	-	rah	-	den
faråfyn unfurls the petals of the heart	fair	-	rah	-	fin
farålisa comes with many	fair	- rah -	lie	-	sah
faråshån size doesn't matter	fair	-	rah	-	shahn

94   The Silver Elves

faråtina eye on the spotlight	fair	-	rah	-	tie	-	nah
faråvåna wishes to reality	fair	-	rah	-	vahn	-	nah
farchåryl awakened by the lore	fair	-			char	-	rill
fardarel flower friend	fair	-			dare	-	real
fardaryn hugs the cushion	fair	-			dare	-	ren
fardrynyl respects the ancients	fair	-			drinn	-	nil
fardynvarėl eyes all alight	fair	-	den	-	vair	-	rell
fareasa in magic dreaming	fair	-	ree	-	a	-	sah
farevyn moves like the wind	fair	-			ree	-	vin
fariåde my door is always open to you	fair	-	rye	-	ah	-	dee
fariådyn settling in	fair	-	rye	-	ah	-	den
faridoryn yawns in the trees	fair	-	rye	-	door	-	ren
farlynde joy of life	fair	-			lynn	-	dee
farlyndre as the stars glisten	fair	-			lynn	-	dree
farlynsa eyes like the sea	fair	-			lynn	-	sah
farnåthyn common trait among elves	fair	-			nah	-	thin
farynådån preceiving glimmer	fair	-	ren	-	nah	-	don

The Book of Elf Names

farynar unconscious motivations	fair	-	ren	-			nair
farynåthel calm center	fair	-	ren	-	nah	-	theal
faryndale awesome power of the earth	fair	-	ren	-	day	-	lee
faryndara taking care of others	fair	-	ren	-	day	-	rah
faryndaryn eternal quest	fair	-	ren	-	dare	-	ren
farynder lord who flies	fair	-	ren			-	deer
faryndil pixie's child	fair	-	ren			-	dial
faryndoleås leaf bearer	fair	-	ren	-	doe	- lee -	ahss
faryndor stands alone	fair	-	ren			-	door
faryndorys makes elixir	fair	-	ren	-	door	-	riss
faryndre seeing ones'elf in others	fair	-	ren			-	dree
faryndreyn things unseen	fair	-	ren	-	dree	-	in
farynnådel true reflection	fair	-	ren	-	nah	-	deal
farynordår keen as an owl	fair	-	ren	-	nor	-	dar
farynrån ready for more	fair	-	ren			-	ron
farynre star wind	fair	-	ren	-	ree		rain
farynsea	fair	-	ren	-	see	-	ah

it is easier to help others when they know not who helped them

faryntha	fair	-	ren	-	thah		
faery seerer							
fårynthel	fah	-	ren	-	theal		
dreams of the realms							
farynthna	fair	-	renth	-	nah		
from the blessed isle							
fåsaråfyn	fah	-	sair	-	rah	-	fin
flows with grace							
fåsaråvor	fah	-	sair	-	rah	-	vour
powers passed down							
fåsare	fah	-	sair	-	ree		
hope that I may rejoin them soon							
fåsareyl	fah	-	sair	-	ree	-	L
hard to see							
fasaryn	fay	-	sair	-	ren		
of faerie blood							
fashåryn	fay	-	shah	-	ren		
faerie fashion							
fatar	fay	-	tayr				
wild dancer							
favarån	fay	-	vair	-	ron		
valient warrior friend							
favåren	fay	-	vah	-	reen		
kin of She							
favaryn	fay	-	vair	-	ren		
realm of infinite possibilities							
faynresa	fay	-	in	-	ree	-	sah
returned from the past							
fazoryn	fay	-	zoar	-	ren		
awakens the realm							
feådarys	fee	-	ah	-	dare	-	riss
always finds a way out							
feådyryn	fee	-	ah	-	der	-	ren
coming to know							

The Book of Elf Names   97

feålåfyn called to serve	fee	-	ah	-	lah	-	fin
feålea premonitions of an elven world	fee	-	ah	-	lee	-	ah
feåmålyl awaits the passage	fee - ah - mah - lil (as in lily)
feånåle wooded water's edge	fe	-	ah	-	anh	-	lee
feånåthel comfort of being alone	fee	-	ah	-	nah	-	theal
feånda elven poise	fee	-	ahn	-	dah
feåndare poise of an enchantress	fee	-	ahn	-	dare	-	ree
feåndora calming hands	fee	-	ahn	-	door	-	rah
feåndre what do they know	fee	-	ahn	-	dree
feåndreyl elves came to play	fee	-	ahn	-	dree	-	L
feåndure healing light	fee	-	ahn	-	dur	-	ree
feåndyryn blackbird's song	fee	-	ahn	-	der	-	ren
feanoryn touching Faerie	fee	-	a	-	nor	-	ren
fearade drawn to elves	fee	-	air	-	ray	-	dee
fearådyn shot with light	fee	-	air	-	rah	-	den
feareyn have always been a thinker	fee	-	air	-	ree	-	in
fearsyn elf mage	fee	-	air	-	sin

fearylyn air of sacred space	fee	-	air	-	rill	-	lynn
fearyn hidden in trees	fee	-		air	-	ren	
feåsåna winter shadow	fee	-	ah	-	sah	-	nah
fedåndys let love slip away	fee	-		don	-	diss	
fedaryn flowers in the hair	fee	-		dare	-	ren	
fedåwyn spirit surrounds us all	fed	-		dah	-	win	
fefåndre strong of heart	fee	-		fahn	-	dree	
fèladreyn loves being elven	fell	-	lay	-	dree	-	in
feladriyn explores the faiths	feel	-	lay	-	dry	-	in
felafyn of all things	feel	-		lay	-	fin	
felana star on a cloud	feel	-		lay	-	nah	
fèlåndys overcomes the fear	fell	-		lahn	-	diss	
felånsa star shines through clouds	feel	-		lahn	-	sah	
felånsar sleeps in the trees	feel	-		lahn	-	sair	
felånsara longs for the trees	fee	-	lahn	-	sair	-	rah
felasynsa gentle healing	fee	-	lay	-	sin	-	sah
felåvyn vibrant life spirit	fee	-		lah	-	vin	

felearyn doesn't quite know what to do with it	fee	-	lee	-	air	-	ren
felefa driven by the moon	fee	-	lee	-	fah		
felefyn now I know what I truly am	fee	-	lee	-	fin		
felefyndra I know what I am	fee	-	lee	-	fin	-	drah
felelondås leaf based motif	fee	-	lee	-	lone	-	dayce
felina wings emerging	fee	-	lie	-	nah		
felonari creates the spirit	fee	-	low	-	nay	-	rye
felynaryn senses their motives	fell	-	lynn	-	nair	-	ren
felynarys deeply attached	fee	-	lynn	-	nair	-	riss
felyndaryn have searched for the truth ever since	fee	-	lynn	-	dare	-	ren
felyndre spreading my magic wherever I go	fee	-	lynn	-	dree		
felynsa searches for the hidden keys	fee	-	lynn	-	sah		
felynsar swimming beneath the stars	fee	-	lynn	-	sair		
felyntas new turning point in life	fee	-	lynn	-	tayce		
femereyn music running through the veins	fee	-	mere	--	ree	-	in
femeryn gets to the root of things	fee	-	mere	-	in		
femoryn lives within	fee	-	more	-	ren		

fenådolyn faery speaker	fee	-	nah	-	doe	-	lynn
fenåmaryn I am what I always believed in	fee	-	nah	-	mare	-	ren
feonoryn not as it had been	fee	-	oh	-	nor	-	ren
feordrys helps the poor	fee	-	or	-	driss		
feore makes it happen	fee	-	or	-	ree		
feorea exotically interesting	fee	-	or	-	ree	-	ah
feoreyl making others happy	fee	-	or	-	ree	-	L
feoreyn honored by their allegiance	fee	-	or	-	ree	-	in
feorsynèl kin of the sidhe	fee	-	or	-	sin	-	nell
feoryn enjoys doing so	fee	-	or	-	ren		
feoryndra fierce in defense	fee	-	or	-	ren	-	drah
feorynsa inner knowing	fee	-	or	-	ren	-	sah
ferynås blue lightening	fee	-	ren	-	nahss		
ferynda it could be	fee	-	ren	-	dah		
feylålyn born within	fee	-	L	-	lah	-	lynn
feyndare collector of memories	fee	-	in	-	dare	-	ree
feyndor moves with nonchalance	fee	-	in	-	door		

feyndre try as hard as I possibly can	fee	-	in	-	dree		
feyndryn lunar powered	fee	-	in	-	drinn		
feynthys snow wolf	fee	-	in	-	this		
fiadadryn so much it hurt	fie	-	a	-	day	-	drinn
fiålea path of discovery	fie	-	ah	-	lee	-	ah
fiålearna wild and free	fie	-	ah	-	lee	- air -	nah
fiålela still do to this day	fie	-	ah	-	lee	-	lah
fiålelyn healing hands	fie	-	ah	-	lee	-	lynn
fialfyn winter's love	fie	-	ale	-	fin		
fiålyndyn wanting to wander forever	fie	-	ah	-	lynn	-	den
fialyryn content to dream	fie	-	ale	-	ler	-	ren
fiåndrys circling back	fie	-	ahn	-	driss		
fiandyryn mind mover	fie	-	ane	-	der	-	ren
fiarfyn loves the flowers	fie	-	air	-	fin		
fiarys faery friend	fie	-	air	-	riss		
fiarzyn seeks to understand	fie	-	air	-	zen		
fidyndra manifesting magic	fie	-	den	-	drah		

102

fielolyn	fie	-	eel	-	low	-	lynn
among the branches							
fiėlowyn	fie	-	l	-	low	-	win
over a long period of time							
fierfyn	fie	-	ear	-			fin
looks from the golden tree							
fileådyn	fie	-	lee	-	ah	-	den
passion to be involved							
fileålyn	fie	-	lee	-	ah	-	lynn
opens a whole new world							
filosyn	fie	-			low	-	sin
keeper of the sacred springs							
filyndanor	fie	-	lynn	-	day	-	nor
always up to something							
fimere	fie	-			mere	-	ree
normal until it all changed							
fimereyn	fie	-	mere	-	ree	-	in
infusing love							
fimeryn	fie	-			mere	-	ren
then I just knew							
finara	fie	-			nay	-	rah
almost from the beginning							
finareyn	fie	-	nair	-	ree	-	in
it makes you wonder							
fineryn	fie	-			near	-	ren
waited all this time							
fiolea	fie	-	oh	-	lee	-	ah
flying leopard							
firrana	fire	-			rain	-	nah
guards the faeries							
fivarvån	fie	-			vair	-	vah
definitely sure							
fiynduryn	fie	-	in	-	dur	-	ren
sound of raindrops falling on leaves							

The Book of Elf Names   103

fodåla feast creator	foe	-	dah	-	lah	
fodilys moon dusted	foe	-	dye	-	liss	
fofalyn talking with the dark	foe	-	fay	-	lynn	
folånåle true blessing	foe	-	lahn	-	nah	-	lee
folaryn deep inside	foe	-	lair	-	ren	
folasiel brings the news	foe	-	lay	-	sigh	-	eel
folavsa touched by the owls	foe	-	lave	-	sah	
folida wandering in the memories of the past	foe	-	lie	-	dah	
folosar swift sword	foe	-	low	-	sair	
fomure I can go on and on about this	foe	-	muir	-	ree	
fondare wish to study my gift	phone	-	dare	-	ree	
fondarėl gets things done now	phone	-	dare	-	rell	
fondarys deep dark woods	phone	-	dare	-	riss	
fondurėl has not aged nor changed at all	phone	-	dur	-	rell	
fonineyl blends in the frost	foe	-	nigh	-	knee	-	L
fonnåvyn remembers the kindred	phone	-	nah	-	vin	
fordårėl drifts in the mist	for	-	dah	-	rell	

forderyn	for	-	deer	-		ren
guides the journeys						
fordryn	for	-				drinn
can be counted on						
foreda	for	-	ree	-		dah
the stars still contain the secrets I must discover						
forèmaryl	for	-	rem	-	mare	- rill
rowan heart						
forjea	for	-	gee	-		ah
unmoved						
formereyn	for	-	mere	-	ree	- in
thinking slightly different than before						
forondyryn	for	-	roan	-	der	- ren
sweet river's flow						
forsarea	for	-	sair	-	ree	- ah
coming home						
forynda	for	-		ren		- dah
it felt like I'd come home						
foryndre	for	-		ren	-	dree led
back to nature						
foryndyn	for	-		ren		- den
helps others to be more						
foryndys	for	-		ren		- diss
moontime						
forynia	for	-		ren	-	nigh - ah
breathing water						
forynsa	for	-		ren		- sah
ages slowly						
foyndål	foe	-		in		- dahl
always in deep thought						
fralådyn	fray	-		lah		- den
proud among the flowers						
franålyn	fray	-		nah		- lynn
I find comfort in things others don't seem to understand						

The Book of Elf Names
105

fratasa hidden shining	fray	-	tay	-	sah		
fråtyndar listens to the earth	frah	-	tin	-	dare		
fredaryn awakening light	free	-	dare	-	ren		
frenåfa silent sounds	free	-	nah	-	fah		
froavor of distant worlds	fro	-	a	-	vour		
fudåndre that tingle in my spine	few	-	don	-	dree		
fůladryn done those activities lots in my life	full	-	lay	-	drinn		
fumereyn magic and mystery have always surrounded me	few	-	mere	-	ree	-	in
furena fireburning	few	-	ree	-	nah		
fureyna shapes the music	few	-	ree	-	in	-	nah
furyndrys as it wouldn't go away	few	-	ren	-	driss		
furynėl represents every thing that I am	few	-	ren	-	nell		
furynmae from a time of old when magic ruled the land	few	-	ren	-	may		
furynsa studies with water fae	few	-	ren	-	sah		
fusolyn stirring fun	few	-	so	-	lynn		
fyereyn mermaid dreams	fee	-	ear	-	ree	-	in
fylådea the journey is just as, if not more important than, the destination	fill	-lah	-	dee	-	ah	

fylådre	fill	-	lah	-	dree	
comes with the north wind						
fyladreyn	fill	-lay	-	dree	-	in
everyday I try to do that						
fyladrys	fill	-lay	-		driss	
longs for more						
fylalensa	fill	-	lay	-	lean	- sah
ever soaring						
fylånådån	fill	-	lah	-	nah	- don
learning more and more each day						
fylånådyl	fill	-lah	-	nah	-	dill
horse running by						
fylåndryn	fill	-	lahn	-	drinn	
mysterious music						
fylea	fill	-	lee	-	ah	
heritage of healing						
fyleånda	fill	-	lee	-	ahn	- dah
friend to the elves						
fylearvyn	fill	-	lee	-	air	- vin
seeker of fun						
fylena	fill	-	lee	-	nah	
pursuing fun						
fylodon	fill	-	low	-	doan	
ever hardy						
fylosaryn	fill	-	low	-	sair	- ren
earth friendly						
fylosi	fill	-	low	-	sigh	
always fun						
fylyndar	fill	-	lynn	-	dare	
don't know what's happening to me						
fylyndea	fill	-	lynn	-	dee	- ah
faery key						
fylyndor	fill	-	lynn	-	door	
shines on stage						

The Book of Elf Names   107

fylyndrea	fill	-	lynn	-	dree	-	ah
left here by mistake							
fylyndreyl	fill	-	lynn	-	dree	-	L
love it and always have							
fylyntheyl	fill	-	lynn	-	thee	-	L
makes perfect sense							
fylynthor f	ill	-	lynn	-	thor		
enriched by the presence of the fae							
fynarfa	fin	-	nair	-	fah		
fragile feather							
fynarfyn	fin	-	nair	-	fin		
finding the way home							
fynaryn	fin-	nair	-	ren			
touches the fae							
fyndålea	fin	-	dah	-	lee	-	ah
even at night							
fyndalfyna	fin	-	dale	-	fin	-	nah
creator of the superb							
fyndalor	fin	-	dale	-	lore		
spell caster							
fyndålyn	fin	-	dah	-	lynn		
little pranks							
fyndara	fin	-	dare	-	rah		
strong link with the nature spirits							
fyndaråfyn	fin	-	dare	-	rah	-	fin
gently glides							
fyndaråvyn	fin	-	dare	-	rah	-	vin
enjoying the ride							
fyndarea	fin	-	dare	-	ree	-	ah
awakens to the magic							
fyndareyl	fin	-	dare	-	ree	-	L
soars above the land							
fyndari	fin	-	dare	-	rye		
feels the land							

fyndarys freedom, love and honor	fin	-	dare	-	riss	
fyndera raven walker	fin	-	dear	-	rah	
fyndorea delicate flower	fin	-	door	-	ree	- ah
fyndradel sky of the sea	fin	-	dray	-	deal	
fyndragor rage for justice	fin	-	dray	-	gore	
fyndråmåra soothes the dragons	fin	- drah	- mah	-	rah	
fyndrayl keeper of the silver leaf	fin	-	dray	-	L	
fyndros spell shifter	fin	-			dross	
fyneryn turns and smiles	fin	-	near	-	ren	

fyngolyd   fin   -   go   -   lid
quick nap (someone who can revive thems'elve with short naps)

fyngolyn a lot like me	fin	-	go	-	lynn
fynladyn excited by the truth	fin	-	lay	-	den
fynmara eyes of the soul	fin	-	mare	-	rah
fynradel faery lover	fin	-	ray	-	dell
fynrasa reaches to the sun	fin	-	ray	-	sah
fynreådyn sea weed	fin	- ree	- ah	-	den
fynriyl fae sight	fin	-	rye	-	L

fynuveyl	fin	-	new	-	vee	-	L
converses with the wild things							
fynvarys	fin	-	vair	-	riss		
nature being							
fynvolyn	fin	-	voe	-	lynn		
out for a good time							
fynvolys	fin	-	voe	-	liss		
flowing clouds							
fynwaryn	fin	-	ware	-	ren		
coming of age							
fynwe	fin	-	wee				
brings joy into life							
fyrynda	fur	-	ren	-	dah		
just coming into it							

ELVES OFTEN ACCUMULATE NAMES THE WAY
SOLDIERS COLLECT MEDALS, ATHLETES
COLLECT TROPHIES, AND BOY SCOUTS
COLLECT BADGES. IN THE END, WE OFTEN
HAVE MORE NAMES THAN THE OLD SPANISH
DONS AND MORE TITLES THAN THE GREAT
EMPORERS. STILL AMOUNG OURS'ELVES, WE
MOST OFTEN GO BY A SIMPLE NICKNAME,
SOMETIMES JUST A SINGLE LETTER AND THE
ONLY TITLES THAT REALLY MATTER TO US
ARE THOSE OF ENDEARMENT.

G

Elven Name and Meaning   **Pronunciation**

Elven Name and Meaning	Pronunciation					
gaåvyn here to help and heal	gay	-	ah	-	vin	
gådånda ancient ways	gah	-	don	-	dah	
gådåndor instant awakening	gah	-	dahn	-	door	
gadåntha golden arrow	gay	-	dahn	-	thah	
gadyndara knows how others are feeling	gay	-	den	-	dare	- rah
gafandyl he calling becomes clearer	gay	-	fane	-	dill	t
gåfarshyn has a feeling about it	gah	-	fair	-	shin	
gafryndor scales of gold	gah	-	frin	-	door	
gålåånådor creating the new	gah	- lah	- ahn	- nah	- door	
gålåare into magic	gah	-	lah	- air	- ree	
galåddrea unique, shiny people	gay	-	lahd	- dree	- ah	
gåladoryn new ballad	gah	-	lay	- door	- ren	
gälådoryn watches the sea	gal	- lah	- door	- ren		
galådreyn mesmerizing eyes	gay	-	lah	- dree	- in	

gåladrys	gah	-	lay	-			driss
out in the wild							
gålålea	gah	-	lah	-	lee	-	ah
sweet serenity							
gålåledra	gah	-	lah	-	lee	-	drah
ponders the meaning of life							
galålyndåshyn	gay	-	lah	-	lynn	-	dah shin
thoughts of hope and magic							
gålålyndor	gah	-	lah	-	lynn	-	door
renews the land							
gålålyndyl	gah	-	lah	-	lynn	-	dill
sparkles like a jewel							
gälåndyn	gal	-	lahn	-			den
patrols the borders							
gålardryn	gah	-	lair	-			drinn
spark of light							
galareasa	gale	-	lair	-	ree	-	a - sah
born of starlight							
galårisa	gale	-	lah	-	rye	-	sah
joyous spirit							
gåleålyn	gah	-	lee	-	ah	-	lynn
could charm the gods themselves							
galeån	gale	-	lee	-			ahn
walks in dreams							
galeåndra	gale	-	lee	-	ahn	-	drah
awakens in dreams							
galedyn	gale	-	lee	-			den
love conquers all							
galidyn	gale	-	lie	-			den
my difference is merely kinship to others							
galona	gale	-	low	-			nah
jewel eye							
galordyn	gale	-	lore	-			den
none other							

galosyndur	gale	-	low	-	sin	-	dur
light shimmering on the sea							
gålosynra	gah	-	low	sin		-	rah
long lost cousin							
galuryn	gale	-		lure		-	ren
deep yearning to know more							
galydeyn	gale	-	lyd	-	dee	-	in
once again							
gälyndara	gal	-	lynn	-	dare	-	rah
powerful chi							
gålynde	gah	-		lynn		-	dee
finally satisfied							
gålyndėl	gah	-		lynn		-	dell
comes from inside me							
gålyndra	gah	-		lynn		-	drah
found much comfort in the folk there							
gälyndre	gal	-		lynn		-	dree
fantastical, whimsical and elvish							
gålyndrea	gah	-	lynn	-	dree	-	ah
deepest mystery							
gålyndys	gah	-		lynn		-	driss
beneath the moon							
gåndäleyl	gahn	-	dawl	-	lee	-	L
free hearted spirit							
gåndålynsėl	gahn	-	dah	-	lynn	-	sell
likes to imagine							
gåndareyn	gahn	-	dare	-	ree	-	in
sees deeper							
gåndariyn	gahn	-	dare	-	rye	-	in
always turn to it for comfort							
gåndarys	gahn	-		dare		-	riss
in other words							
gåndoryn	gahn	-		door		-	ren
peers from a crag							

gåndreyl all my life	gahn	-	dree	-	L		
gånfara breaking free	gahn	-	fair	-	rah		
garathor child of the forest	gayr	-	ray	-	thor		
garåthoreyn plays amid the branches	gayr	-	rah	-	thor	- ree	- in
garåthoryn old child of the forest	gayr	-	rah	-	thor	- in	
garodor sniffs the air	gayr	-	row	-	door		
garyndål open to the currents	gayr	-	ren	-	dahl		
garyndar protects the gate	gayr	-	ren	-	dare		
gåryndari protects the people	gah	-	ren	-	dare	- rye	
gåryndaryn gate keeper	gah	-	ren	-	dare	- ren	
garyndor among the oaks	gayr	-	ren	-	door		
garyndrån fire cheeks	gayr	-	ren	-	drahn		
garyndros heals the dark	gayr	-	ren	-	drowce		
gåthåndryl comes again	gah	-	thahn	-	drill		
gåthsaryn responds to the call	goth	-	sair	-	ren		
gåvändrys described me perfectly	gah	-	van	-	driss		
gåvyndava moves the rain	gah	-	vin	-	day	- vah	

114

gåvyndryn	gah	-	vin	-	drinn
elf wish					

geåjaryn	gee	(like	karate	gi)	-	ah	jair	-	ren
helps where needed									

geålea   gee   -   ah   -   lee   -   ah
now everything seems to make sense

gealyryn   gee   -   ale   -   ler   -   ren
touched by immortals

geåndånor   gee   -   ahn   -   don   -   nor
comes from the east

gearfålyn   gee   -   air   -   fah   –   lynn
out of place in the material world

gearlyn   gee   -   air   -   lynn
beauty emerging

gedåndre   gee   -   don   -   dree
this is what I've been waiting for

geladrys   gee   -   lay   -   driss
my whole life lead up to this moment

gelana   gee   -   lay   -   nah   l
ike being that way

gėlasån   gell   -   lay   -   sahn
saw my past

gelasyn   gee   -   lay   -   sin
of great pride and value

gelela   gee   -   lee   -   lah
knowledge of the heart and soul

gėlena   gell   -   lee   -   nah
always told me we were special

gelordyn   gee   -   lore   -   den
working wonders

gelyndånar   gee   -   lynn   -   dah   -   nair
long known

gėlyndre   gell   -   lynn   -   dree
walks softly

The Book of Elf Names   115

genulyn felt a strange calling	gee	-	new	-	lynn
geondaryn begins the quest	gee	- ohn -	dare	-	ren
geryndålthor protects their own	gee	- ren -	dahl	-	thor
gèsshan holding caution	geese		-		shane
getylana soft furry brown one	gee	- till -	lay	-	nah
giålathån reflection of the dragon	guy	- ah -	lay	-	thahn
gialåvyn twinkle toes	guy	- a -	lah	-	vin
gialyndyn magic steps	guy	- ale -	lynn	-	den
giåndorèl the wisest of them	guy	- ahn -	door	-	rell
gifålon twisting in the air	guy	-	fah	-	lone
giladreyn gasp of realization	guy	- lay -	dree	-	in
gilara favorable sign	guy	-	lair	-	rah
gilarathyn sign of their favor	guy	- lair -	ray	-	thin
gilasyn had an epiphany	guy	-	lay	-	sin
gilea soul flight	guy	-	lee	-	ah
gileådyn awaits a sign from the universe	guy	- lee -	ah	-	den
gileålyn the exotic nature of it is absolutely amazing	guy	- lee -	ah	-	lynn

The Silver Elves

gilelyn	guy	-	lee	-	lynn	
part of another way of life						
gilleådyl	guile	-	lee	-	ah	- dill
loves to explore						
gilodon	guy	-	low	-	doan	
searches for the earth's true secrets						
gilynru	guy	-	lynn	-	rue	
ended up falling for her						
ginarlyn	guy	-	nair	-	lynn	
ups and downs						
givånza	guy	-	von	-	zah	
told thousands of times						
giyndor	guy	-	in	-	door	
of the ancient one						
gladdea	glade	-	dee	-	ah	
feeds the wild ones						
glearathorn	glee	-	air	-	ray	- thorne
knows what's real						

gledarys   glee   -   dare   -   riss
as though there is some part of me that needs to return there

gloreåna	glor	-	ree	-	ahn	- nah
who I will love for life						
gloredyn	glor	-	ree	-	den	
what I have been told						
gloreylyn	glor	-	ree	-	L	- lynn
beautiful rainment						
glorlyndèl	glor	-	lynn	-	dell	
learns the language of the trees						
godåndrea	go	-	don	-	dree	- ah
finds no sadness in being so						
goderea	go	-	dear	-	ree	- ah
has made me feel not so out of place						
golådyn	go	-	lah	-	den	
cat whispers						

The Book of Elf Names

golåndyn saves for the future	go	-	lahn	-	den
golaryn go figure	go	-	lair	-	ren
goleådyn the scent of wood	go	-	lee	-	ah	-	den
gŏlearyn first star of evening	gull	-	lee	-	air	-	ren
goledrea clearer than glass	go	-	lee	-	dree	-	ah
goleyn admires the stars	go	-	lee	-	in
golfyndor seeks the trees	goal	-	fin	-	door
goliåda speaks with eloquence	go	-	lie	-	ah	-	dah
golidyn silver web of energy that connects all fae	go	-	lie	-	den
gomėdėl listens for the sounds of Faerie	go	-	med	-	dell
gondoreyn in the game	gone	-	door	-	ree	-	in
goralyndel lives by instinct	gore	-	ray	-	lynn	-	deal
gordandagor mighty as a bear	gore	-	dane	-	day	-	gore
gordanduryn puckish one	gore	-	dane	-	dur	-	ren
gordåvål shining spear	gore	-	dah	-	vahl
gordondor scans the street	gore	-	doan	-	door
gordonvar glimpses Elfin	gore	-	doan	-	vair

118   The Silver Elves

gorniyn wonderful empowered feeling	gore	-	nigh	-	in
gorvandor scale of a dragon	gore	-	vane	-	door
gorvandryn dragon of gold	gore	-	vane	-	drinn
gorvardryn understands jewels	gore	-	vair	-	drinn
gorvyn deep in the earth	gore		-		vin
goryndål quiet power	gore	-	ren	-	dahl
goryndro streaks across the sky	gore	-	ren	-	dro
gosaryn affinity with elves	go	-	sair	-	ren
goynia speaks for dragons	go	-	in	-	nigh	-	ah

gozynreyl	go	-	zen	-	ree	-	L
in tune with the simple things in life							

graåndor closest to nature	gray	-	ahn	-	door
gradaryn wyzard's spell	gray	-	dare	-	ren
gradoreyn dream day	gray	-	door	-	ree	-	in
gradoryn wyzard light	gray	-	door	-	ren
gragoryn longs for wonder	gray	-	gore	-	ren
grångtori dragon's breath	gran	-	door	-	rye
grangar trusted friend	gran		-		gair

The Book of Elf Names   119

grasyndra elven oaks	gray	-	sin	-	drah		
gravores rises above	gray	-	vour	-	reese		
gravorys finds their own path	gray	-	vour	-	riss		
graynda secret treasures	gray	-	in	-	dah		
greagora graceful in flight	gree	-	a	-	gore	-	rah
gregarůs wings emerge	gree	-	gair	-	russ		
gresådål light shines through	gree	-	sah	-	dahl		
grevondor crouching near	gree	-	vone	-	door		
griåndor attains calm	gry	(rhymes	with	cry)	ahn	-	door
grodandor searches again	grow	-	dane	-	door		
grodandoryl aided by elves	grow	-	dane	-	door	-	rill
grovalor come to help	grow	-	vay	-	lore		
grovalyn curse evil	grow	-	vay	-	lynn		
grunåndiyl elf warmth	grew	-	non	-	dye	-	L
grurasyn heals with hands	grew	-	ray	-	sin		
grymgoryn waist deep	grim	-	gore	-	ren		
gryndonadėl spear of the goddess	grin	-	doe	-	nay	-	dell

grynvåra mixer of potions	grin	-	vah	-	rah		
gulynsa little swift one	goo	-	lynn	-	sah		
gwynriel speaks with eyes	gwenn	-	rye	-	eel		
gydidyn ever since my dream guides came to me	gid	-	dye	-	den		
gyladare cried at their beauty	gill	-	lay	-	dare	-	ree
gyladea covered in dew	gill	-	lay	-	dee	-	ah
gyladra feel magic throughout	gill	-	lay	-	drah		
gyladre too profound for words	gill	-	lay	-	dree		
gylådrea showed me many things	gill	-	lah	-	dree	-	ah
gyladreyn patterns of creation	gill	-	lay	-	dree	-	in
gyladreys priestess of the forest	gill	-	lay	-	dree	-	iss
gyladrys still small voice within	gill	-	lay	-	driss		
gylåladyn hair of silver	gill	-	lah	-	lay	-	den
gylåle high expectations	gill	-	lah	-	lee		
gylånådyl spirit of the coyote	gill	-	lah	-	nah	-	dill
gylardyn grace filled leap	gill	-	lair	-	den		
gylarea dragon eyes	gill	-	lair	-	ree	-	ah

The Book of Elf Names   121

| gylareyn | gill | - | lair | - | ree | - | in |
| soul searcher | | | | | | | |

| gylasyn | gill | - | | lay | - | sin |
| keeps dreaming | | | | | | |

| gyldår | gill | - | dar |
| sounds of nature calling | | | |

| gyldonafyl | gill | - | doan | - | nay | - | fill |
| soothes the wounds | | | | | | | |

| gyldonafyn | gill | - | doan | - | nay | - | fin |
| overcomes the past | | | | | | | |

| gyldracor | gill | - | dray | - | core |
| eye of power | | | | | |

| gyleåla | gill | - | lee | - | ah | - | lah |
| feel in love | | | | | | | |

| gyleålae | gill | - | lee | - | ah | - | lay |
| one of the kind of individuals that ... | | | | | | | |

| gyleålyn | gill | - | lee | - | ah | - | lynn |
| ever onward | | | | | | | |

| gylearyn | gill | - | lee | - | air | - | ren | s |
| eeks the voice | | | | | | | | |

| gyleda | gill | - | lee | - | dah |
| born of enchantment | | | | | |

| gylela | gill | - | lee | - | lah |
| path of enchantment | | | | | |

| gyliåzarn | gill | - | lie | - | ah | - | zairn |
| voice that calms | | | | | | | |

| gylidryn | gill | - | lie | - | drinn |
| cascade of flowers | | | | | |

| gylidyn | gill | - | lie | - | den |
| craving to pursue | | | | | |

| gylodyn | gill | - | low | - | den |
| moonshaper | | | | | |

| gylondar | gill | - | lone | - | dare |
| trusted companion | | | | | |

gylonvafar cavorts wildly	gill	-	lone	-	vay	-	fair
gylordyn swift arrow	gill	-		lore	-		den
gylorvyn shimmering scales	gill	-		lore	-		vin
gylynar have always known	gill	-		lynn	-		nair
gylynareůs streaks beneath the sea	gill	-	lynn	-	nair	- ree -	us
gylyndra prepared to fight to protect those she loves	gill	-		lynn	-		drah
gylyndrae the answer was staring me right in the face	gill	-		lynn	-		dray
gylyndre even though I never did take any classes	gill	-		lynn	-		dree
gylynisa I get whatever I want	gill	-	lynn	-	nigh	-	sah
gynélla leaps high	gen (rhymes with ben, hard "g") nell lah						

AN ELVEN NAME SERVES AS BOTH A
DISGUISE AND A REVELATION. IT GIVES A
HINT OF WHO WE ARE TO OUR OWN KIND
WHILE PROVING CONFUSING TO THOSE WHO
ARE NOT READY FOR THE TRUTH.

H

Elven Name and Meaning	Pronunciation			

hådåndarel
lover in the valleys
hah - dahn - dare - real

hådaryn
sees the illusions
hah - dare - ren

hådrovår
comes back for more
hah - dro - var

hålaåle
understanding the value of friendship
hah - lay - ah - lee

hålådor
one foot in the unseen
hah - lah - door

häladryn
through some sort of portal
hal - lay - drinn

hålådyn
part of the tribe
hah - lah - den

halådyna
returns to the trees
hay - lah - den - nah

hålålea
spreads the peace
hah - lah - lee - ah

hälåndar
sense of family
hal - lahn - dare

halånde
being in their presence
hay - lahn - dee

hålåndor
can reach out and touch other people's minds
hah - lahn - door

hälåryndor
protected by hob - goblins
hal - lah - ren - door

halarys
great personal confidence
hay - lair - riss

haleålyn when I came to	hay	-	lee	-	far	-	ren
hålefåryn deep haven	hah	-	lee	-	fah	-	ren
hålerearyn multi-talented	hah	-	lee	-	ree	-	air	-	ren
hålesyn images of the sea	hah		-		lee		-	sin
halidea graceful archer	hay	-	lie	-	dee	-	ah
halodryn fell to earth	hail		-		low		-	drinn
hålyndarys enchanted smile	hah	-	lynn	-	dare	-	riss
hålyndyn that kinda stuff	hah		-		lynn		-	den
hånålyn never lost my power	hah		-		nah		-	lynn
hånåryth watched over by faeries	hah		-		ah		-	rith
håndareyn called by the gnomes	hahn	-	dare	-	ree	-	in
håndarwe takes a small chance	hahn		-		dare		-	wee
håndrosyl night flyer	hahn		-		dro		-	sill
hånmaryn mystified by Elfin	hahn		-		mare		-	ren
harådaryn pursue relentlessly	hair	-	rah	-	dare	-	ren
håradre always daydreaming	hah		-		ray		-	dre
haranoryn embraces the earth	hair	-	ray	-	nor	-	ren

The Book of Elf Names   125

harårethyn special friend	hair	-	rah	-	wreath	-	thin
haråsyn bright with imagination	hair	-	rah	-	sin		
hårgoryn deep within the earth	har	-	gore	-	ren		
harlåndor returns home	hair	-	lahn	-	door		
harylådyn related to the sea	hair	-	rill	-	lah	-	den
hårynda night time sky	hah	-	ren	-	dah		
haryndår flows through my soul	hair	-	ren	-	dar		
hårynél quintessential gentleman	hah	-	ren	-	nell		
harynteri mist in the morning	hair	-	ren	-	teer	-	rye
hasordyn joy to others	hay	-	soar	-	den		
hasoyndrys loves to discover	hay	-	so	-	in	-	driss
håsyndra joins the dance	hah	-	sin	-	drah		
håvåndurél dangerously close to the edge	hah	-	vahn	-	dur	-	rell
håvånduryn rarely speaks	hah	-	vahn	-	dur	-	ren
havynår among the birds	hay	-	vin	-	nar		
heändre awakens in time	he	-	ann	-	dree		
heåndro chasing dreams	he	-	ahn	-	dro		

hearvyn there for friends	he	-	air	-	vin		
hėladyn dancing naked in the moonlight	hell	-	lay	-	den		
helaryni masters the physical	hell	-	lair	-	ren	-	nigh
hėleålyn drawn to the night sky	hell	-	lee	-	ah	-	lynn
helearvår ravens follow	hell	-	lee	-	air	-	var
hėledreyn noble beliefs	hell	-lee	-	dree	-	in	
helordryn mystic dark	heal	-	lore	-	drinn		
heloreys slow realization	heal	-	lore	-	re	-	iss
hemialyn great interactions	he	-	my	-	a	-	lynn
henarjaryn in a far window	he	-	nair	-	jay	-	ren
heoråvyn continual grace	he	-	or	-	rah	-	vin
heradea not who I was meant to be	he	-	ray	-	dee	-	ah
herador calm soothing nature	he	-	ray	-	door		
herålyn arouses fascination	he	-	rah	-	lynn		
herandanor one with the night	he	-	rain	-	dane	-	nor
herarosyn works with the earth's elementals	he	-	ray	-	row	-	sin
herodyn there to help	he	-	row	-	den		

herordyn far watcher	here	-	or	-	den
herryndånor natural magician	here	-	ren	-	dah	-	nor

herordyn | here | - | or | - | den
far watcher

herryndånor | here | - | ren | - | dah | - | nor
natural magician

herynde | here | - | ren | - | dee
peace among the peoples

hetoreyn | he | - | tour | - | ree | - | in
deeper meaning to life

heynåsar | he | - | in | - | nah | - | sah
longs for the sense of belonging I once had

hiåleåda | high | - | ah | - | lee | - | ah | - | dah
strangely noble

hiåleånda | high | - | ah | - | lee | - | ahn | - | dah
protected by the trees

hiålordre | high | - | ah | - | lore | - | dree
perky and playful

hiasyndra | high | - | a | - | sin | - | drah
fans the flames

hibaryn | high | - | bare | - | ren
drawn to the lore

hidare | high | - | dare | - | ree
light of the glen

hidareyn | high | - | dare | - | ree | - | in
always spinning tales

hidarshyn | high | - | dare | - | shin
spark from the moon

hidaryn | high | - | dare | - | ren
strange but I know it's true

hidarys | high | - | dare | - | riss
bow stringer

hieålyn | high | - | e | - | ah | - | lynn
art comes from the heart

hielodyn | high | - | e | - | low | - | den
my own way

The Silver Elves

hildornyn entwined with nature	heil	-	door	-	nin		
hilela likes to include others	high	-	lee	-	lah		
hiryndal hill scout	high	-	ren	-	dale		
hivara dares to try the new	high	-	vair	-	rah		
hivarådyn silent flight	high	-	vair	-	rah	-	den
hivarasyn limitless possibillities	high	-	vair	-	ray	-	sin
hivosyl learns from the old	high	-	voe	-	sill		
hodåndyryn hidden smile	hoe	-	don	-	der	-	ren
holadys flowing stream	hoe	-	lay	-	diss		
holeali dreams of things that are going to happen	hoe	-	lee	-	a	-	lie
holearna of the nature of the fae	hoe	-	lee	-	air	-	nah
holeyna someone else	hoe	-	lee	-	in	-	nah
holiåle addicted to glitter	hoe	-	lie	-	ah	-	lee
holordys master of earthly realities	hoe	-	lore	-	diss		
honåarla hides in the trees to read	hoe	-	nah	-	air	-	lah
honåndryn feeling like I belong	hoe	-	non	-	drinn		
honaryn wrong to be wasteful	hoe	-	nair	-	ren		

The Book of Elf Names   129

hondare listens to the music of the forest	hone	-	dare	-			ree		
hondereyn when I visit the other world	hone	-	deer	-	ree	-	in		
hondorėl stands out from their peers	hone	-	door	-	rell				
horåndyn becoming quite successful	hoe	-	ron	-	den				
hulåle don't know why	who	-	lah	-	lee				
hulåndor everything seemed far away	who	-	lahn	-	door				
huoreyn likes to stay home	who	-	or	-	ree	-	in		
hurdåndra sings to life	hew-r	-	dahn	-	drah				
huredyn makes friends easily	who	-	ree	-	den				
huryndea we are not alone	who	-	ren	-	dee	-	ah		
huryndėl higher balance	who	-	ren	-	dell				
huryndre it makes so much sense	who	-	ren	-	dree				
huryndyn seems to be basically good	who	-	ren	-	den				
hylålasyn stroked by the enchanted	hill	-	lah	-	lay	-	sin		
hylandėl sees the sign	hill	-	lane	-	dell				
hylasalyn moves objects with her mind	hill	-	lay	-	say	-	lynn		
hylasyn knack for languages	hill	-	lay	-	sin				

hylathyn lifts arms to the rain	hill	-	lay	-		-	thin
hyleylyn in the ranks of the pixies	hill	-	lee	-	L	-	lynn
hylmeryn shouldn't hide it anymore	hill	-	mere	-		-	ren
hylynotha called to remember	hill	-	lynn	-	no	-	thah
hylynsiyl feels the earth	hill	-	lynn	-	sigh	-	L
hymaryn comes about on wings	him	-	mare	-		-	ren
hynårasu guided by the moon	hen	-	nar	-	ray	-	sue
hyndaryn the key to life	hen	-	dare	-		-	ren
hyndårys swift as the wind	hen	-	dar	-		-	riss
hynsadår stirs the leaves	hen	-	say	-		-	dar
hyntårea never ceasing smile	hen	-	tah	-	ree	-	ah
hyråndyryn solitary life	her	-	ron	-	der	-	ren
hyrnavyn related to elves	her	-	nay	-		-	vin
hyrothas at peace in the forest	her	-	row	-		-	thahss
hyrynåsa on the edge of the lake	her	-	ren	-	nah	-	sah
hyryndras needs to know	her	-	ren	-		-	drayce

| hysareyl | hiss | - | sair | - | ree | - | L |

cannot be tamed any longer

| hysylmaryn | hiss | - | sill | - | mare | - | ren |

believes beyond

AN ELF NAME IS AN INVITATION TO THE SPIRIT TO ENTER ONE'S LIFE AND GUIDE ONE.

ELVES THINK THAT OPINIONS ARE LIKE PENNIES. EVEN IF YOU PUT THEM ALL TOGETHER, THEY DON'T USUALLY AMOUNT TO MUCH.

EVERY TIME AN ELF NAME IS SPOKEN, IT IS LIKE A BELL RUNG INTO THE WORLD AWAKENING THE FAE ALL AROUND IT.

1

Elven Name and Meaning	Pronunciation								
iådonyn whirling shadow	eye	-	ah	-	doe	-	nin		
iadoreyl follows the light	eye	-	a	-	door	-	ree	-	L
iadoryn touch of healing	eye	-	a	-	door	-	ren		
iafyndra tongue of wiles	eye	-	a	-	fin	-	drah		
iålea sea song	eye	-	ah	-	lee	-	ah		
ialena flutters nearby	eye	-	a	-	lee	-	nah		
iålosyn hears the call	eye	-	ah	-	low	-	sin		
ialyndor carries the torch	eye	-	a	-	lynn	-	door		
iamordryn says little	eye	-	a	-	more	-	drinn		
iarådyn beneath the silver moon	eye	-	a	-	rah	-	den		
iarea manifests desires	eye	-	a	-	ree	-	ah		
iåreda know that they are real	eye	-	ah	-	ree	-	dah		
iareonda hears what others do not	eye	-	a	-	ree	-	ohn	-	dah
iarnåre everyone says	eye	-	air	-	nah	-	ree		

iaronsa	eye	-	air	-	roan	-	sah
believes in the stories							
iaroyl	eye	-	air	-	row	-	L
one of our own							
iaryn	eye	-	a	-	ren		
never questioned it							
iaryna	eye	-	air	-	ren	-	nah
knew it with more certainty than I've ever known							
iavorel	eye	-	a	-	vour	-	real
sound of faerie							
iåyndra	eye	-	ah	-	in	-	drah
dark wolf							
ibånåder	eye	-	bon	-	nah	-	der
have always loved							
ibanåvyn	eye	-	bane	-	nah	-	vin
longs to cross the sea							
ibareyn	eye	-	bare	-	ree	-	in
it started as a joke							
ibaryn	eye	-	bare		-	in	
with the people							
ibreålor	eye	-	bree	-	ah	-	lore
best companion							
ibrearyn	eye	-	bree	-	air	-	ren
senses what the earth feels							
ibreyl	eye	-	bree		-	L	
defends nature							
icandryl	eye	-	can		-	drill	
married to the sea							
idalodyn	eye	-	day	-	low	-	den
between the forest and the sea							
idånåru	eye	-	don	-	nah	-	rue
growing certainty							
idåndara	eye	-	don	-	dare	-	rah
they each sign to me in their own ways							

idåndoreyl	eye	-	don	-	door	-	ree	-	L
glowing hands									
idändre	eye	-			dan	-			dree
losing track of time									
idare	eye	-			dare	-			ree
shining ones are my protectors									
idarea	eye	-	dare	-	ree	-	ah
ready to emerge									
idarèl	eye	-			dare	-			rell
on the border									
idaronyn	eye	-	dare	-	row	-	nin
works in secret									
idarys	eye	-			dare	-			riss
marked by the fae									
idereïs	eye	-	deer	-	ree	-	iss
the child within is excited									
idereyn	eye	-	deer	-	ree	-	in
hard to put into words									
ideryn	eye	-			deer	-			ren
not part of this world									
idilålar	eye	-	dye	-	lah	-	lair
it suddenly came to me									
idorèl	eye	-			door	-			rell
valued friend									
idoreyl	eye	-	door	-	ree	-	L
pursuit of the mystic									
idorna	eye	-			door	-			nah
dreams of light and power									
idorni	eye	-			door	-			nigh
says what can be									
idorsa	eye	-			door	-			sah
healer of the wind									
idoryn	eye	-			door	-			ren
relieves others of their pain									

The Book of Elf Names   135

idorys giver of the earth	eye	-	door	-	riss		
idranor impressed by their nobility	eye	-	dray	-	nor		
idynaryn eager to learn more	eye	-	den	-	nair	-	ren
idynėl at peace in the night	eye	-	den	-	nell		
ielyn sees the forest through the trees	eye	-	e	-	lynn		
ienådryn you get the picture	eye	-	e	-	nah	-	drinn
ierea people stare as if it's not possible	eye	-	e	-	ree	-	ah
iereyn many secrets we're not normally privy to	eye	-	e	-	ree	-	in
ieryn much other knowledge has come from that realization	eye	-	ear	-	ren		
ifyndra quiet soul	eye	-	fin	-	drah		
ijalo eager to learn	eye	-	jay	-	low		
ijalu become a part of it	eye	-	jay	-	lou		
ijåndra leaf in the stream	eye	-	john	-	drah		
ijaniyl hopes for the light	eye	-	jay	-	nigh	-	L
ijilos sword maker	eye	-	jie	-	lowce		
ijorådåv elf inspired	eye	-	jour	-	rah	-	dahv
ijorna eater of the past	eye	-	jour	-	nah		

ijoru come with us	eye	-	jour	-	rue			
ijynader sad gray eyes	eye	-	jen	-	nay	-	deer	
ikomår more than any other	eye	-	co	-	mar			
iladyn taking care of animals	eye	-	lay	-	den			
iladyryn I've always thought	eye	-	lay	-	der	-	ren	
ilålea something to do with a past life	eye	-lah	-	lee	-	ah		
ilåndre cute one	eye	-lahn	-	dree				
ilarsyn unearthly delight	eye	-	lair	-	sin			
ilasyn climbs the crags	eye	-	lay	-	sin			
ilava dancing leaves	eye	-	lay	-	vah			
ildånådåmer mere a sneaking suspicion	isle	-	dah	-	nah	-	dah	-
ildynarys behind the snake	isle	-	den	-	nair	-	riss	
ilea beautiful script	eye	-	lee	-	ah			
ileåfyn begins the way	eye	-	lee	-	ah	-	fin	
ileålyn looks upon the bright side of life	eye	-	lee	-	ah	-	lynn	
iloshur sees the shadows move	eye	-	low	-	sure			
ilovyndor reaching out	eye	-	low	-	vin	-	door	

The Book of Elf Names   137

iluryn	eye	-	lou	-		ren

iluryn eye - lou - ren
revels in home life

iluvyn eye - lou - vin
bright prompt

ilynlor eye - lynn - lore
made for a greater purpose

ilytheyl eye - lith - thee - L
joy of growing

imarfyn eye - mare - fin
bravely set forth

imarshyn eye - mare - shin
comfortable in whatever situation I find mys'elf

imarsyl eye - mare - sill
odd things happen

imerådor eye - mere - rah - door
loves the ancient songs

imerådyn eye - mere - rah - den
water of the moon

imerdranėl eye - mere - dray - nell
tree that leans from the sea

imeryn eye - mere - ren
drawn to magic

imorasyn eye - more - ray - sin
likes the solitude of the forest

imoreyn eye - more - ree - in
whirling snow

imorfyn eye - more - fin
of the realm

imoru eye - more - rue
that is the honest truth

imorydyn eye - more - rid - den
in the magical fields of healing

imursyn eye - muir - sin
unusual affinity

imuryn	eye	-	muir	-	ren	
voice of the flowers						
imydeyn	eye	-	mid	-	dee	- in
just so mysterious						
imyryn	eye	-	mer	-	ren	
open to all possibilities						
inarasyn	eye	-	nair	-	rah	- sin
heart in flight						
inare	eye	-	nair	-	ree	
I am who I am						
inatålo	eye	-	nay	-	tah	- low
finds her true s'elf						
indalo	ine	-	day	-	low	
whistler on the wind						

inereyl   eye   -   near   -   ree   -   L
glimpses of their shimmer in the garden

inialyn	eye	-	nigh	-	a	- lynn
have always felt					
inidyn	eye	-	nigh	-	den
dancing on air					
inoryn	eye	-	nor	-	ren
though I do not know what					
iorea	eye	-	or	-	ree	- ah
called by the bird's song					
ioreås	eye	-	or	-	ree	- ahss
awoke to birds singing					
iradea	eye	-	ray	-	dee	- ah
mystic magic					
iradra	eye	-	ray	-	drah
my one true home					
irandea	eye	-	rain	-	dee	- ah
nearby woods					
iratha	eye	-	rayth	-	thah
feels the call					

The Book of Elf Names

ireadas loves faerie boys	eye	-	ree	-	a	-	dayce
ireca loves unicorns	eye	-		ree	-	cah	
irekalyn shine of sunset	eye	-	ree	-	kay	-	lynn
irela in tune with nature	eye	-		ree	-	lah	
irethas voice of the raven	eye	-		ree	-	thahss	
irudås what wonderful things the future has in store	eye	-		rue	-	dahss	
irulyn none of it made any sense	eye	-		rue	-	lynn	
irundyn ancient symbol on the palm	eye	-		rune	-	den	
irynca moon lights my path	eye	-		ren	-	cah	
irysyn seeks the high mountain	eye	-		riss	-	sin	
isålalo luck of the stars	eye	-	sah	-	lay	-	low
isalea glows in the forest	eye	-	say	-	lee	-	ah
ïsladyn looks from the trees	is	-		lay	-	den	
isulyn from the silver seas	eye	-		sue	-	lynn	
isylde blood of the fae	eye	-		sill	-	dee	
ïsyndra loyal forever	is	-		sin	-	drah	
itareyn never stops hoping	eye	-	tayr	-	ree	-	in

ivadra	eye	-	vay	-	drah
dreams too real not to exist					
ivälådyn	eye	-	val	-	lay	-	den
short bow					
ivåndare	eye	-	vaughn	-	dare	-	ree
healing meditations					
ivändor	eye	-	van	-	door
knows the woods					
ivarådryn	eye	-	vair	-	rah	-	drinn
redeems magic					
ivarasyn	eye	-	vair	-	ray	-	sin
among the ivy					
ivareyl	eye	-	vair	-	ree	-	L
loves to be free and play					
ivarna	eye	-	vair	-	nah
slow dancer					
ivarodan	eye	-	vair	-	row	-	dane
among the high trees					
ivaru	eye	-	vair	-	rue
burys gold					
ivaryshan	eye	-	vair	-	riss	-	shane
dreams from the past					
ivåsålodyn	eye	-	vah	-	sah	-	low	-	den
inspired by the tales					
ivåshuryn	eye	-	vah	-	shoe	-	ren
feels the flow of the energies					
iveana	eye	-	vee	-	a	-	nah
I can feel it inside me					
iveravyn	eye	-	vee	-	ray	-	vin
healer of the heart					
iversaryn	eye	-	veer	-	say	-	ren
water wings					
iveyndre	eye	-	vee	-	in	-	dree
dreams the truth					

The Book of Elf Names   141

ivondoryn	eye	-	vone	-	door	-	ren

I wish I had their confidence

ivoradyn	eye	-	vour	-	ray	-	den

water breather

ivorånder	eye	-	vour	-	ron	-	deer

taught by the brownies

ivorasyn	eye	-	vour	-	ray	-	sin

amused with what's going on around me

ivoryn	eye	-	vour	-	ren

singing to the trees

ivoryndor	eye	-	vour	-	ren	-	door

protects the innocent

ivynaryn	eye	-	vin	-	nair	-	ren

feels the magic within

ivyndåre	eye	-	vin	-	dah	-	ree

gift of passion

ivyndre	eye	-	vin	-	dree

understands the dragons

ivyraseyl	eye	-	ver	-	ray	-	see	-	L

at the speed of light

iylålyn	eye	-	L	-	lah	-	lynn

sunlight in the woods

iynådyn	eye	-	in	-	nah	-	den

breathes freely in the forest

iynala	eye	-	in	-	nah	-	lah

flattering wings

iynalea	eye	-	in	-	nay	-	lee	-	ah

heals the heart

iyndre	eye	-	in	-	dree

mind of a hawk

iyndreyl	eye	-	in	-	dree	-	L

poetic life style

iyndros	eye	-	in	-	drowce

joyously different

iyndyryn	eye	-	in	-	der	-	ren
builds on high							
izåndryl	eye	-	zahn	-			drill
resists temptation							

WE ELVES FOR THE MOST PART HAVE
NORMAL NAMES THAT WE USE TO PASS
THROUGH THE WORLD OF THE NORMAL FOLK.
SOME MISTAKENLY REFER TO THESE AS OUR
REAL NAMES, BUT THEY REAL-LY DON'T
KNOW WHAT THEY'RE TALKING ABOUT.

J

Elven Name and Meaning	Pronunciation					
jaarlor bears the scars	jay	-	air	-	lore	
jacanta masters the self	jay	-	can	-	tah	
jachale hunts with dragons	jay	-	chah	-	lee	
jåchåndryl accepting them as they are	jah	-	chahn	-	drill	
jåchåntar tossing starlight	jah	-	chahn	-	tayr	
jådafa how I wear my hair	jah	-	day	-	fah	
jådåndafa bridges the gap	jah	-	don	-	day	-	fah
jådåndåle have only recently come to know	jah	-	don	-	dah	-	lee
jådarfyn dragon sage	jah	-	dare	-	fin	
jadaro on a high hill	jay	-	dare	-	row	
jådaryn finds the will power	jah	-	dare	-	ren	
jadyndor knows the way well	jay	-	den	-	door	
jådyråthyn portal to our dreams	jah	-	der	-	rah	-	thin
jafarådys dreams of different worlds	jay	-	fair	-	rah	-	diss

jåfaryn time and again	jah	-	fair	-	ren
jaiålyn awakes to elvish	jay	- eye -	ah	-	lynn
jåile friend you can trust	jah	-	eye	-	lee
jaladorėl awakens joy	jay	- lah -	door	-	rell
jålafar surrounded by roses	jah	-	lah	-	fair
jålale extremely lucky	jah	-	lay	-	lee
jålåndar works with magical creatures	jah	-	lahn	-	dare
jålardor searching for the sense of	jah	-	lair	-	door
jalatoryn dancing till dawn	jay	- lay -	tour	-	ren
jålavyn leave the others to their world	jah	-	lay	-	vin
jålayn wings that sparkle	jah	-	lay	-	in
jålealyn sense of belonging	jah	- lee -	a	-	lynn
jålela wishes to know and learn more	jah	-	lee	-	lah
jåleva sparkling enchantment	jah	-	lee	-	vah
jalonyn love's arrow	jay	-	low	-	nin
jaloriys quick fingers	jay	- lore -	rye	-	iss
jålyndre what convinced me	jah	-	lynn	-	dree

The Book of Elf Names   145

jålynthor	jah	-	lynn	-	thor
I like the way you think					

jåmådraa	jah	-	mah	-	dray	-	ah
walks with beauty							

jåmåhal	jah	-	mah	-	hale
feels certain					

jåmara	jah	-	mare	-	rah
guided by nature					

jåmarwe	jah	-	mare	-	wee
time to focus on my inner power					

jåmereyn	jah	-	mere	-	re	-	in
something more out there							

jåmerwyn	jah		-mere	-	win
also dabbles in other magics					

jameryn	jay	-	mere	-	ren
looking at the stars					

jånådåfur	jah	-	nah	-	dah	-	few-r
creates excitement							

jånåle	jah	-	nah	-	lee
belongs to another time					

jånåndåfa	jah	-	non	-	dah	-	fah
hope to figure things out soon							

jånåndale	jah	-	non	day	-	lee
assists the birth of souls						

jånåvre	jah	-	nah	-	vree
opened my eyes					

jåndåfyr	john	-	dah	-	fur
many reasons present themselves					

jåndåhåru	john	-	dah	-	hah	-	rue
starwind							

jåndålåfyn	john	-	dah	-	lah	-	fin
to make all things equal							

jåndåle	john	-	dah	-	lee
moon over the hills					

jåndåler glides through the forest	john	-	dah	-	leer
jåndålor cloak of shadows	john	-	dah	-	lore
jåndånådur shifting in light	john	-	dah	-	nah	-	dur
jåndar up a tree	john	-		dare
jandareyl sees the light	jane	-	dare	-	ree	-	L
jåndolåfyn quest for truth and understanding	john	-	doe	-	lah	-	fin
jåndoråfyn sound of chimes	john	-	door	-	rah	-	fin
jåndoråmaryn draws closer	john	-	door	-	rah	-	mare	ren
jåndråfår piercing eyes	john	-		drah	-	far
jånvändryn oak root	john	-		van	-	drinn
japålo j protects the sea's treasures	ay	-		pah	-	low
jardondorėl settles to earth	jayr	-	doan	-	door	-	rell
jårėlorys scribbles verse	jah	-	rell	-	lore	-	riss
jasådalu jeweled forehead	jay	-	sah	-	day	-	lou
jasånådro blends with the forest	jay	-	sah	-	nah	-	dro
jåsova sweet beyond measure	jah	-		so	-	vah
jåthåle drawn to peace	jah-		thah	-	lee

The Book of Elf Names   147

jåvådrynsår moon dragon	jah	-	vah	-	drinn	-	sar
jåvåladres seeks to learn from the elven	jah	-	vah	-	lay	-	dreese
jåvålyndre of many talents	jah	-	vah	-	lynn	-	dree
jåvånda sister of the Sidhe	jah	-	vahn	-	dah
javandasa dreams of being	jay	-	vane	-	day	-	sah
javåndoryl noble daughter	jay	-	vaughn	-	door	-	rill
jåvåndreyl calls to them	jah	-	vaughn	-	dree	-	L
jåvändreyn until I realized	jah	-	van	-	dree	-	in
jåvändrys wandering through the shadows	jah		van	-	driss
jåvaryn jumps for joy	jah	-	vair	-	ren
jåvidryl no harm has ever come to me	jah	-	vie	-	drill
jåvynåva sits and marvels	jah	-	vin	-	nah	-	vah
jåvyndryn discovers the truth	jah	-	vin	-	drinn
jåvyndrys walks through the mists	jah	-	vin	-	driss
jåvynre profound love	jah	-	vin	-	ree
jazazyn dreams of elves	jay	-	zay	-	zen
jeåndryn scatters pixie dust	g	-	ahn	-	drinn

jearåvyl decoder of mysteries	g	-	air	-	rah	-	ville
jearvåna memories return	g	-	air	-	vah	-	nah
jearvaryn fades into the surroundings	g	-	air	-	vay	-	ren
jeåvryn something beyond	g	-			ah	-	vrinn
jecändryl takes away the pain	g	-			can	-	drill
jedåndåfa natural animal therapy	g	-	don	-	dah	-	fah
jediyn born of the rhythm	g	-			dye	-	in
jedondafyn smile of the wyzard	g	-	doan	-	dah	-	fin
jedraja dragon armor	g	-			dray	-	jah
jelanu now I feel like I'm home	g	-			lay	-	new
jelodyn bathing in the light	g	-			low	-	den
jeloryn far off places in the mind	g	-			lore	-	ren
jemeryn frolics through the flowers	g	-			mere	-	ren
jenåna only wish to share the joy of that with others	g	-			nah	-	nah
jenarle people have said	g	-			nair	-	lee
jevålynsa unicorn's sigh	g	-	vah	-	lynn	-	sah
jevandoryn center of the fire's storm	g	-	vane	-	door	-	ren

The Book of Elf Names   149

jevåndrys not known to this world	g	-	vaughn	-	driss				
jevarea eternal happiness	g	-	vair	-	ree	-	ah		
jevareyn quest for peace	g	-	vair	-	ree	-	in		
jevarsyn connection to something greater	g	-	vair	-	sin				
jevåsarån rune wyzard	g	-	vah	-	sair	-	ron		
jevåshånu changing back	g	-	vah	-	shah	-	new		
jevasol guided by the stars	g	-	vay	-	soul				
jevåsoråsyn autumn leaf on a summer's breeze	g	-	vah	-	soar	-	rah	-	sin
jeyndara so I could laugh	g	-	in	-	dare	-	rah		
jilale maybe somewhere	ji	-	lay	-	lee				
jilånda if this makes sense	ji	(rhymes	with	high)	lahn	dah	-		
jileålyn artistic, poetic, elegant and quite lovely	ji	-	lee	-	ah	-	lynn		
jilela exceptional hearing	ji	-	lee	-	lah				
jilonafa speaks the ancient tongues	ji	-	low	-	nay	-	fah		
jiloris that eminate from the heart	ji	-	low	-	riss				
jilorvås found the way	ji	-	lore	-	vahss				
jilyndre the meaning of it all	ji	-	lynn	-	dree				

The Silver Elves

jimarys growing wildflowers	ji	-	mare	-	riss	
jinåla elvish personality	ji	-	nah	-	lah	
jinaniyl sister of enchantment	ji	-	nay	-	nigh	-	L
jinareyn breathing the life pulses	ji	-	nay	-	ree	-	in
jinarys he company of trees	ji	-	nair	-	riss	t
jinuryn embraces ones'elf	ji	-	new	-	ren	
jira rose above them	ji	-	rah			
jisala skims the sea	ji	-	say	-	lah	
jisalyn of the undines	ji	-	say	-	lynn	
jivadre memories that feel real	ji	-	vay	-	dree	
jivåndre puts the sunshine in everyone's day	ji	-	vaughn	-	dree	
jivare my whole life has been leading up to this	ji	-	vair	-	ree	
jivarea magical butterfly	ji	-	vair	-	ree	-	ah
jivareyl embraces their shadow	ji	-	vair	-	ree	-	L
jivarna sizzling magic	ji	-	vair	-	nah	
jivarnys intuits the future	ji	-	nair	-	niss	
jivynve easy to approach	ji	-	vin	-	vee	

jiyndårėl	ji	-	in	-	dah	-	rell
one of many							

jobarea	joe	-	bare	-	ree	-	ah
different from anything I've seen							

jodafarna	joe	-	day	-	fair	-	nah
close to home							

jodånde	joe	-	don			-	dee
sees things others don't even suspect exist							

jodaynae	joe	-	day	-	in	-	nay
from another world							

jofarea	joe	-	fair	-	ree	-	ah
shining cloud							

jofylron	joe	-	fill			-	roan
willing to try							

jolädasa	joe	-	lad	-	day	-	sah
joins the play							

joladryl	joe	-	lay			-	drill
no boundaries							

joladrys	joe	-	lay			-	driss
one day I was contacted							

jolara	joe	-	lair			-	rah
connected to the raw and primal forces of nature							

jolardor	joe	-	lair			-	dorr
joy immeasurable							

jolarys	joe	-	lair			-	riss
feels a strong call							

jolasys	joe	-	lay			-	sis
loves the simple life							

joleala	joe	-	lee	-	a	-	lah
without meaning to							

jolear	joe	-	lee			-	air
sings with the true elves							

joledra	joe	-	lee			–	drah
I vowed to myself							

The Silver Elves

jolyndareyn destiny of a smile	joe	-	lynn	-	dare	-	ree	- in
jordrynvar dragon sorcerer	jour	-	drinn	-	vair			
jorela dear to me	jour	-	ree	-	lah			
jorynèl talks to crows	joe	-	ren	-	nell			
jorysylyn never quits	joe	-	riss	-	sill	-	lynn	
jualäryn knows the boundaries	jew	-	a	-	lair	-	ren	
judalys omething out there waiting	jew	-	day	-	liss	s		
judoryn hidden powers	jew	-	door	-	ren			
juèlyn a sense of wonder	jew	-	L	-	in			
juladyn worthy of respect	jew	-	lay	-	den			
juledryn soul link	jew	-	lee	-	drinn			
julyndre contagious personality	jew	-	lynn	-	dree			
junarsyn lucky for others	jew	-	nair	-	sin			
jurådreyl eyes that glow	jew	-	rah	-	dree	-	L	
jurafyn on a quest	jew	-	ray	-	fin			
jurathfa shares the smile	jew	-	rayth	-	fah			
juriaryn all helping all	jew	-	rye	-	air	-	ren	

The Book of Elf Names   153

juridae but then again	jew	-			rye	-	day
juryldrasås dark wind	jew	-	rill	-	dray	-	sahss
jurynadyn shining horn	jew	-	ren	-	nay	-	den
juryndål have always attracted and fascinated me	jew	-			ren	-	dahl
juryndara not there	jew	-	ren	-	dare	-	rah
jurynde eyes opened	jew	-			ren	-	dee
jusåndor as if I was born to it	jew	-			sahn	-	door
jusåndryl doesn't yet realize	jew	-			sahn	-	drill
juylyn summons the elements	jew	-			L	-	lynn
jyfaryn elf eyes	jiff	-			fair	-	ren
jylafa urge to roam	jill	-			lay	-	fah
jylåle thorough in all she does	jill	-			lah	-	lee
jylåneyn explores the hidden truths	jill	-	lah	-	knee	-	in
jylånfe moonlight gave birth	jill	-			lahn	-	fee
jylareyn elfin love	jill	-	lair	-	ree	-	in
jylodare deep abiding affection	jill	-	low	-	dare	-	ree
jylondåfar trimmed with lace	jill	-	lone	-	dah	-	fair

jylvålys majestic strength	jill	-	vah	-	liss
jymari stands by the crashing waters	jim	-	mare	-	rye
jynadyn scared well	gin	-	nay	-	den
jyndala evening sparkles	gin	-	day	-	lah
jyndålåna awakens twilight	gin - dah	-	lah	-	nah
jyndålthor crazy ways	gin	-	dahl	-	thor
jyndalu curiosity for all things	gin	-	day	-	lou
jyndånafa helps others to the light	gin - dah	-	nay	-	fah
jyndaradar slides on air	gin	-	dare	- ray -	dare
jyndåråthyn helped me understand	gin - dar	-	rah	-	thin
jyndardyn remedy is total freedom	gin	-	dare	- den	only
jyndåre quiet dragon	gin	-	dar	-	ree
jyndårea gentle dragon	gin	-	dar	- ree -	ah
jyndareyl dragon's poem	gin	-	dare	- ree -	L
jyndareyn if that is allowed	gin	-	dare	- ree -	in
jyndareys if one listens long enough they will hear what all things have to say	gin	-	dare	- ree -	iss
jyndarfyn nurtures the forest	gin	-	dare	-	fin

jyndari always looking	gin	-	dare	-	rye	
jyndariėl heals with poetry	gin	-	dare	-	rye	-	L
jyndarlor with like purposes and minds	gin	-	dare	-	lore	
jyndaron mythic fire	gin	-	dare	-	roan	
jyndaru deep, pondering thought	gin	-	dare	-	rue	
jyndaryn fierce protector	gin	-	dare	-	ren	
jyndaryn quiet haven	gin	-	dare	-	ren	
jyndasa ready to ride	gin	-	day	-	sah	
jyndasys watching and waiting	gin	-	day	-	sis	
jyndoriel myth to life	gin	-	door	-	rye	-	eel
jyndra silent song	gin		-		drah	
jyndreånyn seek them everywhere	gin	-	dree	-	ah	-	nin
jyndrearyn dark glitter	gin	-	dree	-	air	-	ren
jyndrynėl it's not because of that	gin-		drinn		-	nell
jyndyrïl travels through the dimensions	gin	-	der	-	rill	
jynjååre mushroom faery	gin	-	jah	-	ah	-	ree
jynjåle they seem enchanted	gin	-	jah	-	lee	

156   The Silver Elves

jynjålys gut feeling	gin	-	jah	-	liss		
jynjåra path to wholeness	gin	-	jah	-	rah		
jynjarėl understands much	gin	-	jay	-	rell		
jynjarva powers of the earth	gin	-	jair	-	vah		
jynlada protector of the spirit	gin	-	lay	-	dah		
jyntaleyl turns in the breeze	gin	-	tay	-	lee	-	L
jyntåra circle of life	gin	-	tah	-	rah		
jyntårålyn circle of forgiveness	gin	-	tah	-	rah	-	lynn
jyntareyn elf appeal	gin	-	tair	-	ree	-	in
jyntarys when I touched them	gin	-	tair	-	riss		
jynvala interpreting the elements	gin	-	vay	-	lah		
jynvåra mythic one	gin	-	vah	-	rah		
jynvaråvyn right from the start	gin	-	vair	-	rah	-	vin
jynvarda self confident	gin	-	vair	-	dah		
jynvåre changing reality with dreams	gin	-	vah	-	ree		
jynvårėl night's wisdom	gin	-	vah	-	rell		
jynvårėla hidden among leaves	gin	-	vah	-	rell	-	lah

The Book of Elf Names

jynvaryn elfin host	gin	-		vair	-	ren
jynvåvaryn puddles after storms	gin	-	vah	-	vair	-	ren
jynvidra true passion	gin	-		vie	-	drah
jynvryndrål channels the powers of Elfin	gin	-		vrinn	-	drahl

WHAT DOES IT TAKE TO TREAD THE ELVEN WAY? EVERYTHING YOU HAVE. ALL OF YOUR HEART, ALL OF YOUR SOUL, AND ALL THAT YOU DO EVERY NIGHT AND DAY.

IT IS SAID BY SOME THAT EVERYTIME A BELL RINGS, AN ANGEL GETS HIS WINGS. WE ELVES SAY EVERYTIME AN ELVEN NAME IS SPOKEN, ENCHANTMENTS BURST INTO BEING.

$\mathcal{K}$

Elven Name and Meaning

Pronunciation

kaåndarys bows in reverence	kay	-	ahn	-	dare	-	riss
kabarys if I relax	kay	-	bare	-	riss
kadånåfyr as timid as a wild mouse	kay	-	dah	-	nah	-	fur
kadånåhur ucky to find out early	kay	-	dah	-	nah	-	hew-r l
kalåledra all lonely darkness gone	kay	-	lah	-	lee	-	drah
kalåndor the planes are intertwined with each other	kay	-	lahn	-	door
kalåndys the force that has given me strength to overcome the problems I've faced	kay	-	lahn	-	diss
kalånea tantric enchantress	kay	-	lah	-	knee	-	ah
kalåvår undergoing many changes	kay	-	lah	-	var
kaleådyn ready to protect the forest	kay	-	lee	-	ah	-	den
kaleåfyn feels right	kay	-	lee	-	ah	-	fin
kaleåli extraordinarily clever	kay	-	lee	-	ah	-	lie
kaleålyn songs in the silence	kay	-	lee	-	ah	-	lynn
kalefea with the assistance of the other world	kay	-	lee	-	fee	-	ah

The Book of Elf Names

kalidyna coexist in peace	kay	-	lie	-	den	-	nah
kalithel I heard the voice again	kay	-	lie	-	theal		
kallocnar passes on the elfin lore	kale	-	lowk	-	nair		
kalodåryn sings to thems'elf	kay	-	low	-	dar	-	ren
kalordryn seeks the truth	kay	-	lore	-	drinn		
kalyndara mother was enchanted when she conceived	kay	-	lynn	-	dare	-	rah
kalynmora lady of the shadows	kay	-	lynn	-	more	-	rah
kamareyl striving to improve mys'elf	kay	-	mare	-	ree	-	L
kamyndaryn spinning wildly	kay	-	men	-	dare	-	ren
kanådryn beautiful eyes	kay	-	nah	-	drinn		
kaorålys protects relics	kay	-	or	-	rah	-	liss
karadel touch is healing	kay	-	ray	-	deal		
karador radiant music	kay	-	ray	-	door		
karadyn constant and true	kay	-	ray	-	den		
karåfyn dances naked in the rain	kay	-	rah	-	fin		
karaloryn awakens healed	kay	-	ray	-	lore	-	ren
kareaona powers awakening	kay	-	ree	-	a	-	oh	-	nah

160   The Silver Elves

karearyn	kay	-	ree	-	air	-	ren

finds thems'elves among the elves

kareonra	kay	-	ree	-	ohn	-	rah

sits with the fae among the flowers

kariyna	kay	-	rye	-	in	-	nah

love them all

karuavyn	kay	-	rue	-	a	-	vin

inherits the ring

karudynara	kay	-	rue	-	den	-nair	-	rah

closest to water

karuna	kay	-	rue	-	nah

wild creator

karyldasa kay - rill - day - sah feels the connection

kasåla	kay	-	sah	-	lah

wildling

kazalyn	kay	-	zay	-	lynn

yet to remember

kazynra	kay	-	zen	-	rah

looks for the signs

keåcarona	key	-	ah	-	car	-	row	-	nah

earth light

keåleånda	key	-	ah	-	lee	-	ahn	-	dah

changling found

kealoryn	key	-	a	-	lore	-	ren

laying by the river

kealynsėl	key	-	a	-	lynn	-	sell

eager to start

keånåle	key	-	ah	-	nah	-	lee

spinning moonbeams

keanarlyn	key	-	a	-	nair	-	lynn

unnatural ability

keåndryn	key	-	ahn	-	drinn

just know

keanduryn little white feathers	key	-	ahn	-	dur	-	ren
kearåvėl playfully sexual	key	-	air	-	rah	-	vell
keardåfyn can survive in the elements	key	-	air	-	dah	-	fin
keardåne just in case	key	-	air	-	dah	-	knee
kearlyn wandering eyes	key	-		air	-		lynn
kearlys eases transitions	key	-		air	-		liss
kedålea a good one	key	-	dah	-	lee	-	ah
kelaboryn stepping into the light	key	-	lay	-	boar	-	ren
keladea not that it really matters	key	-	lay	-	dee	-	ah
keladru chills down the spine	key	-		lay	-		drew
keladyn desires to join in love and peace	key	-		lay	-		den
kelåfyn tremendous sense of relief	key	-		lah	-		fin
kėlålyndra runs through the fen in her dreams	kell	-	lah	-	lynn	-	drah
kelanavar keeps the sacred tomes	key	-	lay	-	nay	-	vair
kelåndåle like waking up from a long dream	key	-	lahn	-	dah	-	lee
kelåndanae never be harmed	key	-	lahn	-	day	-	nay
kelandra enchantment by twilight	key	-		lane	-		drah

162   The Silver Elves

kelandryn	key	-	lane	-	drinn		
a lot of pixies							
kėlea	kell	-	lee	-	ah		
teaches calm							
keleavaryn	key	- lee - a -	vair	- ren			
keeps quiet the fire storm							
kėlėtyr	kell	-	let	-	ter		
dreaming with open eyes							
kelodryn	key	-	low	-	drinn		
it is not by chance that I stumbled upon these woods							
kelonyn	key	-	low	-	nin		
spirit of the crossroads							
kelordyn	key	-	lore	-	den		
same situation has happened many times in the past							
kelordys	key	-	lore	-	diss		
magic mind							
kėloreyn	kell	-	lore	- ree	- in		
running through two worlds							
kelorvyn	key	-	lore	-	vin		
attracts people							
kėlynfa	kell	-	lynn	-	fah		
nature's confidant							
kemadryn	key	-	may	-	drinn		
I hope to understand why I am what I am							
kemale	key	-	may	- lee	l		
onging for adventure							
kemålys	key	-	mah	-	liss		
divining fires							
kemarän	key	-	mare	-	ran		
finds the new place							
kemåsyn	key	-	mah	-	sin		
protects the endangered							
kenadlyn	key	-	naid	-	lynn		
measure of magic							

The Book of Elf Names

kenalyn flapping wings	key	-	nay	-	lynn
kenarys ever since I discovered	key	-	nair	-	riss
kentunaa whispers with foxes	keen	-	two	-	nay	-	ah
keoryn shining light of truth	key	-	or	-	ren
keradyn so cool	key	-	ray	-	den
kerana kiss of honey	key	-	air	-	nah
kerarokyn watches from the trees	key	-	ray	-	row	-	ken
kerasa beam of light	key	-	ray	-	sah
keråvåndryl true to their stars	key	-	rah	-	vaughn	-	drill
keriåvyn wonders out loud	key	-	rye	-	ah	-	vin
kerrynde dancing leaves on spiral winds	keyr	-	ren	-	dee
kerrynva that's how I realized	keyr	-	ren	-	vah
kerryson elven warrior maiden	keyr	-	riss	-	sown
kerynatha plays in the stream	key	-	ren	-	nay	-	thah
kerynda dark flower	key	-	ren	-	dah
keryndae silver white	key	-	ren	-	day
keryndaryn dark flower beneath the night sky	key	-	ren	-	dare	-	ren

kerynde	key	-	ren	-	dee

kerynde   key - ren - dee
searching for the bigger picture

kerynladre   key - ren - lay - dree
dream flyer

keryntèl   key - ren - tell
feeling close

kesana   key - say - nah
joy to be near

kevadra   key - vay - drah
feeling sight

kevålaryn   key - vah - lair - ren
cries over the deforestation

kevalryn   key - vale - ren
wander through the woods

kevara   key - vair - rah
my friends will show me the way

kevaryn   key - vair - ren
from the start

kiålea   ki - ah - lee - ah
faery mother

kiånda   ki - ahn - dah
lingering joy

kiåndre   ki - ahn - dree
alive with mystery

kiardra   ki - air - drah
helping me find the answers I need

kiåvådalyn   ki - ah - vah - day - lynn
cares for the strays

kibutre   ki - bew - tree
balancing the scales of justice

kidarys   ki - dare - riss
just seems so beautiful

kilåndyn   ki - lahn - den
full moon mystery

| kilea | ki | - | lee | - | ah | | |
| longing to communicate | | | | | | | |

| kileålae | ki | - | lee | - | ah | - | lay |
| natural side of the world | | | | | | | |

| kileålyn | ki | - | lee | - | ah | - | lynn |
| hitchhiking around the country | | | | | | | |

| kileåvyn | ki | - | lee | - | ah | - | vin |
| meditative visions | | | | | | | |

| kilereyn | ki | - | lee | - | ree | - | in |
| wishful, bountiful and beautiful | | | | | | | |

| kilonshre | ki | - | lone | - | shree | | |
| lady of the wood | | | | | | | |

| kilordyn | ki | - | lore | - | den | | |
| time stood still | | | | | | | |

| kiloshe | ki | - | low | - | shee | | |
| songs of the water | | | | | | | |

| kilynea | ki | - | lynn | - | knee | - | ah |
| love of the moon and stars | | | | | | | |

| kilynle | ki | - | lynn | - | lee | | |
| eventually came to realize | | | | | | | |

| kilynsorsa | ki | - | lynn | - | soar | - | sah |
| energy converging | | | | | | | |

| kimerzyn | ki | - | mere | - | zen | | |
| in the garden at night | | | | | | | |

| kinaryn | ki | - | nair | - | ren | | |
| wonderful to have one as a friend | | | | | | | |

| kirånthor | ki | - | rahn | - | thor | | |
| asserts their self | | | | | | | |

| kirynzar | ki | - | ren | - | zair | | |
| shaded eyes | | | | | | | |

| kivaryn | ki | - | vair | - | ren | | |
| with love there's magic all around | | | | | | | |

| kiynaryn | ki | - | in | - | nair | - | ren |
| glimpses the other | | | | | | | |

kizändra this just clicked	ki	-	zan	-	drah		
kizyndareyn grandmother told me	ki	-	zen	-	dare	-	ree	-	in
kizyndora beautiful starry isle	ki	-	zen	-	door	-	rah
koåndaryn Faery awakens	co	-	ahn	-	dare	-	ren
koåndre refuses to surrender	co	-	ahn	-	dree
koaralys makes dinner for the faeries	co	-	air	-	ray	-	liss
koardåryn from the high trees	co	-	air	-	dah	-	ren
koåthoryn living in the dream state	co	-	ah	-	thor	-	ren
kobåryn such as myself	co	-	bar	-	ren
kodåndor I almost forgot	co	-	don	-	door
kodarfyn opens the portal	co	-	dare	-	fin
kodarlyn looking after what I love most	co	-	dare	-	lynn
kodaryn sounds great to me	co	-	dare	-	ren
kodarys dedicated to the moon	co	-	dare	-	riss
kodåvyn connecting to the source	co	-	dah	-	vin
kodere more than …	co	-	deer	-	ree
kodoryn pretty happy about it	co	-	door	-	ren

The Book of Elf Names

koenåli dragon wings	co	-	e	-	nah	-	lie
kofynėl watched by faeries	co	-	fin			-	nell
koladryn now there is no doubt	co	-	lay			-	drinn
kolådyn speaks of a land long lost	co	-	lah			-	den
kolålyn weaver of sound	co	-	lah			-	lynn
koleåla sensing energy	co	-	lee	-	ah	-	lah
koleåvyn one of the above	co	-	lee	-	ah	-	vin
kolidryn my second home	co	-	lie			-	drinn
kolidyn as I run I become the earth	co	-	lie			-	den
kolvin at home in the field	coal					-	vine
kolvyndyn moonchild	coal	-	vin			-	den
kolyndor gestures of greeting	coal	-	lynn			-	door
komålale sees the unseen	co	-	mah	-	lay	-	lee
komåle naked in the sun	co	-	mah			-	lee
komalyn have always been interested	co	-	may			-	lynn
komaryn dreams that come to pass	co	-	mare			-	ren
komarys arouses my curiosity	co	-	mare			-	riss

komere long awaited	co	-	mere	-	ree		
komiryn easing near	co	-	my	-	ren		
koradre shining dark	co	-	ray	-	dree		
korändryn blending two worlds	co	-	ran	-	drinn		
korathan brings calm	co	-	ray	-	thane		
korearyn driven to do more	co	-	ree	-	air	-	ren
korgånågyl voice of the forest	core	-	gah	-	nah	-	gill
koriyn becoming aware	co	-	rye	-	in		
kornacgryn veins of steel	core	-	nak	(as in naked)	grin		
korynda leprechaun's knot	co	-	ren	-	dah		
koryndal blends with the snow	co	-	ren	-	dale		
koryndar sacred to the sea	co	-	ren	-	dare		
korynėl awaits the cup	co	-	ren	-	nell		
korynsåna edging closer	co	-	ren	-	sah	-	nah
koryntare star gazer	co	-	ren	-	tair	-	ree
koryntyl feel alive for the first time	co	-	ren	-	till		
korysyn clouded star	co	-	riss	-	sin		

kovåndaryn storm on the beach	co	-	vaughn	-	dare	-	ren
kovanduryn bubbles in the water	co	-	vane	-	dur	-	ren
kragare rollicking fun	kray	-	gair	-	ree		
krevarsha followed the path	kree	-	vair	-	shah		
krevashyn when I need to be	kree	-	vay	-	shin		
kromaryn many extraordinary gifts	crow	-	mare	-	ren		
kromoryn old eyes	crow	-	more	-	ren		
krysålys intricate symchronicity	cris	-	sah	-	liss		
krysånådyn then it started	cris	-	sah	-	nah	-	den
krysåndre only younger and cuter	cris	-	sahn	-	dree		
krystana summoned in dreams	cris	-	tay	-	nah		
kryszånde runs with the deer	cris	-	zahn	-	dee		
kuarlyn moved around a lot	cue	-	air	-	lynn		
kudaryn spiraling upwards	cue	-	dare	-	ren		
kuleålu speaks with an accent	cue	-	lee	-	ah	-	lou
kulidyn when the time is right	cue	-	lie	-	den		
kulisyn my feet on the ground	cue	-	lie	-	sin		

The Silver Elves

kulyndyn	cue	-			lyn	-	den
usually when traveling							
kunådea	cue	-	nah	-	dee	-	ah
rather talk than go to war							
kunavyn	cue	-			nay	-	vin
gift of the elves							
kurådyn	cue	-			rah	-	den
these things are most prominent							
kydarys	kid	-			dare	-	iss
spiritual home							
kyélålyn	key	-	L	-	lah	-	lynn
loving the earth							
kylendali	kill	-	lean	-	day	-	lie
safe and warm beneath the moon							
kylorys	kill	-			lore	-	riss
try and do the best I can							
kymeryn	kim	-			mere	-	ren
I cannot explain to you							
kyncara	kin	-			car	-	rah
night gryphon							
kyndala	kin	-			day	-	lah
child of magic							
kyndånådyn	kin	-	dah	-	nah	-	den
on the back of a dragon							
kyndarsyn	kin	-			dare	-	sin
looks deeper							
kyndarthyn	kin	-			dare	-	thin
bright raven							
kyndarvyn	kin	-			dare	-	rin
guards the gates							
kyndaryn	kin	-			dare	-	ren
sways with the music							
kyndaryth	kin	-			dare	-	rith
remembers what's important							

The Book of Elf Names

kyndavae light from within	kin	-	day	-	vay
kyndraa pointy ears unseen	kin	-	dray	-	ah
kyndrayl always sketching	kin	-	dray	-	L
kynjara deep within	kin	-	jay	-	rah
kynrealvyn peeps out	kin	-	ree	-	ale	-	vin
kynsåde wind blowing through the trees	kin	-	dah	-	dee
kynsala born of air	kin	-	say	-	lah
kynzåndrèl another kind	kin	-	zahn	-	drell
kynzardys like home	kin	-	zair	-	diss
kynzare healer of souls	kin	-	zair	-	ree
kynzärèl with the trees	kin	-	zar	-	rell
kynzareyl higher path	kin	-	zair	-	ree	-	L
kynzaru could not resist	kin	-	zay	-	rue
kynzåryn guardian spirit	kin	-	zah	-	ren
kyridynor like a dream	ker	-	rye	-	den	-	nor
kytsumae live proudly	kit	-	sue	-	may
kytsyro song of flowers	kit	-	ser	-	row

ℒ

Elven Name and Meaning | Pronunciation

Elven Name and Meaning							
laådarèl warm breeze	lay	-	ah	-	dare	-	rell
laåfyndèl joins the melee	lay	-	ah	-	fin	-	dell
laåniyn among the sidhe	lay	-	ah	-	nigh	-	in
laaresa pirit speaker	lay	-	air	-	ree	-	sah	s
ladändor told by a wise woman	lay	-	dan	-	door
lådåndor live oak	lah	-	don	-	door
lådånfor walk in fresh air	lah	-	don	-	for
lådånthor tree magic	lah	-	dahn	-	thor
lådardyn seeks the deeper truths	lah	-	dare	-	den
lådarsyn from materials that the forest gave	lah	-	dare	-	sin
lådarys uplifts the oppressed	lah	-	dare	-	riss
lådereyn secret remembraces	lah	-	deer	-	ree	-	in
ladimea tree maiden	lay	-	dye	-	me	-	ah
ladyndre dancing on moonbeams	lay	-	dèn	-	dree

lådynèl	lah	-		den	-		nell
ache to look into their eyes once more

lådynyla	lah	-	den	-	nill	-	lah
magic twin

laènta	lay	-		in	-		tah
full of tricks

låfare	lah	-		fair	-		ree
snow mountain forest

låfaryn	lah	-		fair	-		ren
sharing the gift

låkynvar	lah	-		ken	-		vair
larger than life

lålålea	lah	-	lah	-	lee	-	ah
golden dawn flower

lålea	lah	-		lee	-		ah
since I was a child

låleådyn	lah	-	lee	-	ah	-	den
whispers to the waters

laleålae	lah	-	lee	-	ah	-	lay
increasing excitement

låleålyn	lah	-	lee	-	ah	-	lynn
flower coming into bloom

lalela	lay	-		lee	-		lah
dreams having opened me to the identity of my true self

lalelås	lay	-		lee	-		lahss
I feel I soon will be drawn to do something

lalelyn	lay	-		lee	-		lynn
totally believe

lålelys	lah	-		lee	-		liss
knew it anyway

låliåna	lah	-	lie	-	ah	-	nah
basks in the sun

lålylea	lah	-	lil	-	lee	-	ah
with opened eyes

lalyndae	lay	-	lynn	-	day
doing elvish things together					
lålynder	lah	-	lynn	-	deer
shamanic priestess					
lålyndor	lah	-	lynn	-	door
something greater					
lålyndys	lah	-	lynn	-	diss
communes with the animals spirits					
låmårådyn	lah	-	mah	-	rah	-	den
rides the sundering					
låmordrys	lah	-	more	-	driss
spiked chain					
lånådyre	lah	-	nah	-	der	-	ree
prowls the night					
lånålea	lah	-	nah	-	lee	-	ah
some other magic					
lånarea	lah	-	nair	-	ree	-	ah
no one knows					
lanarsyn	lay	-	nair	-	sin
will defend their rights as my own					
lanaryn	lay	-	nair	-	ren
casting about					
låndåle	lahn	-	dah	-	lee
life adventurous					
låndålor	lahn	-	dah	-	lore
little brother					
låndåloryn	lahn	-	dah	-	lore	-	ren
merges with the earth					
låndareyl	lahn	-	dare	-	ree	-	L
studies in twilight					
l〃ndareyn	lan	-	dare	-	ree	-	in
my parent told me tales of my ancestors					
l〃ndarys	lan	-	dare	-	riss
friend to the trees					

The Book of Elf Names

låndoreyn l spinning light	ahn	-	door	-	ree	-	in
lånfareyn soars over the mountain	lahn	-	fair	-	ree	-	in
lanorea in darkness whispers	lay	-	nor	-	ree	-	ah
lånsåla called from the past	lahn	-	sah	-	lah
lånwyno dawn of understanding	lahn	-	win	-	no
laodarys above the clouds	lay	-	oh	-	dare	-	riss
laowyn always knew	lay	-	oh	-	win
laryndor friend of the wild	lay	-	ren	-	door
låsåbåtha light on the wheel	lah	-	sah	-	bah	-	thah
låsådor blaze of passion	lah	-	sah	-	door
lasodarva awakening youth	lay	-	so	-	dare	-	vah
latånor community oriented	lay	-	tah	-	nor
latåtriyn bit of mischief	lay	-	tah	-	try	-	in
lathånådal rides swiftly	lay	-	thah	-	nah	-	dale
lathdoryn shining sword	layth	-	door	-	ren
latherea feels of trees	lay	-	thee	-	ree	-	ah
låthlorys living with intent	lahth	-	lore	-	riss

176

lauval wielder of the singing sword	lay	-	you	-	vale			
låvåndre magic calls to me	lah	-	vaughn	-	dree			
låvaråshe whispering silence	lah	-	vair	-	rah	-	she	
lavaråshyn quiet kindness	lay	-	vair	-	rah	-	shin	
låvoryn in the right vein	lah	-	vour	-	ren			
lavoryndål black cat	lay	-	vour	-	ren	-	dahl	
låvyndaryn protects the sacred fire	lah	-	vin	-	dare	-	ren	
layndyrèl l sees what others do not see	ay	-	in	-	der	-	rell	
laynylduryn something more to the world	lay	-	in	-	nill	-	dur	- in
leåalwyn circles thrice	lee	-	- ah	-	ale	-	win	
leådadra peace maker	lee	-	ah	-	day	-	drah	
leadarys nature's beauty	lee	-	a	-	dare	-	riss	
leadreyn didn't quite match	lee	-	a	-	dree	-	in	
leådryn new phase in my life	lee	-	ah	-	drinn			
leadynar ever elfin	lee	-	a	-	den	-	nair	
leäfyryn wild card	lee	-	aff	-	fur	-	ren	
leålaa teaches beauty	lee	-	ah	-	lay	-	ah	

The Book of Elf Names   177

leålala so like me	lee	-	ah	-	lay	-	lah	
leålalyn inherited giftedness	lee	-	ah	-	lay	-	lynn	
leålasa silver arrow	lee	-	ah	-	lay	-	sah	
lealdrys through a totally unrelated search	lee	-	ale	-	driss			
leålia have always been fascinated by	lee	-	ah	-	lie	-	ah	
lealolyn flutters by	lee	-	ale	-	low	-	lynn	
lealyn fleet foot	lee	-	a	-	lynn			
leålynara helps people feel good about thems'elves	lee	-	ah	-	lynn	-	nair	- rah
leålynde fleet of thought	lee	-	ah	-	lynn	-	dee	
leålyndrae power of attraction	lee	-	ah	-	lynn	-	dray	
leålyndryn odd sense of knowing	lee	-	ah	-lynn	-	drinn		
leålynva mysterious in my ways of working	lee	-	ah	-	lynn	-	vah	
leåmer heals with the mind	lee	-	ah	-	mere			
leåmynsa frolics in the surf	lee	-	ah	-	men	-	sah	
leånåfe woke up and there was something different about me	lee	-	ah	-	nah	-fee		
leånålea hand extended	lee	-	ahn	-	nah	-	lee	- ah
leanalyn waiting for the magic	lee	-	a	-	nay	-	lynn	

leanånda listens to the whispers of the trees	lee	-	a	-	non	-	dah
leåndåfyn enchantress shining	lee	-	ahn	-	dah	-	fin
leåndar clear in my mind	lee	-	ahn	-	dare		
leånder just felt right	lee	-	ahn	-	deer		
leåndor for honor	lee	-	ahn	-	door		
leåndre they have always loved me	lee	-	ahn	-	dree		
leåndrea eternally loved	lee	-	ahn	-	dree	-	ah
leåndryn loves the supernatural	lee	-	ahn	-	drinn		
leåndrys voice of the spirit	lee	-	ahn	-	driss		
leåndyre music fills my life	lee	-	ahn	-	der		-ree
leanoryn talent unfolding	lee	-	a	-	nor	-	ren
leånthor takes action	lee	-	ahn	-	thor		
leåpena bounces in circles	lee	-	ah	-	pee	-	nah
learådor drawn by mystery	lee	-	air	-	rah	-	door
learådoryn myterious fun	lee	-	air	-	rah	-	door	-	ren
learådre teasy flirt	lee	-	air	-	rah	–	dree
learådryn night fog	lee	-	air	-	rah	-	drinn

The Book of Elf Names

learådyn	lee	-	air	-	rah	-	den	little bit of everything
learåfyl lee going with the flow	-	air	-	rah	-	fill		
learåfyn healing heart	lee	-	air	-	rah	-	fin	
learåle every bit a beautiful elf	lee	-	air	-	rah	-	lee	
leardre spreads with love	lee	-	air	-	dree			
leardreyl hopes to find it	lee	-	air	-	dree	-	L	
leardriyn everquesting	lee	-	air	-	dry	-	in	
leardryn powerful awakening	lee	-	air	-	drinn			
leardrys curious to see	lee	-	air	-	driss			
leardyn just to name a few	lee	-	air	-	den			
leare wishing they were real	lee	-	air	-	ree			
leareyn turns and hisses	lee	-	air	-	ree	-	in	
learfyn underneath it all	lee	-	air	-	fin			
leårfyn guides the healing	lee	-	R	-	fin			
learthyn reaches into the past	lee	-	air	-	thin			
learvyn all life sings	lee	-	air	-	vin			
learynda body talker	lee	-	air	-	ren	-	dah	

learyndarys	lee	-	air	-	ren	-	dare	-	riss
seeks the silence									
leasa	lee	-		a	-		sah		
flowers flourish with her touch									
leåsaryn	lee	-	ah	-	sair	-	ren		
rises from the ashes									
leåthanyn	lee	-	ah	-	thay	-	nin		
realization grows stronger									
leåwyndrèl	lee	-	ah	-	win	-	drell		
perpetually curious									
leawynra	lee	-	a	-	win	-	rah		
begins to stir									
leazora	lee	-	a	-	zoar	-	rah		
golden skin									
lebynas	lee	-		ben	-		nayce		
begins to see									
ledadra	lee	-		day	-		drah		
finding the past									
ledadre	lee	-		day	-		dree		
thinks beyond									
ledånådare	lee	-	don	-	nah	-	dare	-	ree
can't wait to tell them									
ledånådyn	lee	-		don	-nah	-	den		
awaits some knowledge just beyond their grasp									
ledändas	lee	-		dan	-		dayce		
red fox									
ledåndea	lee	-	don	-	dee	-	ah		
seeking the path									
ledåndor	lee	-		don	-		door		
to create what is right for me									
ledåndyryn	lee	-	don	-	der	-	ren		
pure glowing white									
ledaryn	lee	-		dare	-		ren		
before they happen									

The Book of Elf Names   181

ledaryn growing bigger	lee	-	dare	-	ren		
ledarys it felt like I was home	lee	-	dare	-	riss		
ledida of the shade	lee	-	dye	-	dah		
ledonedèl stands with us	lee	-	doe	-	knee	-	dell
lefånde greater purpose	lee	-	fahn	-	dee		
lefyndre called by destiny	lee	-	fin	-	dree		
lelåle moon mother	lee	-	lah	-	lee		
lelalu gifted with spiritual powers	lee	-	lay	-	lou		
lemålyn makes the decision	lee	-	mall	-	lynn		
lemarea floats near the surface	lee	-	mare	-	ree	-	ah
lemareyl feel happier now	lee	-	mare	-	ree	-	L
lemareyn ocean of crystals	lee	-	mare	-	ree	-	in
lemareys hopelessly romantic	lee	-	mare	-	ree	-	iss
lemarys outcast adventure	lee	-	mare	-	riss		
lemere eerie coincidence	lee	-	mere	-	ree		
lemerea bound to me	lee	-	mere	-	ree	-	ah
lemereyl acclaimed elfin beauty	lee	-	mere	-	ree	-	L

lemeryn distant memories	lee	-	mere	-	ren		
lemila listens to feelings	lee	-	my	-	lah		
lenåda dragon healer	lee	-	nah	-	dah		
lenadra first time	lee	-	nay	-	drah		
lenåle can't be around other people too long	lee	-	nah	-	lee		
lenaran touch of feeling	lee	-	nair	-	rain		
lenaråthyn crazy in the nicest sort of way	lee	-	nair	-	rah	-	thin
lenarfyn sensual healing	lee	-	nair	-	fin		
lenåsa feeling connected	lee	-	nah	-	sah		
lenåsyn governed by the moon	lee	-	nah	-	sin		
lenatha holds dear the raindrop	lee	-	nay	-	thah		
leniyl healing trance	lee	-	nigh	-	L		
lenothas loved Faery since childhood	lee	-	no		thayce		
leoleyn called by the Sidhe	lee	-	oh	-	lee	-	in
leŏndaryn accepts the cup	lee	-	un	-	dare	-	ren
lesadoreyl little sister of the dragons	lee	-	say	-	door	-	ree	-	L
leshåndėl grew apart	lee	-	shahn	-	dell		

The Book of Elf Names

leshynca always there	lee	-	shin	-	cah	
lesola sea spray	lee	-	so	-	lah	
lesolale my heart rejoices	lee	-	so	-	lay	-	lee
lethoryn amazing regenerative capabilities	let	-	thor	-	ren	
levåldre longing heart	lee	-	val	-	dree	
levånådån filled with desire	lee	-	vah	-	nah	-	don
levåndryn around the next bend	lee	-	vaughn	-	drinn	
levara beast speaker	lee	-	vair	-	rah	
levaradre senses their spirit	lee	-	vair	-	ray	-	dree
levaryn a love of magic	lee	-	vair	-	ren	
levarys described my feelings exactly	lee	-	vair	-	riss	
levyndryn most unusual	lee	-	vin	-	drinn	
levynwarel one with the forest	lee	-	vin	-	wear	-	rell
leylna soul magic	lee	-	L	-	nah	
leyndrasha blood red cherry blossom	lee	-	in	-	dray	-	shah
leyndrys more than you realize	lee	-	in	-	driss	
leyndyre dreams that are like memories	lee	-	in	-	der	-	ree

liålajyn	lie	-	ah	-	lay	-	gin
magic dreamer							
liålea	lie	-	ah	-	lee	-	ah
knows with certainty							
liåleålyn	lie	-	ah	-	lee	-	ah	-	lynn
soul awakening							
liålefyn	lie	-	ah	-	lee	-	fin
set free							
liåleyn	lie	-	ah	-	lee	-	in
love being free							
liålyn	lie	-	ah	-	lynn
they will never see what I see							
lidarys	lie	-	dare	-	riss
from the time I was able to remember							
lidoryn	lie	-	door	-	ren
leafy friend							
lifyndra	lie	-	fin	-	drah
spins on toes							
lijåmae	lie	-	jah	-	may
master of the masks							
lilaneatha	lie	-	lay	-	knee	-	a	-	thah
of those days							
lileryn	lie	-	leer	-	ren
memories and dreams							
limereyl	lie	-	mere	-	ree	-	L
music is a language of its own							
linåneda	lie	-	nah	-	knee	-	dah
honing one's abilities							
linaråshyn	lie	-	nair	-	rah	-	shin
dancing by moonlight							
linårea	lie	-	nah	-	ree	-	ah
my favorite place							
linarys	lie	-	nair	-	riss
born of the forest							

linävra naturally good with a bow	lie		-nav		-	rah
lindelore brings news	line	-	dee	-	lore	-	ree
linera words can't describe it	lie	-	near		-	rah
linerys loves to dance	lie	-	near		-	riss
liorthyn feel them all around	lie	-	or		-	thin
lirelyn sleek cat of dreams	lie	-	ree		-	lynn
lisyndoryn rises with the mist	lie	-	sin	-	door	-	ren
litarea full moon shining bright	lie	-	tay	-	ree	-	ah
litaryn adopted by the people	lie	-	tay		-	ren
litosodyn feather light	lie	-	toe	-	so	-	den
livånoryn distant flicker	lie	-	vah	-	nor	-	ren
livaryn ocean of dreams	lie	-	vair		-	ren
liynda love of sports	lie	-	in		-	dah
loåcar scouting ahead	low	-	ah		-	car
loale senses through twilight	low	-	ale		-	lee
loålea shines with laughter	low	-	ah	-	lee	-	ah
loclathyn surrounded by the wee folk	lowk	-	lay		-	thin

186

lodåndryn	low	-	don	-	drinn

the dreams were so real to me

lodändyn	low	-	dan	-	den

awakens wonder

lodarfyn	low	-	dare	-	fin

all the earth speaks to me

loderyn	low	-	deer	-	ren

something magical in me waiting to be unleashed

lodoryn	low	-	door	-	ren

growing certain

lofåndår	low	-	fahn	-	dar

longs to understand

lofareyl	low	-	fay	-	ree	-	L

faery dreaming

lofarjyn	low	-	fair	-	gin

thin blade

lohacha	low	-	hay	-	chah

twilight's melody

lohedryn	low	-	he	-	drinn

awakening seeker

lokefyn	low	-	key	-	fin

as always

lokelfyn	low	-	keal	-	fin

not of the world

lokeryn	low	-	key	-	ren

calling to me

lokynca	low	-	kin	-	cah

keeper of the watch

lokynfari	low	-	ken	-	fair	-	rye

silver sunset

lokynta	low	-	ken	-	tah

coming back

loleåle	low	-	lee	-	ah	-	lee

truly adore everything about them

lolela gift of song	low	-	lee	-	lah		
lolelyn faerie curious	low	-	lee	-	lynn		
lolethea told me I would one day come to know mys'elf	low	-	lee	-	thee	-	ah
lolylea had a realization	low	-	lil	-	lee	-	ah
lolyndys place in the soul that feels like home	low	-	lynn	-	diss		
lolynle wave of bliss	low	-	lynn	-	lee		
lolynthor presence of the Divine	low	-	lynn	-	thor		
lolynza longed for magic	low	-	lynn	-	zah		
lolynzea like a curtain was lifted	low	-	lynn	-	zee	-	ah
lomålyn loves every beauty	low	-	mah	-	lynn		
lonardre then the realization came	low	-	nair	-	dree		
londrayl fair chance	lone	-	dray	-	L		
loradyn seeks to know	low	-	ray	-	den		
loråvyn tools for power	low	-	rah	-	vin		
lordåndu dictates of spirit	lore	-	don	-	dew		
lordånėl streak of silver	lore	-	don	-	nell		
lordarshyn moves in shadow	lore	-	dare	-	shin		

188   The Silver Elves

loryndorèl beyond boundaries	lore	-	ren	-	door	-	rell
losode rising from the dark	low	-	so	-	dee		
lotåsa loves to read	low	-	tah	-	sah		
lothladreys warrior of the spirit	lowth	-	lay	-	dree	-	iss
lothladyn fun and carefree	lowth	-	lay	-	den		
lothnarys moondrawn	lowth	-	nair	-	riss		
lotynear time has come	low	-	tin	-	knee	-	air
lovaarfa one with us	low	-	vay	-	air	-	fah
lovara dream's eye	low	-	vair	-	rah		
lovarys sense of justice	low	-	vair	-	riss		
lovynsa in the cool of the trees	low	-	vin	-	sah		
loynadèl valiant heart	low	-	in	-	nay	-	dell
loyndarys reminds us to love	low	-	in	-	dare	-	riss
loyndor living life to the fullest	low	-	in	-	door		
luarådryn raised among the elves	lou	-	air	-	rah	-	drinn
luardre stirring vibrating power	lou	-	air	-	dree		
luare radiates a kind of glow	lou	-	air	-	ree		

luarne pixie mark	lou	-	air	-	vin		
luarvyn riding the currents	lou	-	air	-	vin		
luåvynron horned dragon	lou	-	ah	-	vin	-	roan
ludinyn soothed by nature	lou	-	dye	-	nin		
ludonfari dragon faerie blue	lou	-	doan	-	fair	-	rye
lufidra rare beauty	lou	-	fie	-	drah		
lukyntri checks it out	lou	-	ken	-	try		
lulåndålae true friends	lou	-	lahn	-	dah	-	lay
lulelyn to further my understanding	lou	-	lee	-	lynn		
lunåda runs with the hounds	lou	-	nah	-	dah		
lunåfaryn light that shines at sunset	lou	-	nah	-	fair	-	ren
lunånda vowed to protect it at almost any cost	lou	-	non	-	dah		
lunara light eye	lou	-	nair	-	rah		
lunaråfyn will stay with me for the rest of my life	lou	-	nair	-	rah	-	fin
lunarea innocent and childlike face	lou	-	nair	-	ree	-	ah
lunarfyn awakens enchantment	lou	-	nair	-	fin		
lunarthyn very whimsical family	lou	-	nair	-	thin		

lunarys always desires to go home	lou	-	nair	-	riss		
luneda happy all the time	lou	-	knee	-	dah		
lunida dark smile	lou	-	nigh	-	dah		
lunorys along the path	lou	-	nor	-	riss		
luparådyn faery wolk	lou	-	pair	-	rah	-	den
lurådreyl not like all the rest	lou	-	rah	-	dree	-	L
lurynasa draws one close	lou	-	ren	-	nay	-	sah
lusania near to the flowers	lou	-	say	-	nigh	-	ah
lutheyl from another time	lou	-	thee	-	L		
luvyndre caretaker of the elders	lou	-	vin	-	dree		
luynva protects those near	lou	-	in	-	vah		
lydåla kind of odd actually	lyd	-	dah	-	lah		
lyldonyn begins to know	lil	-	doe	-	nin		
lyleålyn small, spritely and glittery	lil	-	lee	-	ah	-	lynn
lyledyn born of the fen	lil	-	lee	-	den		
lylela blue jewel	lil		lee	-	lah		
lylyndea divines the future	lil	-	lynn	-	dee	-	ah

lymåndre	limb	-	mahn	-	dree		
then I realized it was magic							
lymerdryn	limb	-	mere	-	drin		
light in the dark							
lynåle	lynn	-	ah	-	lee		
called in dreams							
lyndaa	lynn	-	day	-	ah		
vision of healing							
lyndålos	lynn	-	dah	-	loos		
sleep of dreams							
lyndaråsyn	lynn	-	dare	-	rah	-	sin
eye of the faerie							
lyndare	lynn	-	dare	-	ree		
wanders through fields of flowers							
lyndarea	lynn	-	dare	-	ree	-	ah
it must be real somewhere							
lyndareyl	lynn	-	dare	-	ree	-	L
heralds the new							
lyndareys	lynn	-	dare	-	ree	-	iss
roaming the forest							
lyndaryn	lynn	-	dare	-	ren		
the elusives							
lyndor	lynn	-	door				
quick to decide in times of need							
lyndoryn	lynn	-	door	-	ren		
acts quicklly in times of need							
lyndreåne	lynn	-	dree	-	ah	-	knee
all things new							
lyndylae	lynn	-	dill	-	lay		
tree love							
lynsidar	lynn	-	sigh	-	dare		
true to nature							
lynvoryn	lynn	-	vour	-	ren		
flower touch							

The Silver Elves

lytåre	lit	-	tah	-	ree
elf call					

lyvåndyryn	liv	-	vaughn	-	der	-	ren
lost in daydreams and music							

> AN ELF NAME IS THE FAE'S PERSONAL MANTRA. ONE CAN CHANT IT REPETITIVELY TO FOCUS ONE'S AWARENESS AND INCREASE ONE'S PERSONAL POWER OR THE ELF CAN CHANT ANOTHER'S NAME TO EMPOWER THAT PARTICULAR ELF.

> THE ELVES SAY A GOOD EDUCATION LUBRICATES THE MIND SO ALL ONE'S PREJUDICES AND PRECONCEPTIONS SLIP OUT AND AWAY.

ℳ

Elven Name and Meaning	Pronunciation			
maareyn runs with the wind	may	- air	- ree	- in
maarpari bringer of delight	may	- air	- pair	- rye
maaryshon packed with power	may	- air	- riss	- shown
maåyldorn certain aim	may	- ah	- L	- dorn
måchåndre tree singer	mah	- chahn	- dree	
måcharyna dedicated to help	mah	- char	- ren	- nah
madålysyn dusk's whisper	may	- dah	- liss	- sin
mådrava dazzling radiance	mah	- dray	- vah	
mådravyn searching ones'elf	mah	- dray	- vin	
mådrea gift of seeing other's past lives	mah	- dree	- ah	
madreyl of the woods	may	- dree	- L	
mådrylys sailing the open waters stirs my soul	mah	- drill	- liss	
mådrynel soon to be	mah	- drinn	- neal	
maharyn open to learn	may	- hair	- ren	

majåla magic mom	may	-	jah	-	lah		
majyndor branch to branch	may	-	gin	-	door		
majynteyl comes from the ancients	may	-	gin	-	tee	-	L
måleåla when the weather allows	mah	-	lee	-	ah	-	lah
måliys passion for swimming	mah	-	lie	-	iss		
måloreyn sudden shiver	mah	-	lore	-	ree	-	in
måloyndra tree drawn	mah	-	low	-	in	-	drah
målyndor inter-relatedness of the cosmic whole	mah	-	lynn	-	door		
målyndra knows what's important	mah	-	lynn	-	drah		
malyndre always known but not remembered	may	-	lynn	-	dree		
målynle intense in detail	mah	-	lynn	-	lee		
mamådryn hard to explain	may	-	mah	-	drinn		
mamareyl the pull of Faerie	may	-	mare	-	ree	-	L
mamareyn miracles happen	may	-	mare	-	ree	-	in
måmareys laughter a must	mah	-	mare	-	ree	-	iss
mamaryn ives in a tree	may	-	mare	-	ren	l	
måmerfyn intense recollection	mah	-	mere	-	fin		

mameroa hidden things	may	-	mere	-	row	-	ah
mameryn strange light in my eyes	may	-	mere	-	ren		
måmora mysteriously childlike	mah	-	more	-	rah		
måmorea do like them though	mah	-	more	-	ree	-	ah
mamorvyn enchanting mystery	may	-	more	-	vin		
måmoryn just out of reach	mah	-	more	-	ren		
manaryn lover	may	-	nair	-	ren	dragon	
måndåfyn wishing I was like them	mahn	-	dah	-	fin		
måndåle ready to accept	mahn	-	dah	-	lee		

måndori   mahn   -   door   -   rye
have guided me een when I refused their help

manerdra awakens the flowers	may	-	near	-	drah			
månjålåfår walks in elfin light	mahn	-	jah	-	lah	-	far	
månjordur proud to be elven	mahn	-	jour	-	dur			
månridor hazy light	mahn	-	rye	-	door			
maordrys prancing wildly	may	-	or	-	driss			
maråchåryn awakens to joy	may	-	rah	-	char	-	ren	
marådaa summons the horses	may	-	rah	-	day	-	ah	

marådor bring life into balance	may	-	rah	-	door	
marådyn waving pan	may	-	rah	-	den	
marågana fairy's promise	may	-	rah	-	gay	- nah
marågyle home of dreams	may	-	rah	-	gill	- lee
marålodyn tree whisper	may	-	rah	-	low	- den
maråndyn little beings tending the fruit trees	may	-	rahn	-	den	
måräntor fondness for cats	mah	-	ran	-	tour	
maråre serves the sisters	may	-	rah	-	ree	
marårelyn of the green	may	-	rah	-	ree	- lynn
måråtél darting eyes	mah	-	rah	-	tell	
maråthelys the way I really am	may	-	rah	-	thee	- liss
mårathyn waters of the world	mah-		ray	-	thin	
mareåle it is my life	may	-	ree	-	ah	- lee
måreåna amidst the music	mah	-	ree	-	ah	- nah
mareasa mind power	mare	-	ree	-	a	- sah
marechyn sea feather	mare	-	re	-	chin	
marethyn keeper of strays	mare	-	ree	-	thin	

måreyl golden wings	mah	-	ree	-	L	
måreylys something to hold on to	mah	-	ree	-	L	- liss
måreynda moon on water	mah	-	ree	-	in	- dah
mariåda know how to tap it	mah	-	rye	-	ah	- dah
maridor lush forest	mare	-	rye	-	door	
marieyl I belong in a world like that	mare	-	rye	-	e	- L
mårieyn moves with grace	mah	-	rye	-	e	- in
marïnre to bring the magic back	mah	-	ren	-	ree	
maritheyl nature's salvation	may	-	rye	-	thee	- L
mariyl guardian of those in need	mare	-	rye	-	L	
mariyla flys above the sea	mare	-	rye	-	L	- lah
marnynål reminds them of thems'elves	mare	-	ini	-	nal	
martåndor dancing dwarf	mare	-	than	-	door	
måryleyn arrow of faith	mar	-	L	-	lee	- in
marynåla ice blue eyes	mare	-	ren	-	nah	- lah
marynartha duets with birds	mare	-	ren	-	nair	- thah
marynarwe sheds tears of fellowship	mare	-	ren	-	nair	- we

marynåryn	mare	-	ren	-nah	-	ren	
there are still spirits of wonder in the world							
maryndana	mare	-	ren	-	day	-nah	
spiritually connected							
maryndåth	mare	-	ren	-	dahth		
sorting it out							
maryndor	mare	-	ren	-	door		
heart of the company							
maryndyn	mare	-	ren	-	den		
brings healing							
maryndys	mare	-	ren	-	diss		
goes out of their way to make others smile							
mårynthor	mah	-	ren	-	thor		
transition to the next realm							
maryntor	mare	-	ren	-	tour		
prancing on the green							
marynvål	mare	-	ren	-	vahl		
sylvan quick							
marynvar	mare	-	ren	-	vair		
taking refuge in Faerie							
marysthel	mare	-	riss	-	theal		
invisible presence							
mathelyn	may	-	thee	-	lynn		
blessed with the gift of art							
måvare	mah	-	vair	-	ree		
better than what the world has to offer							
meåndarys	me	-	ahn	-	dare	-	riss
otherworldly beauty							
mearana	me	-	air	-	a	-	nah
trick of the sea							
mearmore	me	-	air	-	more	-	ree
weather working							
medarfyn	me	-	dare	-	fin		
watch, listen and learn							

mejåle	me	-	jah	-	lee	
mystical purpose						
melåtara	me	-	lah	-	tair	-	rah
making love to the ocean						
meleïs	me	-	lee	-	iss	
near the stream						
mèlelea	mell	-	lee	-	lee	-	ah
not afraid to be mys'elf						
mèleyn	mell	-	lee	-	in	
drawn to the trees						
mèlvorn	mell	-	vorn			
hidden star						
mèlynsea	mell	-	lynn	-	see	-	ah
earth child						
memarsa	me	-	mare	-	sah	
they accepted me as one of their own						
memaryn	me	-	mare	-	ren	
light in the void						
menarådyn	me	-	nair	-	rah	-	den
astral playmates						
menothyn	me	-	no	-	thin	
served by the littles						
merådån	mere	-	rah	-	don	
feels so natural and pure						
merådyn	mere	-	rah	-	den	
silvered blade						
meråre	mere	-	rah	-	ree	
come and take me home						
meråtèlyn	mere	-	rah	-	tell	-	lynn
smile of an angel						
merathås	mere	-	ray	-	thahss	
twirls in the garden						
meråthyna	mere	-	ah	-	thin	-	nah
awaiting each day eagerly imagining all that can come to be						

mercandra nature's grounds keeper	mere	-	can	-	drah	
merearyn found the ken of long ago	mere	-	ree	-	air	-	ren
meretha making dreams real	mere	-	ree	-	thah	
mereynde seeks the silence	mere	-	ree	-	in	-	dee
meriåde ever present feeling	mere	-	rye	-	ah	-	dee
mernatharyl more than expected	mere	-	nay	-	thair	-	rill
mervareyn flung far away from home	mere	-	vair	-	ree	-	in
merynåda my calling	mere	-	ren	-	nah	-	dah
merynarea glides gracefully	mere	-	ren	-	nair	-	ree	-	ah
merynåtha sleek skin	mere	-	ren	-	nah	-	thah
merynåthe great joy in all that is magic	mere	-	ren	-	nah	-	thee
meryndånae going forward	mere	-	ren	-	dah	-	nay
meryndatha in love with the water	mere	-	ren	-	day	-	thah
meryndra hill top watchtower	mere	-	ren	-	drah	
meryndre I know this may sound strange	mere	-	ren	-	dree	
meryne fire and darkness	mere	-	ren	-	knee	
merynifyn that's what started it all	mere	-	ren	-	nigh	-	fin

The Book of Elf Names

meryniyl one too many times	mere	-	ren	-	nigh	-	L	
merynosa magic of the mind	mere	-	ren	-	no	-	sah	
merynsar tree shadow	mere	-		ren	-		sair	
merynthe language of shadows	mere	-		ren	-		thee	
merynva life renewed	mere	-		ren	-		vah	
merysi moon faery	mere	-		ren	-		sigh	
metholyn tends to shimmer	me	-		tho	-		lynn	
metholys serenely beautiful	me	-		tho	-		liss	
methra dreams come alive	me	-					thrah	
mezmerys very close to water	mez	-		mere	-		riss	
mialea ventures boldly	my	-	a	-	lee	-	lah	
miåleala always try to get what I want	my	-	ah	-	lee	-	a	-	lah
miåndor strange charisma	my	-		ahn	-		door	
miaråryn come to greet me	my	-	air	-	ah	-	ren	
miårasa reaching in	my	-	ah	-	ray	-	sah	
miardyn circle of protection	my	-		air	-		den	
miåreäl everyone thought I was different	my	-	ah	-	ree	-	al	

202   The Silver Elves

miaresa blending together	my	-	air	-	ree	-	sah
miartha letting things go unsaid	my	-	air	-	thah
miasolyn among the leaves	my	-	a	-	so	-	lynn
midålea nothing more to say	my	-	dah	-	lee	-	ah
midåndåle my greatest wish	my	-	don	-	dah	-	lee
midava only just begun the journey	my	-	day	-	vah
midoryn all of a sudden	my	-	door	-	ren
mijålyn plays with pixies	my	-	jah	-	lynn
miladea always tries to help	my	-	lay	-	dee	-	ah
milånda feels intentions	my	-	lahn	-	dah
milåndea every little thing	my	-	lahn	-	dee	-	ah
milazarna sits on the edge	my	-	lay	-	zair	-	nah
mileåla shadow in the eyes	my	-	lee	-	ah	-	lah
mileåryn magical little creatures	my	-	lee	-	ah	-	ren
milofyn from chaos, order	my	-	low	-	fin
milogarda protecter of the mist	my	-	low	-	gair	-	dah
milozara spits fire	my	-	low	-	zair	-	rah

The Book of Elf Names

milozor sees trouble ahead	my - with soar)	low -	zoar	(rhymes
milyndar mixer of herbs	my -	lynn -	dare	
milyneyl learning to love	my -	lynn -	knee -	L
milynsa ancient seal	my -	lynn -	sah	
milynta growing awareness	my -	lynn -	tah	
mimarys when I first heard	my -	mare -	riss	
miora among her people	my -	or -	rah	
miorådre of water born	my -	or -	rah -	dree
miorayl inherently beautiful	my -	or -	ray -	L
miordryn never want to leave	my -	or -	drinn	
miråsynara song is louder there	my - rah -	sin -	nair -	rah
mïresa I've always been what I am	mer -	ree -	sah	
mirynda stillness as if everything had become frozen	my -	ren -	dah	
mitaleo mighty warrior	my -	tay -	lee -	oh
miyndyryn commanded by honor	my -	in -	der -	ren
moiryndor birds on shoulder	mo -	eye -	ren -	door
momeryn always the clever one	mo -	mere -	ren	

mondale only word to describe me	moan	-	day	-	lee		
mondalea born of dreams	moan	-	day	-	lee	-	ah
mondave flits in shadows	moan	-	day	-	vee		
mondåwe embraces the inner child	moan	-	dah	-	wee		
mondrovål begins again	moan	-	dro	-	val		
morådaa exuberant life	more	-	rah	-	day	-	ah
moradavor awaiting the chance	more	-	ray	-	day	-	vour
morådoryn seeks to become	more	-	rah	-	door	-	ren
moråfe magic vibrations	more	-	rah	-	fee		
morårea she is guiding me in my life	more	-	ah	-	ree	-	ah
morårynda shines among the trees	more	-	rah	-	ren	-	dah
moråvådyn feels elfin growing within	more	-	rah	-	vah	-	den
moråvaryl smallest star around	more	-	rah	-	vair	-	rill
mordån desires to heal the wrongs	more		-		don		
mordaryn I have written before	more	-	dare	-	ren		
mordrasys heals the wounded	more	-	dray	-	sis		
moreada accept no substitutes	more	-	ree	-	a	-	dah

The Book of Elf Names

moreåna	more	-	ree	-	ah	-	nah
has traveled the long lonely road							
moreändra	more	-	re	-	ann	-	drah
wants to be real							
moreardra	more	-	ree	-	air	-	drah
skipping spritely							
morearna	more	-	ree	-	air	-	nah
loves the dance							
morearyn	more	-	ree	-	air	-	ren
fire on the sea							
morefyn	more	-	ree	-		-	fin
dream born							
morefynėl	more	-	ree	-	fin	-	nell
makes love to the Divine							
morenar	more	-	ree	-		-	nair
raven hawk							
morerasyl	more	-	ree	-	a	-	sill
comfortable under the trees							
moreyn	more	-	ree	-		-	in
keeps it all in order							
morfaryn	more	-	fair	-		-	ren
meadow of silver flowers							
morfyndru	more	-	fin	-		-	drew
master of the air							
morfyndryn	more	-	fin	-		-	drinn
connection to things unseen							
moriarėl	more	-	rye	-	air	-	rell
loves to sketch							
morqåniar	more	-	qwan	-	nigh	-	air
brings forth the child							
morsarys	more	-	sair	-		-	riss
skin of green							
mortålea	more	-	tah	-	lee	-	ah
deep in conversation							

206   The Silver Elves

morwyn	more	-		win
dream of things of which others never think				

morwyndar   more - win - dare
loves the land

morwyndare   more - win - dare - ree
sensual fulfillment

morwyndre   more - win - dree
feels like I'm one of them

morwyndwyn   more - wind - win
can't quite put my finger on it

morynåsa   more - nah - sah
sees beyond

morynda   more - ren - dah
awaits the future

moryndal   more - ren - dale
connection to the other realms

moryndar   more - ren - dare
waits to see

moryndari   more - ren - dare - rye
feels the future

moryndarys   more - ren - dare - riss
behind the mask

moryndėl   more - ren - dell
attracted to elves

morynfa   more - ren - fah
magical pearl

moryngåsa   more - ren - gah - sah
softly shimmers

morynsa   more - ren - sah
upon meeting

morynvådån   more - ren - vah - don
sits reading in the trees

morynvar   more - ren - vair
don't know how I came to this

The Book of Elf Names   207

mothrasèl	moe	-	thray	-	sell
nature's child					

movaryn	moe	-	vair	-	ren
glides with beauty					

murdarys	muir	-	dare	-	riss
one of the few					

murearyn	mew	-	ree	-	air	-	ren
life's meaning is unique to each being							

muredyn	mew	-	ree	-	den
discovered at last					

muretha	mew	-	ree	-	thah
sings a song of enchantment					

murnåtha	muir	-	nah	-	thah
especially the old faery tales					

murynda	mew	-	ren	-	dah
tease me by hiding my things					

myåthen	may	-	ah	-	theen
became it					

mydrasa	mid	-	dray	-	sah
very new to the idea					

myladea	mill	-	lay	-	dee	-	ah
trying to do the best that I can							

myladlosa	mill	-	laid	-	low	-	so
joyous heart							

mylåndre	mill	-	lan	-	dree
passion for the moon					

mylånthås	mill	-	lahn	-	thahss
wind in the hair					

mylånthe	mill	-	lahn	-	thee
see the good things					

mylathån	mill	-	lay	-	thahn	tiger
beneath the moon						

mylathos	mill	-	lay	-	thoss
takes comfort in the magic					

mylathyn jewel finder	mill	-	lay	-	thin		
mylesyna eats the dream berry	mill	-	lee	-	sin	-	nah
mylorthan as good as any	mill	-	lore	-	thane		
myloryn soul song	mill	-	lore	-	ren		
mylyndea encountered the sacred realm	mill	-	lynn	-	dee	-	ah
mynadra this place feels like home to me	men	-	nay	-	drah		
mynadre dream sight	men	-	nay	-	dree		
mynala mind feeler	men	-	nay	-	lah		
mynåle in love with oak trees	men	-	nah	-	lee		
mynalyn playing to the trees	men	-	nay	-	lynn		
myndånådėl betwixt and between	men	-	don	-nah	-	dell	
myndånåtha delicate cheeks	men	-	don	-	nah	-	thah
myndare something else	men	-	dare	-	ree		
myrada moon maiden	mer	-	ray	-	dah		
myradea reaches across the barriers	mer	-	ray	-	dee	-	ah
myrådor willow warrior	mer	-	rah	-	door		
myråqe emerges from the shadows	mer	-	rah	-	qwee		

myrasa shadow cat	mer	-	ray	-	sah		
myrdyndrys helps the lost	mer	-	den	-	driss		
myrona cat's shadow	mer	-	row	-	nah		
myrqåara aura of mystery	mer	-	qwah	-	air	-	rah
myrynatha strokes the cat	mer	-	ren	-	nay	-	thah
myrynathea cat dragon	mer	-	ren	-	nay	-	thee	-	ah
myrynsa cat like	mer	-	ren	-	sah		
myryntor sense of connectedness to all things	mer	-	ren	-	tour		
myrynvålona cat of bright colors	mer	-	ren	-	vah	-	low	-	nah
myrytor of the cats	mer	-	rit	-	tour		
mystorea emerges from the fog	miss	-	tour	-	ree	-	ah
mythoryn thinks ahead	myth	-	thor	-	ren		
mythrondar silver crest	myth	-	roan	-	dare		
mythrynda that's about it	myth	-	ren	-	dah		

$\mathcal{N}$

Elven Name and Meaning	Pronunciation						
naåvynfår remembers old friends	nay	-	ah	-	vin	-	far
nåbeyna peeks over the hedge	nah	-	be	-	in	-	nah
nadaleyn lest we forget	nay	-	day	-	lee	-	in
nådändar soul filled with light	nah	-	dan	-	dare		
nådåndayl golden leaf	nah	-	dahn	-	day	-	L
nådåndor my mate decided	nah	-	dahn	-	door		
nådånko half and half	nah	-	dahn	-	co		
nådårasa beauty unseen	nah	-	dar	-	rah	-	sah
nådare scent of Faerie	nah	-	dare	-	re	-	in
nådareyn that answered a lot of question	nah	-	dare	-	ree	-	in
nådarfyn on the money	nah	-	dare	-	fin		
nådarsyn ocean's beauty	nah	-	dare	-	sin		
nadaryth dragon's tongue	nay	-	dare	-	rith		
nådåthareyn amidst the beauty	nah	-	dah	-	thay	-	re	-	in

nådoreyn	nah	-	door	-	ree	-	in
flawless and graceful movement							
nådorys	nah	-	door	-	riss		
contemplating the heavens							
nåduran	nah	-	dur	-	rain		
gliding by							
nådyndor	nah	-	den	-	door		
wild shadow							
nåerys	nah	-	ear	-	riss		
dives deep							
nafåndur	nay	-	fan	-	dur		
lights the candles							
nåfyndor	nah	-	fin	-	door		
fog clearing							
någåror	nah	-	gar	-	or		
channels anger							
nälådanu	nawl (rhymes with owl) lah - dane - new -						
enraged by cruelty							
nålåfidoryn	nahl	-	lah	-	fie	-	door	-	ren
fantasy in green and grey							
nalana	nay	-	lay	-	nah		
in gossamer green							
nålåndrys	nah	-	lahn	-	driss		
sun through the leaves							
nålare	nah	-	lair	-	ree		
moves with the ease of the wind							
nålåwyndre	nah	-	lah	-	win	-	dree
really, really like them							
nåldåndyryn	nahl	-	don	-	der	-	ren
paces of magic and mystery							
naldoryn	nail	-	door	-	ren		
has forgotten							
naleåna	nail	-	lee	-	ah	-	nah
through the ages							

nåleånda *I know as soon as I walk in a room*	nah	-	lee	-	ahn	-	dah
nåleare *right on time*	nah	-	lee	-	air	-	ree
nalearyn *treads without leaving footprints*	nay	-	lee	-	air	-	ren
naleforêl *under the magic moon*	nay	-	lee	-	for	-	rell
nalerea *opened my mind to it*	nay	-	lee	-	ree	-	ah
nalerthyn *this time I wasn't afraid*	nay	-	leer	-	thin		
nalilea *on the rise*	nay	-	lie	-	lee	-	ah
nålodorus *rhymer of truth*	nah	-	low	-	door	-	youse
nålokanyn *born of the sky*	nah	-	low	-	kay	-	nin
nalorvådorn *point of love's awakening*	nay	-	lore	-	vah	-	dorn
nalynarle *sheds the flesh*	nay	-	lynn	-	nair	-	lee
nålynas *listening to the sea*	nahl	-	lynn	-	nayce		
nalyndre *mystic dreams*	nay	-	lynn	-	dree		
nålynle *following the signs*	nah	-	lynn	-	lee		
namartha *in the faerie's garden*	nay	-	mare	-	thah		
nåmartheyl *reflecting in the moonlight*	mah	-	mare	-	thee	-	L
nåmåsa *near the border*	nah	-	mah	-	sah		

nåmåsha in the secret valley	nah	-	mah	-	shah
namea feels it in the wind	nay	-	me	-	ah
namera sees the goodness	may	-	mere	-	rah
nåmorjyn little said	nah	-	more	-	gin
nanadålsa dives back	nay	-	nay	-	dahl	-	sah
nandaorda on the stage	nayn	-	day	-	or	-	dah
nåndåresa wishing willow	non	-	dah	-	ree	-	sah
nåndarethån holds the honor	non	-	dare	-	ree	-	thahn
nåndearyn sweet smell	non	-	dee	-	air	-	ren
nandorėl wiser with age	nane	-	door	-	rell
nåndoreyn heals in dreams	non	-	door	-	ree	-	in
nånduryn makes a great meal	non	-	dur	-	ren
naobilyn yearns to be closer	nay	-	oh	-	by	-	lynn
naordor new opportunities	nay	-	or	-	door
naore neverending greenery	nay	-	or	-	ree
naoresa always elfin	nay	-	or	-	ree	-	sah
naråkyndryn healer of the shadows	nay	-	rah	-	ken	-	drinn

214   The Silver Elves

narareyl shifting speeds	nay	-	ray	-	ree	-	L
narathvyn slips it through	nay	-		rayth	-		vin
narilos softly sounding	nay	-		rye	-		lowce
narthandor dreams of snow	nair	-		thane	-		door
naryndari from the others	nair	-	ren	-	dare	-	rye
naryniel I hope that helps	nair	-	ren	-	nigh	-	L
nåsari drop of golden water	nah	-		sair	-		rye
nåshåman single horn	nah	-		shah	-		mane
nasyryn moves unseen	nay	-		sir	-		ren
nåtålana mystery unraveling	nah	-	tah	-	lay	-	nah
natarbyn ready for battle	nay	-		tair	-		ben
nataryn not of normals	nay	-		tair	-		ren
nåthålon silence of the mystery	nah	-		thah	-		lone
natharyn jewel of the stars	nay	-		thay	-		ren
nathdunågår does no harm	nayth	-	dune	-	nah	-	gar
nathoryn strange dreams	nay	-		thor	-		ren
nathyndra tuned into the other world	nay	-		thin	-		drah

The Book of Elf Names

nåvålåsha	nah	-	vah	-	lah	-	shah
swift, gentle, kind, friendly and loving							
nåvaleyn	nah	-	vay	-	lee	-	in
crystal ball gazer							
nåvalfwyn	nah	-	vale	-	fwinn		
definite peace of mind							
nåvändåle	nah	-	van	-	dah	-	lee
practical compassion							
nåvåndre	nah	-	vaughn	-	dree		
things just clicked							
navarådys	nay	-	vair	-	rah	-	diss
swimming naked in a cold lake							
nåvaråsel	nah	-	vair	-	reh	-	sell
sensually aware							
navaråvyn	nay	-	vair	-	rah	-	vin
song of silence							
nåvare	nah	-	vair	-	ree		
drawn to the elfin ways							
nåvåreåva	nah	-	vah	-	ree	-	ah	-	vah
belongs elsewhere							
navarshuryn	nay	-	vair	-	sure	-	ren
steps into the astral plane							
navarys	nay	-	vair	-	riss		
sees the night							
navėleyn	nay	-	vell	-	lee	-	in
mad though it seems							
nåvoråthyn	nah	-	vour	-	rah	-	thin
from another realm							
navoreyl	nay	-	vour	-	re	-	L
powers unleashed							
navoreyn	nay	-	vour	-	ree	-	in
power of water							
nåvorthas	nah	-	vour	-	thayce		
deeply inclined							

nåvynde will try anything once	nah	-	vin	-	dee	
nåvyndre called by the Earth	nah	-	vin	-	dree	
nawatyl home camper	nay	-	way	-	till	
neadranyn long wisdom	knee	-	a	-	dray	-	nin
neådyna utterly devoted	knee	-	ah	-	den	-	nah
neåle helps the littles	knee	-	ah	-	lee	
neålea close to the wee folk	knee	-	ah	-	lee	-	ah
neålelyn night moon magic	knee	-	ah	lee	-	lynn	
nealeyn pure heart	knee	-	a	-	lee	-	in
neåmånva connects deeply	knee	-	ah	-	mon	-	vah
neåmara thrist to know the mysteries of the world	knee	-	ah	-	mare	-	rah
neånåma the voices are really speaking	knee	-	ah	-	nah	-	mah
neåndrys wishes to be one	knee	-	ahn	-	driss	
neanduryn on the road to adventure	knee	-	ahn	-	dur	-	ren
neåndyre shadow's whisper	knee	-	ahn	-	der	-	-ree
neåndyri watches from the shadows	knee	-	ahn	-	der	-	rye
neåneron care deeply for animals	knee	-	ah	-	near	-	roan

The Book of Elf Names   217

neangar	knee	-		ain	-		gair
passes the wisdom							
nearådyn	knee	-	air	-	rah	-	den
learns all they can							
nearålyn	knee	-	air	-	rah	-	lynn
love is thicker than blood							
nearavyn	knee	-	air	-	ray	-	vin
rising skyward							
nearea	knee	-	air	-	ree	-	ah
silver eyes							
neårefyn	knee	-	ah	-	ree	-	fin
needs a nudge							
neåreyn	knee	-	ah	-	ree	-	in
peers out							
nearlyn	knee	-		air	-		lynn
emerges from the sea							
nearyn	knee	-		air	-		ren
slips through the forest							
neatharyn	knee	-	a	-	thay	-	ren
settles on the tide							
neåvåshål	knee	-	ah	-	vah	-	shahl
at home in the water							
necalor	knee	-		cah	-		lore
deep in earth							
necatoryn	knee	-	cah	-	tour	-	ren
silent thunder							
nedåndryn	knee	-		don	-		drinn
shifts into bird form							
nedaryn	knee	-		dare	-		ren
would love to stop the pain							
nefånde	knee	-		fahn	-		dee
heals the past							
néfrade	nef	-		fray	-		dee
floats slowly across the water							

nelasana	knee	-	lay	-	say	- nah
look of the green						
nelasyn	knee	-	lay	-	sin	
just the way I live						
neliålyn	knee	-	lie	-	ah	- lynn
deep appreciation from others						
nėlynde	nell	-	lynn	-	dee	
speaks to the spirits						
nemäleyn	knee	-	mal	-	lee	- in
breathing in the air deeply						
nemålyn	knee	-	mah	-	lynn	
plays the fool						
nemålys	knee	-	mah	-	liss	
power in the hands						
nemaryn	knee	-	mare	-	ren	
closest to the Sidhe						
nemoryn	knee	-	more	-	ren	
senses what they feel						
nenanduryn	knee	-nane	-	dur	-	ren
sees the lady of the stars						
nenareyl	knee	-	nair	-	ree	- eel
dragon faery						
nenarmåre	knee	-	nair	-	mah	- ree
compassion's calling						
nenavia	knee	-	nay	-	vie	- ah
the bridge between						
neolynasa	knee	- oh -	lynn	- nay -	sah	
elf song						
nermådån	near	-	mah	-	dahn	
wish to lift the veil that divides the worlds						
neshiel	knee	-	shy	-	eel	
high flyer						
nesidara	knee	-	sigh	-	dare	- rah
shimmering eye						

The Book of Elf Names

nethyndre	knee	-	thin	-	dree		
protects the weak							
nevadrys	knee	-	a	-	driss		
feel them around me							
nevålådån	knee	-	vah	-	lah	-	don
hiding in the trees							
nevåladryn	knee	-	vah	-	lay	-	drinn
to find out all I can							
nevålys	knee		vahl	-	liss		
walked away without an injury							
nevåndor	knee	-	vaughn	-	door		
stirring in the belly							
nevåndre	knee	-	vaughn	-	dree		
heals melancholy							
nevåndreyl	knee	-	vaughn	-	dree	-	L
melancholy dreams							
nevaråryn	knee	-	vair	-	rah	-	ren
completely loving							
neviadyn	knee	-	vie	-	a	-	den
water wonder							
nevondre	knee	-	vone	-	dree		
favorite place							
nevondreyn	knee	-	vone	-	dree	-	in
sensual attraction							
nevonduryn	knee	-	vone	-	dur	-	ren
have always believed							
nevordås	knee	-	vour	-	dahss		
forced to believe in destiny							
nevorsyn	knee		-vour	-	sin		
ache that never goes away							
niåada	nigh	-	ah	-	a	-	dah
horse in the stream							
niådålyn	nigh	-	ah	-	dah	-	lynn
passionate for them							

niålea wept at their beauty	nigh	-	ah	-	lee	-	ah
niåledyn night slips her arms around me	nigh	ah	-	lee	-	den	
niåleon elf attraction	nigh	-	ah	-	lee	-	ohn
niåloyn from the rocks	nigh	-	ah	-	low	-	in
niålyndyn fights for the cause	nigh	-	ah	-	lynn	-	den
niålynsėl close to the meadow	nigh	-	ah	-	lynn	-	sell
niåmynta protects small creatures	nigh	-	ah	-	men	-	tah
niåndrys drawn to me	nigh	-	ahn	-	driss		
niåndyra stands firm for their beliefs	nigh	-	ahn	-	der	-	rah
niaosa found in the woods	nigh	-	a	-	oh	-	sah
nibardyn secret spot by the waterfall	nigh	-	bare	-	den		
nidaarvyn desires freedom	nigh	-	day	-	air	-	vin
nidarathyn raise ambient magic levels	nigh	-	dare	-	ray	thin	
nidarfyn begins to believe	nigh	-	dare	-	fin		
nidarva learning to control thoughts	nigh	-	dare	-	vah		
nidarys last but not least	nigh	-	dare	-	riss		
nidasa wood shadow	nigh	-	day	-	sah		

The Book of Elf Names

nidynåfyn ice elf	nigh	-	den	-nah	-	fin	
nifålosor bringing villains to heel	nigh	-	fah	-	low	-	soar
nigålys bears the golden rod	nigh	-	gah	-	lyss		
nigyleyn beauty of life	nigh	-	gill	-	lee	-	in
nilåndyn hears colors	nigh	-	lahn	-	den		
nileåde listens wisely	nigh	-lee	-	ah	-	dee	
nileåfyn it was so right	night	-	lee	-	ah	-	fin
nileålyn after a long search	nigh	-	lee	-	ah	-	lynn
niloara rescued from pain	nigh	-	low	-	air	-	rah
nilole enchanted song	nigh	-	low	-	lee		
nilolyn true seeker	nigh	-	low	-	lynn		
nilosvar twinkling smile	nigh	-	lowce	-	vair		
nilotharyn feels the warmth	nigh	-	low	-	thay	-	ren
nilovor shaping energy	nigh	-	low	-	vour		
nilylys fighting for what's right	nigh	-	lil	-	lyss		
nilynsa shining rider	nigh	-	lynn	-	sah		
nilyrshura bright rider	nigh	-	ler	-	shoe	-	rah

nimora   nigh - more - rah
so much joy it is painful

nimordyn   nigh - more - den
born of beauty

nimoryn   nigh - more - ren
close to the earth

nimorys   nigh - more - riss
innocent love

nimythra   nigh - myth - thrah
doesn't yet dare

ninara   nigh - nair - rah
sends good vibes to everyone

ninona   nigh - no - nah
pain and struggles make me stronger

niondriėl   nigh - ohn - dry - L
fashions jewels

niordyn   nigh - or - den
red haired deer

niråndea   nigh - rahn - dee - ah
somewhere in the arcs of space

niselea   nigh - see - lee - ah
gentle touch

nividra   nigh - vie - drah
storm whisperer

nodaryn   no - dare - ren
strong till the end

noėtėlor   no - et - tell - lore
searching endlessly

nogaryn   no - gair - ren
to his self

noidyna   no - eye - den - nah
comes from within

nolåndor   no - lahn - door
moment I hit puberty

The Book of Elf Names

nolaryn turns to light	no	-	lay	-			ren
nolasyn awakens to ones'elf	no	-	lay	-			sin
noldareyn pixie smile	knoll	-	dare	-	ree	-	in
nomereyn have always wanted	no	-	mere	-	ree	-	in
nontocaryn marked by magic	non	-	to	-	car	-	ren
nonynpari finds the other	non	-	nin	-	pair	-	rye
norådoryn escapes to other worlds	nor	-	rah	-	door	-	ren
noråndor see them in the fire	nor	-	rahn	-			door
nordador pixie wild	nor	-	day	-			door
noreådyn protected from harm	nor	-	ree	-	ah	-	den
noreala angel with a human face	nor	-	ree	-	a	-	lah
norearyn wants to know how	nor	-	ree	-	air	-	ren
noreåta well, then where did it come from?	nor	-	ree	-	ah	-	tah
noriėlys knows for certain	nor	-	rye	-	L	-	liss
noriyndor at home on the sea	nor	-	rye	-	in	-	door
norvåndåri protects their friends	nor	-	von	-	dah	-	rye
noryndarel extraordinary fascination	nor	-	ren	-	dare	-	real

noryndarys beyond human	nor	-	ren	-	dare	-	riss
noryndåva snow leopard's laugh	nor	-	ren	-	dah	-	vah
noryndåve finds the courage	nor	-	ren	-	dah	-	vee
noryndea in love with the romantic life	nor	-	ren	-	dee	-	ah
noryndor touched a faerie	nor	-	ren	-	door		
noryndys fun and perky	nor	-	ren	-	diss		
norynthel spiritual well being	nor	-	ren	-	theal		
nostatra heart that understands	no	-	stay	-	trah		
nowynli delves into the new	no	-	win	-	lie		
nuarådyn realized my calling	new	-	air	-	rah	-	den
nuare feels nature within	new	-	air	-	ree		
nudalyn educated by the sea	new	-	day	-	lynn		
nularyn song of the sea	new	-	lair	-	ren		
nulordyn it all seemed to fit	new	-	lore	-	den		
nulosyn biggest priority right now	new	-	low	-	sin		
nulynve all of life is magical	new	-	lynn	-	vee		
numynaryn no ill not balanced with light	new	-	men	-	nair	-	ren

nunåla black rose	new	-	nah	-	lah	
nureyn just not positive	new	-	ree	-	in	
nurisyn realized daily I was different	new	-	rye	-	sin	
nurovyn an even deeper interest	new	-	row	-	vin	
nurudyn gives of herself completely	new	-	rue	-	den	
nuterasa nimble fingers	new	-	tier	-	ray	- sah
nuthandarys wonderful willow	new	-	thane	-	dare	- riss
nuvereyl silver branch	new	-	veer	-	ree	- L
nuvondryn growing powers	new	-	vone	–	drinn	
nybåndor natural weapons	nib	-	bon	–	door	
nylådea looking for the way back home	nill	-	lah	- dee	– ah	
nylea each day is exciting	nill	-	lee	-	ah	
nymbara drawn to the twilight	nim	-	bare	-	rah	
nymrafyn seeks the warmth	nim	-	ray	-	fin	
nyshcama healing soul	nish	-	cah	-	mah	

O

Elven Name and Meaning	Pronunciation			
oåndanèl hears voice calling	oh	ahn	day	nell
obeånda it's okay to join us now	oh	bee	ahn	dah
odålea dark wanderer	oh	dah	lee	ah
odånådor magic musician	oh	don	nah	door
odånådyl flashes a smile	oh	don	nah	dill
odånåle so glad I found you	oh	don	nah	lee
odånålys plays the part	oh	don	nah	liss
odånåvyl in the high wind	oh	don	nah	ville
odaryn sense of purpose	oh	dare		ren
odarys stars singing to the earth's music	oh	dare		riss
odèleyn something good is going to happen	oh	dell	lee	in
odenådyn I wonder why	oh	dee	nah	den
oderyn can create whatever I desire with my thoughts	oh	deer		ren
odilyn all my troubles just disappeared	oh	dye		lynn

odonådèl beneath the hill fort	oh	-	doe	-	nah	-	dell
odonadur elf in the big city	oh	-	doe	-	nay	-	dur
odureyn others of my kind	oh	-	dur	-	ree	-	in
oduryn laying on the mossy rocks	oh	-		dur		-	ren
oeråle lives with books	oh	-	ear	-	rah	-	lee
oewyn crest of the wave	oh	-		e		-	win
ofåndyryn long walks beneath the full moon	oh	-	fahn	-	der	-	ren
ofaradyn wildly unique	oh	-	fair	-	ray	-	den
ofarna sensual earth	oh	-		fair		-	nah
ofelyn vague attraction	oh	-		fee		-	lynn
ofyndåryn no joke	oh	-	fin	-	dah	-	ren
ofyndere tiger of the crystal wind	oh	-	fin	-	deer	-	ree
okidyn loved by everybody	oh	-		ki		-	den
olådrys called to the green mound	oh	-		lah		-	driss
olåndara thought of getting one, too	oh	-	lahn	-	dare	-	rah
olandarèl feathers unseen	oh	-	lane	-	dare	-	rell
olåse a lot more living to do	oh	-		lah		-	see

228   The Silver Elves

olåsyn	oh	-	lah	-	sin
have learned much from them					

oleådryn	oh	-	lee	-	ah	-	drinn
patterns of the waylands							

oleålu	oh	-	lee	-	ah	-	lou
different level of knowledge							

olealyn	oh	-	lee	-	a	-	lynn
always pretty much loved							

oleånyn	oh	-	lee	-	ah	-	nin
I love to sit and look at them							

olearyn	oh	-	lee	-	air	-	ren
at the front							

olemare	oh	-	lee	-	mare	-	ree
gods smiled on me							

olenaryn	oh	-	lee	-	nair	-	ren
loves to be near water							

olialyn	oh	-	lie	-	a	-	lynn
hums secrets of magic							

olydra	oh	-	lyd	-	drah
speaks without words					

olyndålo	oh	-	lynn	-	dah	-	low
somewhere down deep							

olyndåsa	oh	-	lynn	-	dah	-	sah
called by the stories							

omåldor	oh	-	mahl	-	door
senses people's feeling before they are aware of them					

omålyn	oh	-	mah	-	lynn
learns to heal					

omånåle	oh	-	mon	-	nah	-	lee
terrible longing							

omarådyn	oh	-	mare	-	rah	-	den
light from hands							

omarålyn	oh	-	mare	-	rah	-	lynn
healing spirit							

The Book of Elf Names

omarzyn	oh	-	mare	-	zen			
speaks in riddles								
omële	oh	-	mell	-	lee			
together we managed to …								
omera	oh	-	mere	-	rah			
in my heart I feel one with them								
omeradyn	oh	-	mere	-	ray	-	den	
distant laughter								
omereyl	oh	-	mere	-	re	-	L	rides
fast and free								
omiåle	oh	-	my	-	ah	-	lee	
beneath the whispering hazel								
omikyn	oh	-	my	-	ken			
touching all								
omilyn	oh	-	my	-	lynn			
awakened from the coating that covered the true s'elf								
omireyl	oh	-	my	-	ree	-	L	
glitter and glitz								
omita	oh	-	my	-	tah			
there for us								
omiyl	oh	-	my	-	L			
twin flames								
omore	oh	-	more	-	ree			
dances with the flowers								
omorole	oh	-	more	-	row	-	lee	
if you will								
omuryn	oh	-	muir	-	ren			
innocence of an elf								
onaleal	oh	-	nay	-	lee	-	ale	
tender blossom								
onalyn	oh	-	nay	-	lynn			
a series of dreams								
onånda	oh	-	non	-	dah			
treasures the power								

onaråfyn inner goddess	oh	-	nair	-	rah	-	fin
onareyl nature's imagination	oh	-	nair	-ree	-	L	
onareyn bears a dragon's stone	oh	-	nair	-	ree	-	in
onarynėl one of the family	oh	-	nair	-	ren	-	nell
ondålyn one of many waiting	ohn	-	dah	-	lynn		
ondåma mysterious shade	ohn	-	dah	-	mah		
ŏndåryleon looking to share	on - dah - rill - lee - on						
ondeåndåfa sees before the others	ohn - dee - ahn - dah - fah						
ondeåndėl feels their pain	ohn	-	dee	-	ahn	-	dell
ondonadėl light caster	ohn	-	doe	-	nay	-	dell
oneåle when I awoke	oh	-	knee	-	ah	-	lee
onereyl caught my attention	oh	-	knee	-	ree	-	L
onerlyn to heal those around me	oh	-	near	-	lynn		
oniåda I was the only one that could see them	oh - nigh - ah - dah						
oniåle drawn to it	oh	-	nigh	-	ah	-	lee
oniålys ikes the idea	oh - nigh - ah - liss l						
onilyn after much searching and prayer	oh	-nigh	-	lynn			

The Book of Elf Names

onire	oh	-	nigh	-			ree
chaser of wisdom							
oniyn	oh	-	nigh	-		in	s
peaks in melodic tones							
onoreyn	oh	-	nor	-	ree	-	in
my whole life							
onqidra	ohn	-	qwi	-			drah
comes as a friend							
onureyn	oh	-	new	-	ree	-	in
that's where I belong							
oradreyn	oh	-	ray	-	dree	-	in
sees the beauty in the smallest leaf							
oradyn	oh	-	ray	-			den
a mission still unknown to me							
oraleyn	oh	-	ray	-	lee	-	in
song of the pen							
oraluva	oh	-	ray	-	lou	-	vah
golden moon hawk							
orändåvar	oh	-	ran	-	dah	-	vair
learning the arcana							
oraråvyn	oh	-	ray	-	rah	-	vin
behind the waterfall							
oråreånda	oh	-	rah	-	ree	-	ahn	-	dah
senses the coming							
orarynda	oh	-	ray	-	ren	-	dah
crow's song							
oraryndala	oh	-	ray	-	ren	-	day	-	lah
ready to learn							
orasyn	oh	-	ray	-			sin
overwhelming fascination							
oravyndal	oh	-	ray	-	vin	-	dale
of other worlds							
ordålea	or	-	dah	-	lee	-	ah
everyone needs to be free							

ordathålyn mutual love	or	-	day	-	thah	-	lynn
ordynala delicate form	or	-	den	-	nay	-	lah
oreadyn awakens the others	or	-	ree	-	a	-	den
orealyn awakened by nature	or	-	ree	-	a	-	lynn
orearyn at one with nature	or	-	ree	-	air	-	ren
oreåvyn awakens those ready	or	-	ree	-	ah	-	vin
oredynél golden smile	or	-	ree	-	den	-	nell
orejala golden laughter	or	-	ree	-	jay	-	lah
orelyn in the silence in the sunshine	or	-	ree	-	lynn		
oresa the outer edge	or	-	ree	-	sah		
orevaryn always there without a moment's hesitation	or	-	ree	-	vair	-	ren
oreyndél beyond the normal	or	-	ree	-	in	-	dell
orialyn I have my suspicions	or	-	rye	-	a	-	lynn
orilena forever yours	or	-	rye	-	lee	-	nah
oriryndaryn shapes gold	or	-	rye	-	ren	-	dare - ren
orlodyn multiphased	or	-	low	-	den		
ormålea cannot block it out any longer	or	-	mah	-	lee	-	ah

orona	oh	-	row	-	nah		
field of desires							
oronea	oh	-	row	-	knee	-	ah
child of nature							
orryndasha	or	-	ren	-	day	-	shah
caressed by the rain							
orudyn	or	-	rue	-	den		
where did you learn to speak my language							
orushyn	or	-	rue	-	shin		
pale, white skin							
orvynador	or	-	vin	-	nay	-	door
calms the spirit							
orvyndål	or	-	vin	-	dahl		
song smith							
orwyndėl	or	-	win	-	dell		
stands beyond							
orylea	or	-	rill	-	lee	-	ah
seeking to become whole							
oryndåfa	or	-	ren	-	dah	-	fah
rides a unicorn							
oryndår	or	-	ren	-	dar		
mysteries seen							
orynde	or	-	ren	-	dee	helps	
others who are willing to see							
oryndea	or	-	ren	-	dee	-	ah
helps others to see the truth							
oryndor	or	-	ren	-	door		
guardian of the fifth gate							
oryndyn	or	-	ren	-	den		
impossible truth							
orynle	or	-	ren	-	lee		
warms one to one's toes							
orynvådalo	or	-	ren	-	vah	-	day	-	low
trilled with life							

orynvar gives back more than he gets	or	-			ren	-			vair	

orynvar   or   -   ren   -   vair
gives back more than he gets

orynvidor   or   -   ren   -   vie   -   door
trusts his senses

osåla   oh   -   sah   -   lah
straight on till morning

osalala   oh   -   say   -   lay   -   lah
chants in the ancient tongue

osåleara   oh   -   sah   -   lee   -   air   -   rah
by the statue on the hill

osånådyn   oh   -   sah   -   nah   -   den
flowing heart

oseåna   oh   -   see   -   ah   -   nah
light upon the sea foam

oseyndar   oh   -   see   -   in   -   dare
broad appreciation

osheara   oh   -   she   -   air   -   rah
safe in the sea

oshuryn   oh   -   sure   -   ren
pretty lucky

osolore   oh   -   so   -   lore   -   ree
sensual dancer

osondaru   oh   -   sewn   -   dare   -   rue
dragon thoughts

osunåle   oh   -   sue   -   nah   -   lee
just strolling along

osuryn   oh   -   sue   -   ren
helped by the wolves

ovåndåre   oh   -   vaughn   -dah   -   ree
patter of rain

ovaresyn   oh   -   vair   -   ree   -   sin
ever seeking to be better

ovareyl   oh   -   vair   -   ree   -   L
dreams among the trees

The Book of Elf Names

ovarsusen feeling elfish	oh	-	vair	-	sue	-	scene
ovaryn carrier of secrets	oh	-	vair	-	sin
ovoradyn never alone	oh	-	vour	-	ray	-	den
owynia true to the Mother	oh	-	win	-	nigh	-	ah
oyla admired the love	oh	-	L	-	lah
oyndrås beyond the veil	oh	-	in	-	drahss
oyndure always seeks the truth	oh	-	in	-	dur	-	ree
ozåndrea senses the illusion	oh	-	zahn	-	dree	-	ah

𝒫

Elven Name and Meaning

Pronunciation

Elven Name and Meaning	Pronunciation					
pådardryn best memory of my whole life	pah	-	dare	-	drinn	
pådoreyn elvish witch	pah	-	door	-	ree	-	in
pådyndor sees the lights	pah	-	den	-	door	
påfardåcor never forgotten	pah	-	fair	-	dah	-	core
paladore tries to understand	pay	-	lay	-	door	-	ree
palådori illuminated on the stage	pay	-	lah	-	door	-	rye
pålådorys understands the trees	pah	-lah	-	door	-	riss
påladreyn strong longing to be connected	pah	-	lay	-	dree	-	in
påladrys that tale always struck a cord with me	pah	-	lay	-	driss
pålådyndor among the best	pah	-	lah	-	den	-	door
päladyryn rush of excitement	pal	-	lay	-	der	-	ren
palafyndra easing closer	pay	-	lay	-	fin	-	drah
pålålyndra dream of things that seem so real but cannot be of this lifetime	pah	-	lah	-	lynn	-	drah
påländar rhyme is the reason	pah	-	lahn	-	dare

pälåndor captures the light	pal	-	lahn			-	door
palasea castle in the mist	pay	-	lay	-	see	-	ah
päläsiryn hears a call when near an older forest	pal	-	lah	-	sire	-	ren
pålasyn flash of silver	pah	-	lay			-	sin
paldalan lavender faery	pale	-	day			-	lane
paldalo knew from before	pale	-	day			-	low
palelashåna just might be	pay	-	lee	-	lay	- shah -	nah
palentra seeker of sorcery	pay	-	lean			-	trah
palesyndra standing near	pay	-	lee	-	sin	-	drah
paletaryn stands out	pay	-	lee	-	tair	-	ren
palevåntral soft bark	pay	-	lee	-	vaughn	-	trail
pålolidyn yearns for rebirth	pah	-	low	-	lie	-	den
paltalan on their own path	pale	-	tay			-	lane
påltora one who sets things aright	pahl	-	tour			-	rah
pålyndåre watches the sea waves	pay	-	lynn	-	dar	-	ree
palynder hears the voice	pay	-	lynn			-	deer
pålyndor hiding out on a cold winter day	pah	-	lynn			-	door

pålyndreador awaits the return	pah	-	lynn	-	dree	-	a	- door
palyndyr dark shiny one	pay	-	lynn	-	der			
palynsa irridescent beauty	pay	-	lynn	-	sah			
palynta whispering woods	pay	-	lynn	-	tah			
palyntareyl called to the woods	pay	-	lynn	-	tair	-	ree	- L
pålyntåryn sees with the heart	pah	-	lynn	-	tar	-	ren	
pandåle starting to discover who I am	pain	-	dah	-	lee			
påndålea have never gotten it out of my head	pahn	-	dah	-	lee	-	ah	
påndålyn set apart	pahn	-	dah	-	lynn			
påndrågor among the secret texts	pahn	-	drah	-	gore			
pånvådoryn light on her feet	pahn	-	vah	-	door	-	ren	
pånvåndorån born with a sword in their hand	pahn	-	vaughn		door		rahn	
påpåle would like to help	pah	-	pah	-	lee			
parådathyn skips happily	pair	-	rah	-	day	-	thin	
parådryn full wind	pair	-	rah	-	drinn			
paråfyndro from the beginning	pair	-	rah	-	fin	-	dro	
parålena secret magic	pair	-	rah	-	lee	-	nah	

The Book of Elf Names

påreåryn it happened overnight	pah	-	ree	-	ah	-	ren
parelåndra pair touched by light		-	ree	-	lahn	-	drah
parelosyn one with the sea	pair	-	ree	-	low	-	sin
parevondryl pair oak meadow		-	ree	-	vone	-	drill
parondoryn deeply, passionately, wonderfully	pair	-	roan	-	door	-	ren
paruvyn bringer of the inner truth	pair	-	rue	-	vin
parydea holds the mirror	pair	-	rid	-dee	-	ah
parynala can play an instrument	pair	-	ren	-	nay	-	lah
parynda sits in the glen	pair	-	ren	-	dah
paryndåla born of the glen	pair	-	ren	-	dah	-	lah
paryndålås dragon of the glen	pair	-	ren	-	dah	-	lahss
paryndamer guided by the signs	pair	-	ren	-	day	-	mere
paryndarys pair sits for hours waiting for wild life		-	ren	-	dare	-	riss
paryndas sleeps under the stars	pair	-	ren	-	dayce
paryndåthås great to have one	pair	-	ren	-	dah	-	thahss
paryndel passing by	pair	-	ren	-	deal
paryndir tunes in	pair	-	ren	-	dire

240

paryndolf	pair	-	ren	-			dole-f
sense of meaning							

päthåleyl	pat	-	thah	-	lee	-	L
at peace among the trees							

pathynra	pay	-	thin	-	rah
cat of many colors					

peålea	pee	-	ah	-	lee	-	ah
awesome people							

peåndålyn	pee	-	ahn	-	dah	-	lynn
filled with hope							

peazaleyn	pee	-	a	-	zay	-	lee	-	in
really has a choice									

pedålyn	ped	-	dah	-	lynn
chosen by the sacred mother					

pedånawyn	ped	-	dah	-	nay	-	win
whether they deserve it or not							

pedåwyn	pee	-	dah	-	win
can fend for thems'elves					

peladåryn	pell	-	lay	-	dah	-	ren
I was more than I had been led to believe							

pelålyndarys	pell	-	lah	-	lynn	-	dare	-
heart of light	riss							

pelåndås	pell	-	lahn	-	dahss
breathes beneath the waters					

pelea	pell	-	lee	-	ah
gifts of the heart					

peledynda	pell	-	lee	-	den	-	dah
sister of our sister							

peleländros	pell	-	lee	-	lan	-	drowce
studies humans							

pelonu	pell	-	low	-	new
spent much time practicing					

pelordas	pell	-	lore	-	dayce
ready to embark upon the great journey of my life					

The Book of Elf Names

pėlynsåndrys scent of magic	pell	-	lynn	-	sahn	-	driss
pėlyntari seeks the way	pell	-	lynn	-	tair	-	rye
pemeryn followed by a light	pee	-	mere	-	ren		
pendrasa soothed by the fair	peen	-	dray	-	sah		
pennala jumps in with both feet	peen	-	nay	-	lah		
peoreyl off venturing in the woods	pee	-	or	-	ree	-	L
peravol drawn to beauty and sensuality	pee	-	ray	-	vole		
perondåna just curious	pee	-	roan	-	dah	-	nah
pertholas hill dweller	peer	-	thoo	-	lace		
perynatha time draws nigh	peer	-	ren	-	nay	-	thah
perynathe most favorite memory	peer	-ren	-	nay	-	thee	
peryndeyn knows instinctively	peer	-	ren	-	dee	-	in
perynsa on the bottom of the sea	peer	-	ren	-	sah		
perynsyndori mood of the sea	peer	-	ren	-	sin	-	door	-	rye
perynter faith in the morrow	peer	-	ren	-	tier		
perynvar music of remembering	peer	-	ren	-	vair		
pialea plays with words	pie	-	a	-	lee	-	ah

piåndåru	pie	-	ahn	-	dah	-	rue
yearns for the certain place							

piåreyn	pie	-ah	-	ree	-	in
it makes me weep						

piåsereyn	pie	-	ah	-	seer	-	ree	-	in
beneath the flowers									

pidånda	pie	-	don	-	dah
knew without having studied the subject					

pidrasys	pie	-	dray	-	sis
gracefully serious					

pikasa	pie	-	kay	-	sah
impish smile					

pilyndea	pie	-	lynn	-	dee	-	ah
one hundred percent sure							

pinadra	pie	-	nay	-	drah
natural talent					

pinardryn	pie	-	nair	-	drinn
sister to naiads					

pirerreyn	pie	-	rear	-	ree	-	in
long time coming							

pirule	pie	-	rue	-	lee
high curiosity					

pitharyn	pie	-	thay	-	ren
reads about them					

podånder	poe	-	don	-	deer
changes every day					

polale	poe	-	lay	-	lee
far away star					

polåndar	poe	-	lahn	-	dare
you just accept it					

polarun	poe	-	lair	-	rune
have a lot of exploring to do					

poleare	poe	-	lee	-	air	-	ree
trys to help							

The Book of Elf Names

polinafar	poe	-	lie	-	nay	-	fair
one of many names							
ponåålyn	poe	-	nah	-	ah	-	lynn
sweet and pure at heart							
pondarådon	pone (rhymes with bone) dare - rah – doan						
skillful wood elf							
pondåreda	pone	-	dah	-	ree	-	dah
feels like a dragon							
pondareyn	pone	-	dare	-	ree	-	in
drawn to Elfin							
ponfynaryn	pone	-	fin	-	nair	-	ren
safe in the forest							
poreånda	pour	-	ree	-	ahn	-	dah
from the time I was a child							
poriålyn	pour	-	rye	-	ah	-	lynn
spins like a top							
poroduri	pour	-	row	-	dur	-	rye
pixie ears							
porulyn	pour	-	rue	-	lynn		
happiest when creating something							
poryndåryn	pour	-	ren	-	dar	-	ren
realized I knew most of it already							
praådynor	pray	-	ah	-	den	-	nor
I'll know when I come across it							
pralaryn	pray	-	lair	-	ren		
phantom wolf							
predåsyn	pre	-	dah	-	sin		
cares for the wounded							
prelasa	pre	-	lay	-	sah		
questing for truth							
prilåndryn	pry	-	lahn	-	drinn		
found what fits best							
purådor	pure	-	rah	-	door		
varys in belief							

244

puriådėl	pure	-	rye	-	ah	-	dell
we have much in common							
puryndaa	pure	-	ren	-	day	-	ah
physically challenging activities							
pyksalea	pick	-	say	-	lee	-	ah
born on a cloud							
pyksåna	pick	-	sah			-	nah
bright and blushing							
pymerys	pim	-	mere			-	ris
power of the fae							
pynadoryn	pin	-	nay	-	door	-	ren
born of mystery							
pynatha	pin	-	nay			-	thah
essence of the earth							
pyndala	pin	-	day			-	lah
just starting to realize all this							
pyndånåfa	pin	-	don	-	nah	-	fah
guides the child							
pyndånåle	pin	-	don	-	nah	-	lee
did not feel my soul was complete							
pyndarådyn	pin	-	dare	-	rah	-	den
born this way							
pyryndor	per	-	ren			-	door
words of power							

Q

Elven Name and Meaning	Pronunciation						
qådåloryn as long as I can remember	qwah	-	dah	-	lore	-	ren
qådalys in any way possible	qwah	-		day	-		liss
qålådoryn have never stopped believing	qwah	-	lah	-	door	-	ren
qålådreyl well of light	qwah	-	lah	-	dree	-	L
qalamera never gives up	qway	-	lay	-	mere	-	ah
qålåndar light hearted	qwah	-		lahn	-		dare
qålånde unique gift	qwah	-		lahn	-		dee
qåledånde don't want to be recognized or thanked	qwah	-	lee	-	don	-	dee
qalela called by the fae	qway	-		lee	-		lah
qålmålyn awakening psychic	qwahl	-		mah	-		lynn
qalyndareån moon on forehead	qway	-	lynn	-	dare	-	ree	ahn
qålyndre swan maiden	qwah	-		lynn	-		dree
qålyndri all I want to be	qwah	-		lynn	-		dry
qåmalys if and when	qway	-		may	-		liss

qåndålådyn shadowed eyes	qwan	-	dah	-	lah	-	den
qåndåle world weaver	qwan	-	dah		lee		
qåndalys mate seeker	qwan	-	day	-	liss		
qåndaråsyn walks on air	qwan	-	dare	-	rah	-	sin
qåndare place for them	qwan	-	dare		ree		
qandarea let fate decide	qwain	-	dare	-	ree	-	ah
qandareon fire witch	qwain	-	dare	-	ree	-	ohn
qåndareyl joining in with merriment and song	qwan	-	dare	-	ree	-	L
qandareys extremely loyal	qwain	-	dare	-	ree	-	iss
qåndaryn shares truth	qwan	-	dare		ren		
qåndarynfyl in the company of truth	qwan	-	dare	-	ren	-	fill
qandėleyn watches the golden fire	qwain	-	dell	-	lee	-	in
qandori in the deep caverns	qwain	-	door		rye		
qåntaryn it's just the way it is	qwah	-	tair	-	ren		
qåntarys near the water	qwah	-	tair	-	riss		
qareyn wand maker	qway	-	ree	-	in		
qarthänådån memories of other places	qway	-	than	-	nah	-	don

The Book of Elf Names

qåtareyn close to the family	qwah	-	tair	-	ree	-	in
qåvålalo as simple as that	qwah	-	vah	-	lay	-	low
qavånåvyn drifts away	qway	-	vaughn	-	nah	-	vin
qåvåndåryn protects the earth and all her creatures	qwah	-	vaughn	-	dah	-	ren
qavondra pays attention to the sacred messages	qway	-	vone			-	drah
qåvylådån listens to the stories of the trees	qwah	-	ville	-	lah	-	don
qåvyndål called to travel	qwah	-	vin			-	dahl
qåvyndålys on the far reaches	qwah	-	vin	-	dah	-	liss
qeåduryn hopelessly committed	qwee	-	ah	-	dur	-	ren
qeåladyn survives on their own	qwee	-	ah	-	lay	-	den
qeånaryn walks in Elfin in dreams	qwee	-	ah	-	nair	-	ren
qeånduryn there were hints	qwee	-	ahn	-	dur	-	ren
qearadyn starting a new life	qwee	-	air	-	rah	-	den
qedånda my gosh, it can't be true	qwee	-	don			-	dah	oh
qedarea made many of my plans turn to dust	qwee	-	dare	-	ree	-	ah
qėlala where the earth is treasured and spirit honored	qwee	-	lay			-	lah
qėlåndarån light hearted elf	qwee	-	lahn	-	dare	-	ron

qëlathynor guided by the spirit	qwee	-	lay	-	thin	-	nor
qëleryn went through a period of denial	qwee	-	leer	-	ren		
qemarys light footed and agile	qwee	-	mare	-	riss		
qenashyn silent beauty	qwee	-	nay	-	shin		
qendålyn music saved my life	qwee	-	dah	-	lynn		
qenifålen in the palace of vines	qwee	-	nigh	-	fah	-	lean
qevålana vision calls	qwee	-	vah	-	lay	-	nah
qevåndor elfin hunter	qwee	-	von	-	door		
qeyndareyn tremendous talents and abilities	qwee	-	in	-	dare	-	ree	-	in
qiafyryn seeks adventure	qwi	-	a	-	fur	-	ren
qiala iquid one	qwi	-	a	-	lah	l	
qiåna come in a hurry	qwi	-	ah	-	nah		
qidånåfyle slides down the rope	qwi	-	don	-	nah	-	fill	-	lee
qidånåfyn don't know how I do it	qwi	-	don	-nah	-	fin	
qidåndor several different kinds	qwi	-	don	-	door		
qidånle hungry for more	qwi	-	don	-	lee		
qidantha guides who are helping us	qwi	-	dane	-	thah		

The Book of Elf Names

qidarfyn	qwi	-	dare	-	fin
mysterious magic					
qidarsa	qwi	-	dare	-	sah
taking the next steps					
qidarshyn	qwi	-	dare	-	shin
concentrates on faery					
qidarve	qwi	-	dare	-	vee
seen on the face					
qidarvyn	qwi	-	dare	-	vin
have lived this life many times					
qidaryn	qwi	-	dare	-	ren
called to the realms					
qidarys	qwi	-	dare	-	riss
bush baby					
qidåvyn	qwi	-	dah	-	vin
lots of love inside to give to others					

qideadyn	qwi	-	dee	-	a	-	den
friend of the weather							
qidoniyl	qwi	-	doan	-	nigh	-	L
from the clift							

qidynsha	qwi	-	den	-	shah
childlike smile					
qidynta	qwi	-	den	-	tah
poses with a smile					

qifynyryn	qwi	-	fin	-	ner	-	ren
rather like an elf							
qilodarshyn	qwi	-	low	-	dare	-	shin
talks to them with great ease							
qinånålyn	qwi	-	ah	-	nah	-	lynn
unique and special							

qineryn	qwi	-	near	-	ren
stars are the eyes of the mother					

qinoreyn	qwi	-	nor	-	ree	-	in
surreally rational							

The Silver Elves

qivadryn elvish spells	qwi	-	vay	-	drinn
qivåloryn feels the trees talking	qwi	-	vah	-	lore	-	ren
qivarys needs the peace of nature	qwi	-	vair	-	riss
qivereyn learns by intuition	qwi	-	veer	-	ree	-	in
qiwylyn something unique for my own	qwi	-	will	-	lynn
qoadrys dryad's wink	qwo	-	a	-	driss
qoaduryn difficult to explain	qwo	-	a	-	dur	-	ren
qodåndor master of the forest realm	qwo	-	don	-	door
qodåråthyn in my own world	qwo	-	dah	-	rah	-	thin
qodavyn very pretty elf maid	qwo	-	day	-	vin
qoladyn beckons me to drink	qwo	-	lay	-	den
qolorys cat person	qwo	-	lore	-	riss
qonåda ever since I was a toddler	qwo	-	nah	-	dah
qonadål crystal wings	qwo	-	nay	-	dahl
qorånde on the brink of possibility	qwo	-	ron	-	dee
qorantor explores the wild	qwo	-	rain	-	tour
qoryndar I walk with the wind in my hair	qwo	-	ren	-	dare

The Book of Elf Names   251

qoryntaryn seeks the syndaryn	qwo	-	ren	-	tair	-	ren
quaryn covered in faery dust	Q	-		air		-	ren
quarys deep magic	Q	-		air		-	riss
qudoryn have all but lost faith	Q	-		door		-	ren
qunaryn able to see	Q	-		nair		-	ren
quoryn gift of powers	Q	-		or		-	ren
qureålyn help others realize	Q	-	ree	-	ah	-	lynn
qureta rarely confides in anyone	Q	-		ree		-	tah
quvådoryl paler shade of blue	Q	-	vah	-	door	-	rill
quvorådyn tree vine	Q	-	vour	-	rah	-	den
quvorvyn clear night sky	Q	-		vour		-	vin
quvorys don't know where they came from	Q	-		vour		-	riss
qyctålyn ahead of the others	quick	-		tah		-	lynn
qyladea join your family	qwill	-	lay	-	dee	-	ah
qylorys wandering divine	qwill	-		lore		-	riss
qylyndru sees spirits	qwill	-		lynn		-	drew
qyndåfa offers the nectar	quinn	-		dah		-	fah

qyndarådynsa plays the role	quinn sah	-	dare	-	rah	-	den -
qyndaryn incessant scribbler	quinn	-	dare	-	ren		
qyndina fluent in the tonque	quinn	-	dye	-	nah		
qynvåna quick foot	quinn	-	vah	-	nah		
qynvara observes the rites	quinn	-	vair	-	rah		
qynzarådån passes it on to the children	quinn	-	zair	-	rah	-	don
qytåndra I want to reclaim my heritage	quit	-	than	-	drah		

---

*THE DIFFERENCE BETWEEN THE ELVISH AND
MOST OTHER FOLKS IS OUR HOMES ARE FILLED
WITH SINGING, DANCING, LOVE, AND
LAUGHTER AND THEIRS ARE OFTEN SUBJECT
TO THE INTERMITTEN DIN OF YELLING,
FIGHTING, COMPLAINING, AND MUTUAL
RECRIMINATION. IT'S THAT SIMPLE.*

—OBSERVATIONS BY THE ELVES

R

Elven Name and Meaning	Pronunciation			
raådaos clear to be seen	ray - ah - day - ohss			
raälåryn luck and good fortune never fail me	ray - al - lah - ren			
raalåsyn disappears behind a tree	ray - a - lah - sin			
raåndånél protected by the fae	ray - ahn - dah - nell			
råarleyn of few words	rah - air - lee - in			
rådålae shine brightly	rah - dah - lay			
radålea more interested in	ray - dah - lee - ah			
radålyn almost golden	ray - dah - lynn			
rådånda drawn to the woods	rah - don - dah			
rådåndor somewhere in that area	rah - don - door			
radåndryn now I embrace it	ray - don - drinn			
radånfa joyous revelation	ray - don - fah			
radaryn true to their heart	ray - dare - ren			
rådonåfor shade of the eagle	rah - doan - nah - for			

rådoragor listens to the trees	rah	-	doe	-	ray	-	gore
radynvår song seeker	ray	-			den	-	var
radynvårys holds the orb	ray	-	den	-	vah	-	riss
rafåle elfin ways of magic	ray	-			fah	-	lee
ragŏndor elegant warrior	ray	-			gone	-	door
rajorůs on the look out	ray	-			jour	-	roos
rakorjyn protective wing	ray	-			core	-	gin
råleleyn energetic dancing	rah	-	lee	-	lee	-	in
råltilyn sleep watcher	rah	-			tie	-	lynn
ralyn glimmering jewel	ray				-		lynn
ralyndåmeŏn the music rises	ray	-	lynn-	dah	-	me	-	on
råmynsor born of old	rah	-			men	-	soar
råndågorys keeps own counsel	ron	-	dah	-	gore	-	riss
råndålea green thumb and good luck	ron	-	dah	-	lee	-	ah
ränpåre beneath the rain	ran	-			pah	-	ree
ränvaryn just not sure yet	ran	-			vair	-	ren
rasånå one with nature	ray	-			sah	-	nah

rasuvala awakens the light	ray	-	sue	-	vay	-	lah
rasyndor tree of crystal	ray	-	sin	-	door
ratålbyndor the number of the kingfisher	ray	-	tall	-	ben	-	door
rathareyn shielded by the sun	ray	-	thay	-	ree	-	in
råthrynde sees the dangers	roth	-	ren	-	dee
ratisana starts anew	ray	-	tie	-	say	-	nah
råvådea deeper appreciation	rah	-	vah	-	dee	-	ah
råvåleda spreads joy, love and magic	rah	-	vah	-	lee	-	dah
råvålolyn craves the waters	rah	-	vah	-	low	-	lynn
ravålyndre love talker	ray	-	vah	-	lynn	-	dree
råvånda stands in the rain	rah	-	vaughn	-	dah
råvåndåle getting close	rah	-	vaughn	-	dah	-	lee
råvåndålys embraced me gently	rah	-	vaughn	-	dah	-	liss
råvåndaryn spreads good luck	rah	-	vaughn	-	dare	-	ren
ravandre caresses the flowers	ray	-	vane	-	dree
råvåndre longs for the woods	rah	-	vaughn	-	dree
ravandrèl keen focus	ray	-	vane	-	drell

The Silver Elves

råvändreyl ponders the mysteries	rah	-	van	-	dree	-	L
råvändryn messages from the eagles	rah	-	van	-	drinn		
ravåndyl faery born	ray	-	vaughn	-	dill		
ravånsa can only die of a broken heart	ray	-	vaughn	-	sah		
råveåndėl dragon shadow	rah	-	vee	-	ahn	-	dell
råvoreyn sought by others	rah	-	vour	-	ree	-	in
råvynåle assists the trees	rah	-	vin	-	nah	-	lee
råvyndre true form	rah	-	vin	-	dree		
råvynėl looks deep into the soul	rah	-	vin	-	nell		
rayndasyl realizes the truth	ray	-	in	-	day	-	sill
reådåndre by the light of the silver moon	ree	-	ah	-	don	-	dree
reådora heals by touch	ree	-	ah	-	door	-	rah
reålasa messages from nature spirits	ree	-	ah	-	lay	-	sah
reålosyn always welcome	ree	-	ah	-	low	-	sin
reånådyn changes the world	ree	-	ahn	-	nah	-	den
reånålyn dynamic spontaneous experience	ree	-	ahn	-	nah	-	lynn
reånåtharea creates the sound	ree	-	ahn	-	nah	-	thay - ree ah

reånda raven wolf	ree	-	ahn	-	dah	
reåndafa wolf runner	ree	-	ahn	-	day	- fah
reåndåfe run and be free	ree	-	ahn	-	dah	- fee
reåndasys feels the music	ree	-	ahn	-	day	- sis
reånthara much adored	ree	-	ahn	-	thay	- rah
reårynda reflected in still water	ree	-	ah	-	ren	- dah
rearzyn poet's tongue	ree	-	air	-	zen	
reåseyl bringing calm	ree	-	ah	-	see	- L

reåthådan   ree - ah - thah - dane
not just a figment of the imagination

reathådyn longing for someone like me	ree	-	a	-	thah	- den
reathyna wild gypsy elf	ree	-	a	-	thin	- nah
reåvifyn dark storm	ree	-	ah	-	vie	- fin
recondasa height of shade	ree	-	con	-	day	- sah
recorådyn shade of the shadows	ree	-	core	-	rah	- den
redånare my history is a hard one	ree	-	don	-	nair	- ree
redånashan dream voyager	ree	-	fon	-	nay	- shane
redånde answers with a song	ree	-	don	-	dee	

redånva	ree	-	don	-	vah	

slowly regaining memories of past life events

redarea	ree	-	dare	-	ree	-	ah

helps as many as possible

redarthyn	ree	-	drae	-	thin

water witch

redåva	ree	-	dah	-	vah

in love with two

reedåniyl	ree	-	e	-	dom	-	nigh	-	L

yearning to be set free

regåndål	ree	-	gahn	-	dahl

lost but found

reisa	ree	-	eye	-	sah

priestess of the silk

relmareyn	reel	-	mare	-	ree	-	in

view of the valleys

rėlyna	rell	-	lynn	-	nah

voice of the meadow

remeråfyn	ree	-	mere	-	rah	-	fin

never known why

remeråle	ree	-	mere	-	rah	-	lee

power stored within

remerålyn	ree	-	mere	-	rah	-	lynn

dragon keeper

remeråve	ree	-	mere	-	rah	-	vee

renews the earth

remerayl	ree	-	mere	-	ray	-	L

bursting with compassion

remerdra	ree	-	mere	-	drah

drawn down to the source

remerdre	ree	-	mere	-	dree

innocent and childlike

remerea	ree	-	mere	-	ree	-	ah

have been chosen

The Book of Elf Names

remereyn flys through the trees	ree	-	mere	-	ree	-	in
remerthyn memories of what will be	ree	-	mere	-			thin
remerys finding out	ree	-	mere	-			riss
renånda everything is related to everything	re	-	non	-			dah
renåvyn truly magical	ree	-	nah	-			vin
reondåryl unlocks the secrets of the mind	ree	-	ohn	-	dah	-	rill
reondre soars in the clouds	ree	-	ohn	-			dree
rermeråthe true great love	rear	-	mere	-	rah	-	thee
resåle sun patch	ree	-	sah	-			lee
resällea instinctively knows	ree	-	sal	-	lee	-	ah
resåna awakening touch	ree	-	sahn	-			nah
resåndre tingling all over	ree	-	sahn	-			dree
reshåla filled with bounce	ree	-	shah	-			lah
reshånåfa in the twinkling of an eye	ree	-	shah	-	nah	-	fah
resoldas loves the large trees	ree	-	soul	-			dayce
resyldur underground in the very dark	ree	-	sill	-			dur
resylea creates fun	ree	-	sill	-	lee	-	ah

rethyndryl strong of will	ree	-	thin	-		drill
revalyn it pains me to see them destroyed	ree	-	vay	-		lynn
revalynthe nature's advocate	ree	-	vay	-	lynn	-	thee
revåna protector of the sacred waters	ree	-	vaughn	-		nah
revånådil comfortable in the woods	ree	-	vaughn	-	nah	-	dial
revanadyn cannot be tamed	ree	-	vay	-	nay	-	den
revånåshåd escapes into Elfin	ree	-	vaughn	-	nah	-	shod
revåndar blue spirit dancer	ree	-	vaughn	-		dare
revändre calmly waiting	ree	-	van	-		dree
revåndreyl awaits the magic	ree	-	vaughn	-	dree	-L
revandreyn exploring the realms of the mind	ree	-	vane	-	dree	-	in
revandryn has earned the right	ree	-	vane	-		drinn
revåndrys wolf eyes	ree	-	vaughn	-		driss
revarådryn on the move	ree	-	vair	-	rah	-	drinn
revaradyn meets elves in the fores	ree	-	vair	-ray	-	den
revarasyn extremely powerful presence in my life	ree	-	vair	-	ray	-	sin
revarfyn trying to learn as much as I can	ree	-	vair	-		fin

revashsuryn living in symbiosis with nature	ree	-	vaysh	-	sue	-	ren
revyndreyl shaman of the soul	ree	-	vin	-	dree	-	L
reyndal feathered dragon	ree	-		in	-	dale	
reyndara hidden wonder	ree	-		in	-	dare	- rah
reyndre close to the angels	ree	-		in	-	dree	
riabälryn except I've always ...	rye - a - bowel (said as bow-L) - ren						
riadora placed among them	rye	-	a	-	door	-	rah
riadoryn from the mist of the sea	rye	-	a	-	door	-	ren
rialynel deeds to do	rye	-	a	-	lynn	-	neal
riånådyn weaver of time	rye	-	ah	-	nah	-	den
riasynda takes the leap	rye	-	a	-	sin	-	dah
riavynor inner magic	rye	-	a	-	vin	-	nor
rigylosena two of one realm	rye	-	gill	-	low	- see - nah	
rimaryl joy of the wind	rye	-		mare	-	rill	
rimeryn feels oneness with the spirit world	rye	-		mere	-	ren	
rinoryn sees through the darkness	rye	-		nor	-	ren	
riodryndår fire of awakening	rye	-	oh	-	drinn	-	dar

The Silver Elves

riozarul darts away	rye	-	oh	-	zair	-	rule
rithyndre called to lead	rye	-	thin			-	dree
rivånådån need to explore	rye	-	vaughn	-	nah	-	don
rivånår quick camp	rye	-	vaughn			-	nar
rivändor trained from an early age	rye	-	van			-	door
rivändrea continues the journey	rye	-	van	-	dree	-	ah
rivåndryn loved by nature	rye	-	vaughn			-	drinn
rivarådyn what it once was	rye	-	vair	-	rah	-	den
riynadel among the wee creatures	rye	-	in	-	nay	-	dell
riyndåle seeks the Divine	rye	-	in	-	dah	-	lee
roåtina stares at the clouds	row	-	ah	-	tie	-	nah
robaryn bright bringer	row	-	bare			-	ren
rocajyndare little seer	row	-	cah	-	gin	-	dare	ree
rodånåwyn holds a more secure belief	row	-	don	-	nah	-	win
rodåndalys wandering starlight	row	-	don	-	day	-	liss
rodåndreyl a certain love for stars	row	-	don	-	dree	-	L
rodånduryn surrounded by elves	row	-	don	-	dur	-	ren

The Book of Elf Names

rodurvaryn dragon rider	row	-	dur	-	vay	-	ren
rodynadre buzzing with life	row	-	den	-	nay	-	dree
rodynavyn love of the arts	row	-	den	-nay	-	vin	
rodyndar caretaker of the holy grove	row	-	den	-	dare		
rogaryn something really special	row	-	gair	-	ren		
rogeradyn velvet tunic	row	-	gear	-	ray	-	den
romarthyn unspoken acknowledgement	row	-	mare	-	thin		
romere otherworldly desires	row	-	mere	-	ree		
romeryn yearns for community	row	-	mere	-	ren		

ronåla   row - nah - lah
wanders the forest trying to find one's s'elf and one's powers

ronåndål defends honor	row	-	non	-	dahl		
ronazaer trees' rage	row	-	nay	-	zay	-	ear
rondareän still in touch	roan	-	dare	-	re	-	ann
rorråtor wild call	roar	-	rah	-	tour		
rothalyn laughter among the trees	row	-	thay	-	lynn		

rovånådyn   row - vaughn - nah - den
as soon as I looked to her eyes I recognized mys'elf

rovarådyn   row - vair - rah - den
something other than human

The Silver Elves

rovaryshan child at heart	row	-	vair	-	riss	-	shane
roviålyn little bit of each	row	-	vie	-	ah	-	lynn
rovyndre part of it	row	-		vin	-		dree
royndålfar flower talker	row	-	in	-	dahl	-	fair
royngårdor dragon rider's smile	row	-	in	-	gar	-	door
ruara loved by dogs	rue	-		air	-		rah
ruareyn soul ascending	rue	-	air	-	ree	-	in
ruarfyn student of nature	rue	-		air	-		fin
rudareŏn amidst the veils	rue	-	dare	-	ree	-	on

rudåryn   rue   -   dar   -   ren
extremely sensitive to all that happens around me

rudåvea when the trees rustle	rue	-	dah	-	vee	-	ah
rudŏnvor chasing surf	rue	-		dun	-		vour
ruladyn tendency to shyness	rue	-		lay	-		den
rulålys returns to the forest	rue	-		lah	-		liss
rulitawyn clever wordster	rue	-	lie	-	tay	-	win
rulynde pulled from within	rue	-		lynn	-		dee
runarthys black water pearl	rue	-		nair	-		thiss

The Book of Elf Names

rureålyn something calling from nature	rue	-	ree	-	ah	-	lynn
rushata ever about	rue	-	shay	-	tah		
ruthalys beneath the hill	rue	-	thay	-	liss		
ruthåndor calming presence	rue	-	thahn	-	door		
ruthele strongly focuses	rue	-	thee	-	lee		
ruvånåde a light came to me	rue	-	vaughn	-	nah	-	dee
ruvareyl eye of the sun star	rue	-	vair	-	ree	-	L
ruvorådyn stumbled upon	rue	-	vour	-	reh	-	den
ruvordryn love reveals the path	rue	-	vour	-	drinn		
ruvorna way of the healer	rue	-	vour	-	nah		
ruvoryn blessed touch	rue	-	vour	-	ren		
rydålys hears the piper	rid	-	dah	-	liss		
rylåndor don't know what happened	rill	-	lahn	-	door		
rylordryn love of things mystical	rill	-	lore	-	drinn		
rymardyn I ignore them and go my own way	rim	-	mare	-	den		
rymyrėl kin to the deer	rim	-	mer	-	rell		
rynareyn selected by nature	ren	-	nair	-	ree	-	in

ryndålasa seeing the beauty	ren	-	dah	-	lay	-	sah
ryndalea many scars	ren	-	day	-	lee	-	ah
ryndålos seeker of the secrets of horse and unicorn	ren	-	dah	-	lowse		
ryndalys here at last	ren	-	day	-	liss		
ryndåndor explores the shadows	ren	-	don	-	door		
ryndånefål drawn to dragons	ren	-	don	-	knee	-	fall
ryndåneyl to magic drawn	ren	-	don	-	knee	-	L

ryndår   ren   -   dar
one who has the power to change a being's chemisty by understanding them

ryndareyn stars in the eyes	ren	-	dare	-	ree	-	in
ryndarys windswept tree	ren	-	dare	-	riss		
rynderyn talks with animals	ren	-	deer	-	ren		
ryndoråfyn wants to go with	ren	-	door	-	rah	-	fin
ryndoråvår protects the groves	ren	-	door	-	rah	-	var
ryndoreyn eager for the quest	ren	-	door	-	ree	-	in

ryndornadur ren - door - nay - dur at the feet of dragons

ryndorvyn ever since I was a child	ren	-	door	-	vin		
ryndoryn sea healer	ren	-	door	-	ren		

The Book of Elf Names   267

ryngaronda fierce ally	ren	-	gair	-	roan	-	dah
rynradon feels our own	ren	-	ray	-	doan		
rynravyn this is me	ren	-	ray	-	vin		
rynresa in the action	ren	-	ree	-	sah		
ryntara remembers home	ren	-	tair	-	rah		
ryntårys deep in the soul	ren	-	tah	-	riss		
ryntaryth guided by the trees	ren	-	tair	-	rith		
ryntere makes me happy	ren	-	teir	-	ree		
rynvådra dreams of adventure	ren	-	vah	-	drah		
rynvynvarna in the circle of the Goddess	ren	-	vin	-	vair	-	nah
rysadonu sent to help	riss	-	say	-	doe	-	new
rysaryn pushed to Faerie	ris	-	sair	-	ren		

> *IF YOU'RE GIVEN AN ELF NAME, CHERISH IT.*
> *IT CONTAINS MORE MAGIC THAN MOST*
> *NORMAL FOLKS EXPERIENCE IN A LIFETIME.*

S

Elven Name and Meaning	Pronunciation							
sådånåthyn began to be guided by it	sah	-	don	-	nah	-	thin	
sådåndre gliding colors	sah	-	don	-	dree			
sådåndyryn have scars to prove it	sah	-	don	-	der	-	ren	
sådånle awakens hearts	sah	-	don	-	lee			
sådånodas fiercely loyal	sah	-	don	-	no	-	dayce	
sådyndre windtalker	dah	-	den	-	dree			
sadyndrys like you guys	say	-	den	-	driss			
sådynrys within touching distance	sah	-	den	-	riss			
safir love calls	say	-	fire					
sålådrea hear them in the wind	sah	-	lah	-	dree	-	ah	
sålådyndra faeries whisper	sah	-	lah	-	den	-	drah	
sålåladryn belongs to nature	sah	-	lah	-	lay	-	drinn	
sälåmåndrea drawn to things of a fiery nature	sal	-	lah	-	mon	-	dree	- ah
sålåndryn singer of songs	sah	-	lahn	-	drinn			

sålmareyn loved by many	sahl	-	mare	-	ree	-	in
salofyna humming wings	say	-	low	-	fin	-	nah
sålorys ever sharing	sah	-	lore	-	riss		
sålyndas it was meant to be	sah	-	lynn	-	dayce		
salyndra guided warrior	say	-	lynn	-	drah		
sålyndre mutual recognition	sah	-	lynn	-	dree		
sålyndreyn they need us as much as we need them	sah	-	lynn	-	dree	-	in
sanamor looked up to	say	-	nay	-	nore		
sånardreyn heart that knows	sah	-	nair	-	dree	-	in
såndåre healing power of beauty	sahn	-	dah	-	ree		
såndarėl arrives in times of need	sahn	-	dare	-	rell		
såndåsa resonates with one upon meeting	sahn	-	dah	-	sah		
sandor not as others	sane	-	door				
sandorea free as a bird	sane	-	door	-	ree	-	ah
såndråfålås twilight awakening	sahn	-	drah	-	fah	-	lahss
sandrafena rising of the dawn	sane	-	dray	-	dee	-	nah
såndrea everything it stands for	sahn	-	dree	-	ah		

såndynae called over	sahn	-	den	-	nay			
sånedra will cherish it so much	sah	-	knee	-	drah			
sånrasa elven loyal	sahn	-	ray	-	sah			
såntåloreyn ancient of ancients	san	-	tah	-	lore	-	ree	-	in
sårådath calms the animals	sah	-	rah	-	dayth			
saråsa starfire	say	-	rah	-	sah			
saresyn shining light	say	-	ree	-	sin			
saridea enchantress' smile	say	-	rye	-	dee	-	ah	
sårilor dream traveler	sah	-	rye	-	lore			
sariosa shining sorcery	say	-	rye	-	oh	-	sah	
sarniryndor sees what's true	sair	-	nigh	-	ren	-	door	
sarynalos sea maiden's smile	sair	-	ren	-	nay	-	lowce	
saryndålyn yearns for the sea	sair	-	ren	-	dah	-	lynn	
saryndarsa beneath the waves	sair	-	ren	-	dare	-	sah	
saryndaryn one of the children	sair	-	ren	-	dare	-	ren	
saryndor shadowed by the spirit	sair	-	ren	-	door			
såvaråsyn knows this to be true	sah	-	vair	-	rah	-	sin	

såvaryndås	sah	-	vair	-	ren	-	dahss
awaits the news							

sealåryn	see	-	a	-	lah	-	ren
I sing to the trees							

seåndil	see	-	ahn	-	dial
harp singer					

seåndor	see	-	ahn	-	door
grant me this great favor					

seåndre s	ee	-	ahn	-	dree
has an invitation					

seareyn	see	-	air	-	ree	-	in
circles overhead							

sedåndor	see	-	don	-	door
fell in love with the strength of the trees and the peacefulness of their shade					

sedandre	see	-	dane	-	dree
wisdom's child					

sedaryn	see	-	dare	-	ren
always been there for me					

sedasra	see	-	dayce	-	rah
fascinated by water					

sedathyn	see	-	day	-	thin
pencils in hand					

sedramea	see	-	drah	-	me	-	ah
loves to give							

seleändre	see	-	lee	-	ann	-	dree
just found out today							

selelyn	see	-	lee	-	lynn
near running water					

sèloryn	sell	-	lore	-	ren
foolishly fell in love					

selyndrea	see	-	lynn	-	dree	-	ah
visions of things that may come to pass							

semaryn close to the crossing	see	-		mare	-	ren
senafyn extraordinarily sensitive	see	-		nay	-	fin
senålea then I had strange dreams	see	-	nah	-	lee	-	ah
senamåre staying true to the vision	see	-	nay	-	mah	-	ree
senaryn switched at birth	see	-		nair	-	ren
senarys restores the balance	see	-		nair	-	riss
serana weaver of mist	see	-		ray	-	nah
seravar keen for adventure	see	-		ray	-	vair
serynåtha free spirited love	see	-	ren	-	nah	-	thah
sevaryn feels the others around	see	-		vair	-	ren
seyndånål elf fingers	see	-	in	-	dah	-	nahl
shaåndåru born to it	shay	-	ahn	-	dah	-	rue
shådåks one who stirs me	shah			-		docs
shådåndåla the wind sings with me	shah	-	don	-	dah	-	lah
shadara little good spells	shay	-	dare	-	rah
shådarys drawn to the woods at night	shah	-	dare	-	riss
shadrafar calls from the sea	shay	-	dray	-	fair

The Book of Elf Names   273

shadrafena elfin glowing face	shay	-	dray	-	fee	-	nah
shadrea beneath the waterfall	shay	-	dree	-	ah
shadryna runes on shoulder	shay	-	drinn	-	nah
shaladare tends the healing waters	shay	-	lay	-	dare	-	ree
shälådaryn called to the sea	shall	-	lah	-	dare	-	ren
shålådyndara arrives from the east	shah rah	-	lah	-	den	-	dare -
shålasa standing near the edge	shah	-	lay	-	sah
shålisän whispered secrets	shah	-	lie	-	s-ann
shandalafar glides above the ground	shane	-	day	-	lay	-	fair
shandarea rising to the surface	shane	-	dare	-	ree	-	ah
shandrafyn returns to joy	shane	-	drah	-	fin
shandrasa keeper of the elixirs	shane	-	dray	-	sah
shåndreyl that is where I am now	shahn	-	dree	-	L
sharålelyn ever seeks the truth	share	-	rah	-	lee	-	lynn
sharasèl shining elf	share	-	ray	-	sell
shariada quiet grace	share	-	rye	-	a	-	dah
shåryndår flows in the blood	shah	-	ren	-	dar

The Silver Elves

sharyndara stems the tide	share	-	ren	-	dare	-	rah
sheåndåru of the faery family	she	-	ahn	-	dah	-	rue
shedånala song of twilight	she	-	don	-	nay	-	lah
shedåneyl golden flower	she	-	don	-	knee	-	L
shialea shy fall of contradiction		-	a	-	lee	-	ah
shiarådyn off the beaten path	shy	-	air	-	rah	-	den
shiaråvyn repeats the spell	shy	-	air	-	rah	-	vin
shiareyl gathering faeries	shy	-	air	-	ree	-	L
shiaryn as for this lifetime	shy	-	air	-	ren		
shilathfyn looks for the others	shy	-	layth	-	fin		
shinaryn pea pod pixie	shy	-	nair	-	ren		
shodarna wish to understand them	show	-	dare	-	nah		
shodarnaru seeking their own	show	-	dare	-	nay	-	rue
shondra power of the mystic bayou	shown	-	drah				
shoredarèl blends with the sunset	show	-	ree	-	dare	-	rell
shrearadon blends with the trees	shree	-	air	-	rah	-	doan
shrevalyn winged variety	shree	-	vay	-	lynn		

shurondora sea song sounding	sure	-	roan	-	door	-	rah	
shuryndaarea would like to	sure ah	-	ren	-	day	-	air	- ree -
shyladreyn steps into the dream	shill	-	lay	-	dree	-	in	
shyndånåru shadow turning	shin	-	dah	-	nah	-	rue	
shyndaråfyn old blood	shin	-	dare	-	rah	-	fin	
shyndareyn went wandering for awhile	shin	-	dare	-	ree	-	in	
shyndaryn ancient child	shin	-	dare	-	ren			
shyndera mighty soul	shin	-	deer	-	rah			
shyndrosa hip shot (one who is accurate at shooting without needing to aim)	shin	-	dro	-	sah			
shyndryn strong of spirit	shin	-	drinn					
siådarlyn views the unseen	sigh	-	ah	-	dare	-	lynn	
sialonia ever young	sigh	-	a	-	low	-	nigh	- ah
siåndreyl you know this	sigh	-	ahn	-	dree	-	L	
siånza living the life elfin	sigh	-	ahn	-	zah			
siareyl shining sea	sigh	-	air	-	ree	-	L	
siåroen awakening glow	sigh	-	ah	-	row	-	een	
siåsyndar longing for the unknown	sigh	-	ah	-	sin	-	dare	

siåsyndra whispers the music	sigh	-	ah	-	sin	-	drah
sibaryn a life of protecting others	sigh	-	bare		ren		
sidarån hangs upside down	sigh	-	dare	-	ron		
sidaråthyn tranquil waters	sigh	-	dare	-	rah	-	thin
sidaråvyn struggling to understand	sigh	-	dare	-	rah	-	vin
sidareyn ancient sword fighting techniques	sigh	-	dare	-	ree	-	in
sidarvyn born of shadow	sigh	-	dare	-	vin		
sidaryn feel like I should be one	sigh	-	dare	-	ren		
sijador gleaming sword	sigh	-	jay	-	door		
silåndor beyond day to day	sigh	-	lahn	-	door		
silandys blends wherever they go	sigh	-	lane	-	diss		
sileda soft touch	sigh	-	lee	-	dah		
siledalyn velvet touch	sigh	-	lee	-	day	-	lynn
silosys sleek waves	sigh	-	low	-	sis		
silyndor sea runner	sigh	-	lynn	-	door		
silyndre sunlight dancing around me	sigh	-	lynn	-	dree		
silyndryn not at all like other people	sigh	-	lynn	-	drinn		

silyntar	sigh	-	lynn	-	tair		
waits in silence							
simareyl	sigh	-	mare	-	ree	-	L
under the dark shade of the old grove							
sinsåryn	sign	-	sah	-	ren		
reads hearts							
siresa	sigh	-	ree	-	sah		
became very interested							
siresyn	sigh	-	ree	-	sin		
secrets shared							
sirondar	sigh	-	roan	-	dare		
remembers the time							
sirydea	sigh	-	rid	-	dee	-	ah
for that I am forever grateful							
sisynara	sigh	-	sin	-	nair	-	rah
dew on the leaves							
sisyndår	sigh	-	sin	-	dar		
melded with it							
siynardås	sigh	-	in	-	nair	-	dahss
loves the open spaces							
siyndas	sigh	-	in	-	dayce		
homesick for Elfin							
skinari	sky	-	nair	-	rye		
out for fun							
skorånål	score	-	ron	-	nahl		
brings to life							
soåfyn	sew	-	a	-	fin		
feather soft							
soarys	sew	-	air	-	riss		
I don't know beyond that							
sodeålyn	sew	-	dee	-	ah	-	lynn
so peaceful and beautiful							
sodoralyn	sew	-	door	-	ray	-	lynn
now you understand							

sodoryn dream mastery	sew	-	door	-	ren	
sodridea magic flows around them	sew	-	dry	-	dree	-	ah
sodynėl rune writing on sand	sew		-den	-	nell	
sofishyn brings form to life	sew	-	fie	-	shin	
soladeyn world walker	sew	-	lay	-	dee	-	in
solasyn what is important is how we deal with it	sew	-	lay	-	sin	
solesa sending thoughts	sew	-	lee	-	sah	
solesyn haven't tried them out yet	sew	-	lee	-	sin	
solisea surfing the wind	sew	-	lie	-	see	-	ah
solosor breeze glider	sew	-	low	-	soar	
solynde mysteries abound	sew	-	lynn	-	dee	
solynder realizing a new life	sew	-	lynn	-	deer	
solyndre brings healing	sew	-	lynn	-	dree	
solynsa flew away	sew	-	lynn	-	sah	
solynse struck home	sew	-	ynn	-	see	
somådålwe untouched by bitterness	sew	-	mah	-	dahl	-	wee
sonååle since a very young age	sew	-	nah	-	ah	-	lee

sonåndryn	sew	-	non	-	drinn
went off on their own					
sonara	sew	-	nay	-	rah
friend of dragons					
sondråna	sewn	-	drah	-	nah
spots the eagles					
sorådolyn	soar	-	rah	-	doe	-	lynn
sister of the dolphins					
sordåndryl	soar	-	don	-	drill
very strange old other					
sorèla	soar	-	rell	-	lah
friend to elves					
sorèlsys	soar	-	rell	-	sis
smooth as the calm sea					
sorsyndår	soar	-	sin	-	dar
star on cheek					
sorynara	soar	-	ren	-	nair	-	rah
heard the flowers laughing					
sorynvala	soar	-	ren	-	vay	-	lah
can be trusted					
sorynzar	soar	-	ren	-	zair
automatically knew					
sorynze	soar	-	ren	-	zee
special powers					
sorzaryn	soar	-	zair	-	ren
shining blade					
soven	sew	-		veen
sweet song					
sovoryn	sew	-	vour	-	ren
from the mist					
sovyndra	sew	-	vin	-	drah
dancing in the raindrops					
stylason	still	-	lay	-	sewn
soft yet powerful					

The Silver Elves

sudåndryn shields the earth	sue	-	dahn	-	drinn	
sudarys heals with a smile	sue	-	dare	-	riss	
suladyn argent wind	sue	-	lay	-	den	
sunålyn concentrating deep inside	sue	-	nah	-	lynn	
sunånda thirsts for knowledge	sue	-	non	-	dah	
sundålys seeks the holy	soon	-	dah	-	liss	
sundaresa feels the current	soon	-	dare	-	ree	- sah
sunidae beckoning me	sue	-	nigh	-	day	
sunidyn dolphins call	sue	-	nigh	-	den	
sunväla voice of the trees	soon	-	val	-	lah	
sunvåsa rises to the sun	soon	-	vah	-	sah	
sureåthyn the result was startling	sue	-	ree	-	ah	- thin
suretha that's pretty much it	sue	-	ree	-	thah	
susholyn whisper sleep	sue	-	show	-	lynn	
susynara from the sea	sue	-	sin	-	nair	- rah
suvådra for the longest time	sue	-	vah	-	drah	
suvånådan goes around dancing	sue	-	vaughn	-	nah	- dane

The Book of Elf Names   281

suzynra	sue	-	zen	-	rah
white lotus star					

sydalthyn	sid	-	dale	-	thin
my heart has guided me					

sydåndyn	sid	-	don	-	den
instinctual knowledge					

sylådyn	sill	-	lah	-	den
kin to birds					

sylasyndra sill - lay - sin - drah busy around the hearth

sylathyn	sill	-	lay	-	thin
faerie's laughter					

sylbaryn	sill	-	bare	-	ren
still believe					

sylete	sill	-	lee	-	tee
waking dream					

syleynsa	sill	-	lee	-	in	-	sah
among the faery children							

sylsalea	sill	-	say	-	lee	-	ah
amidst the pouring rain							

sylvadreyl	sill	-	vay	-	dree	-	L
robes of silver							

sylvånys	sill	-	vaughn	-	niss
desires to be one with the magic					

sylynea	sill	-	lynn	-	knee	-ah
gets the fun started					

sylynsa	sill	-	lynn	-	sah
creator of fun					

symålea	sim	-	ah	-	lee	-	ah
air walker							

synåndys	sin	--	nahn	-	diss
help them to help thems'elves					

synbåzor	sin	-	bah	-	zoar	(rhymes
in touch with the littles	with soar)					

syndålyn	sin	-	dah	-	lynn		
daughter of the dragonflies							
syndålys	sin	-	dah	-	liss		
shining soul							
syndaråfyn	sin	-	dare	-	rah	-	fin
called by the trees							
syndaråle	sin	-	dare	-	rah	-	lee
befriends the friendless							
syndaras	sin	-	dare	-	race		
among the people							
syndaråthån	sin-	dare	-	rah	-	thahn	
circle of truth							
syndarathyn	sin	-	dare	-	ray	-	thin
lives for dreaming							
syndare	sin	-	dare	-	ree		
born for a purpose							
syndarea	sin	-	dare	-	ree	-	ah
always by myself							
syndaresa	sin	-	dare	-	ree	-	sah
affinity with the magical							
syndarethyn	sin	-	dare	-	ree	-	thin
ever childlike							
syndareyn	sin	-	dare	-	ree	-	in
comes together							
syndarfyn	sin	-	dare	-	fin		
seeking the truth ever since							
syndarthyn	sin	-	dare	-	thin		
required for a meaningful existence							
syndaru	sin	-	dare	-	rue		
on her own							
syndaryn	sin	-	dare	-	ren		
expresses the self freely							
syndårys	sin	-	dar	-	riss		
elf bow							

syndaryth ever exploring	sin	-	dare	-	rith		
syndasys entranced by the forest	sin	-	day	-	sis		
syndatha never stopped	sin	-	day	-	thah		
syndathyn friend to the fae	sin	-	day	-	thin		
syndåva faint giggling among the trees	sin	-	dah	-	vah		
synderea want to know the real me	sin-	deer	-	ree	-	ah	
syndoryn hidden away	sin	-	door	-	ren		
syndra born of the deep wood	sin		-		drah		
syndramis delving in the deep wood	sin	-	dray	-	mice		
syndrayl spreading pixie dust	sin	-	dray	-	L		
syndrea dreaming awake	sin	-	dree	-	ah		
syndreyl came soon after	sin	-	dree	-	L		
syndreyla rising above the darkness	sin	-	dree	-	L	-	lah
syndrynås direction finder	sin	-	drinn	-	nahss		
synjarea passion for the trees	sin	-	jay	-	ree	-	ah
synjynare free as the breeze	sin	-	gin	-	nair	-	ree
synjynari speaks in verse	sin	-	gin	-	nair	-	rye

The Silver Elves

synridyn gaze of the wyzard	sin	-	rye	-	den	
synsålåryn from the palace of the stars	sin	-	sah	-	lah	- ren
synsarådyn solutions that work	sin-	say	-	rah	-	den
synsare masked by the sea	sin	-	. say	-	ree	
synsårea elfin maskėd	sin	-	sah	-	ree	- ah
synsareyl everything has a use and a purpose	sin-	say	-	ree	-	L
synsåsor wave sparkle	sin-	sah	-	soar		
synsynara yet to see	sin-	sin	-	nair	-	rah
syrändar my soul tells me so	sir	-	ran	-	dare	
syredyn rises and falls with the tide	sir	-	ree	-	den	
syrladre eventful life	sir	-	lay	-	dree	
syrlidysyn clear sailing	sir	-	lie	-	diss	- sin
syrtynara shining shade	sir	-	tin	-	nair	- rah
syryahyr gathers the kin	sir	-	ray	-	ah	- her
syryntha far away land	sir	-	ren	-	thah	
syrynve finally have found my true path	sir	-	ren	-	vee	

sysaryn	sis	-	say	-	ren
touched by angels					

sysashon	sis	-	say	-	shown
clothes that flow when you walk					

WHEN ELVES DO MARTIAL ARTS, WE OFTEN
DO JUDO, JUJITSU, AKIDO, CAPOEIRA, KUNG
FU, AND OTHER FLOWING FORMS. SOME
MIGHT ASK IF ELVES HAVE MAGIC THEN WHY
WOULD THEY BOTHER WITH MARTIAL ARTS,
BUT ELVES WILL TELL YOU MARTIAL ARTS
ARE MAGIC. BUT THEN TO THE ELVES,
NEARLY EVERYTHING IS MAGIC. OR IF IT IS
NOT, THEY WILL MAKE IT SO.

The Silver Elves

$\mathcal{T}$

Elven Name and Meaning	Pronunciation							
tåbareyn for a few years	tah	-	bare	-	ree	-	in	
tabris voyager resting	tay		-				brice	
tåcaryndar one of the leaves	tah	-	car	-	ren	-	dare	
tadånåfyl twists in circles	tay	-	don	-	nah	-	fill	
tadåndåder by a twist of fate	tay	-	don	-	dah	-	deer	
tagåndor running with others like mys'elf	tay		-	gone		-	door	
tågaryn moss covered	tah		-	gair		-	ren	
tåhalor on the steppes	tah		-	hay		-	lore	
tålådån the being inside	tah		-	lah		-	don	
taladarna great reconteur	tay	-	lay	-	dare	-	nah	
tåladoreyn speaker of the hidden things	tah	-	lay	-	door	-	ree	- in
tålåladrys my own spiritual wholeness will guide me there	tah	-	lah	-	lay	-	driss	
talåle heals with salves	tay		-	lah		-	lee	
tälålyndrea her nature provides	towl (rhymes with dowel) - lah - lynn – dree – ah							

talånvor to make greater or more beautiful	tay	-	lahn	-	vour	
tålare cat singer	tah	-	lair	-	ree	
tålåreyl peeks though the bushes	tah	-	lah	-	ree	- L
tålårynde stands among the stones	tah	-	lah	-	ren	- dee
tålarys great fondness	tah	-	lair	-	riss	
tälaseyn unexplained memories	towl	-	lay	-	see	- in
talasoryn searching the sea	tail	-	lay	-	soar	- ren
tålåvadrys memories returned in a rush	tah	-	lah	-	vay	- driss
tålavea something to believe in	tah	-	lay	-	vee	- ah
tålåvedre creates peace	tah	-	lah	-	vee	- dree
tälåvere watches as they enter the world	towl	-	lah	-	veer	- ree
talavyndaron light of foot	tay	- lay	- vin	- dare	- roan	
talazyndar beautiful speaker	tay	- lay	- zen	- dare		
täldaråthyn it sounds foolish but it's true	towl	-	dare	-	rah	- thin
tåldareon looks for the future	tall	-	dare	-	ree	- on
tåleåla slowly memories begin to unfold	tah	-	lee	-	ah	- lah
tåleålyn drawn to the stories	tah	-	lee	-	ah	- lynn

The Silver Elves

tåleåre wise beyond their years	tah	-	lee	-	ah	-	ree
talena soaring high	tay	-	lee	-	nah
tåleynda finally able to put a name to it	tah	-	lee	-	in	-	dah
talomyr much to say	tay	-	low	-	mer
talriejyn doesn't give up	tail	-	rye	-	e	-	gin
tålynarfyn duty to share	tah	-	lynn	-	nair	-	fin
tålyndar hawk of elsewhere	tah	-	lynn	-	dare
talyndårys shadow hawk	tay	-	lynn	-	dar	-	riss
tålyndayl plucks at the strings	tah	-	lynn	-	day	-	L
talyndor ever since I was born	tay	-	lynn	-	door
tålyndra dream dancer	tah	-	lynn	-	drah
tålyndreyn all one ever needs comes from within	tah	-	lynn	-	dree	-	in
tålyndrys searches the archives	tah	-	lynn	-	driss
talynjor hawk of peace	tay	-	lynn	-	jour
tåmyndalfor heart of magic	tah	-	men	-	dale	-	for
tanala mourns the trees	tay	-	nay	-	lah
tånåryl intense love for all things	tah	-	nah	-	rill

tånåsea	tah	-	nah	-	see	-	ah
feet hardly touch the ground							
tånåsila	tah	-	nah	-	sigh	-	lah
hair of sun							
tåndålaon	tahn	-	dah	-	lay	-	ohn
of forest lake							
tåndareyn	tahn	-	dare	-	ree	-	in
wise for their age							
tångåri	tahn	-	gah	-	rye		
waits and watches							
tångariyl	tahn	-	gay	-	rye	-	L
running free							
tängylys	tan	-	gill	-	liss		
hinting at the secrets							
tåntåleys	tahn	-	tah	-	lee	-	iss
obsessed with learning							
tåntålynsa	tahn	-	tah	-	lynn	-	sah
healing with flowers							
taoryndar	tay	-	or	-	ren	-	dare
wants to believe							
tarafyndor	tay	-	ray	-	fin	-	door
song of earth							
tarålea	tay	-	rah	-	lee	-	ah
swift as love							
taråsidra	tay	-	rah	-	sigh	-	drah
elfin beauty							
taråthyn	tay	-	rah	-	thin		
sardonic laugh							
taredra	tay	-	ree	-	drah		
sense of honor							
tareoryn	tay	-	ree	-	or	-	ren
it gives me a feeling I can't place							
targondor	tair	-	gohn	-	door		
riding the storm							

taruvyn invisible friend	tay	-	rue	-	vin		
taryndal song of magic	tay	-	ren	-	dale		
tåryndala for a moment	tar	-	ren	-	day	-	lah
taryndålėl moves in silence	tay	-	ren	-	dah	-	lell
taryndålor sings of true magic	tay	-	ren	-	dah	-	lore
taryndalos dragon warrior	tay	-	ren	-	day	-	lowce
taryndålval it started with a dream	tay	-	ren	-	dahl	-	vale
taryndarsys beneath the high hill	tay	-	ren	-	dare	-	sis
tarynde heals the soul	tay	-	ren	-	dee		
taryndėl moss covered paths	tay	-	ren	-	dell		
taryndre unique point of view	tay	-	ren	-	dree		
tåryndryl sunset on the river	tah	-	ren	-	drill		
taryndyl mild light	tay	-	ren	-	dill		
tarynori dream walker	tay	-	ren	-	nor	-	rye
tårynratår masked for the hunt	tah-	ren	-	ray	-	tar	
tarynryl gathers others	tay	-	ren	-	rill		
tarynva out of the corner of the eye	tay	-	ren	-	vah		

The Book of Elf Names

tåshånåda dressed like the trees	tah	-	shan	-	nah	-	dah
tasoora dusty jewel	tay	-	so	-	or	-	rah
tåsudåri stirs the branches	tah	-	sue	-	dar	-	rye
tåsudre making mirth	tah	-	sue	-	dree
tatåtyn dark moon	tay	-	tah	-	tin
tayyndar well graced	tay	-	yin	-	dare
tåzyndåra indigo child	tah	-	zen	-	dah	-	rah
tåzyndėl against all odds	tah	-	zen	-	dell
teådartha among the mystical stones	tee	-	ah	-	dare	-	thah
teadryn rich in nature	tee	-	a	-	drinn
teåladi incredible power for attracting people	tee	-	ah	-	lay	-	dye
teålile stirs the magic	tee	-	ah	-	lie	-	lee
tealosyn stirs the song	tee	-	a	-	low	-	sin
tealyndas weaves in wood	tee	-	a	-	lynn	-	dayce
teålynde shadow shine	tee	-	ah	-	lynn	-	dee
teåndålys creates the way	tee	-	ahn	-	dah	-	liss
teändora real and true	tee	-	ann	-	door	-	rah

teåndre	tee	-	ahn	-	dree	
wishing it would come true						
teånthel	tee	-	ahn	-	theal	
mother's light						
teårasa	tee	-	ah	-	ray	-	sah
hugs the trees						
tearona	tee	-	air	-	row	-	nah
hair of wind						
tearvyn	tee	-	air	-	vin	
carries the weight of the lost forests like a stone in the chest						
tearyn	tee	-	air	-	ren	
plays with unicorns						
teavor	tee	-	a	-	vour	
strives for patience						
tedånda	tee	-	don	-	dah	
slips though the woods						
tedarea	tee	-	dare	-	ree	-	ah
if you know what I mean						
tedareyl	tee	-	dare	-	ree	-	L
feeding faeries						
tedays	tee	-	day	-	iss	
crystal clear						
tedorea	tee	-	door	-	ree	-	ah
strives to help people be happy						
telådas	tell	-	lah	-	dayce	
but it is often necessary						
teladea	tee	-	lay	-	dee	-	ah
what we are meant to do						
telåndryn	tee	-	lahn	-	drinn	
far more than anyone I know						
telåndrys	tee	-	lahn	-	driss	
reconnecting myself						
telareyn	tee	-	lair	-	ree	-	in
senses the truth						

The Book of Elf Names   293

telasyndra happily spinning	tee	-	lay	-	sin	-	drah
tėlelela running wild in the forest	tell	-	lee	-	lee	-	lah
tėlpareån long remembering	tell	-	pair	-	ree	-	ahn
tėlperea sees the future	tell	-	peer	-	ree	-	ah
tėlůsyn remembers the magic	tell	-	loose	-	sin		
tėlvyndara glimmer of hope	tell	-	vin	-	dare	-	rah
telynde talked and talked	tee	-	lynn	-	dee		
tėlynko earth digger	tell	-	lynn	-	co		
telynta my elvish powers came alive	tee	-	lynn	-	tah		
telyntasa fire red hair	tee	-	lynn	-	tay	-	sah
temaryn water is my shelter	tee	-	mare	-	ren		
tenalyn meditates standing	tee	-	nay	-	lynn		
tenarsa born of mist	tee	-	nair	-	sah		
tenaryn heals all with kindness	tee	-	nair	-	ren		
teoralyn feel like I belong	tee	-	or	-	ray	-	lynn
teryndale gifts of precognition	tier	-	ren	-	day	-	lee
teryndava so everyone says	tier	-	ren	-	day	-	vah

The Silver Elves

teryndor mystic conjuror	tier	-	ren	-	door		
tevålea feeling of heaviness lifts	tee	-	vah	-	lee	-	ah
tevåndre path of healing	tee	-	vahn	-	dree		
teylyn dark fortress	tee	-	L	-	lynn		
teynothas loves the voice of the trees	tee	-	in	-	no	-	thayce
teynrodas mother of laughter	tee	-	in	-	row	-	dayce
thaåfyna living vine	thay	-	ah	-	fin	-	nah
thaåfyndre beginning to see	thay	-	ah	-	fin	-	dree
thagryndar willing to risk	thay	-	grin	-	dare		
thånaryn or something else entirely	thah	-	nair	-	ren		
thånere good judge of character	thah	-	near	-	ree		
thaorlyn strong of purpose	thay	-	or	-	lynn		
thårana watches over ...	thah	-	ray	-	nah		
tharynda hears the faeries whisper	thay	-	ren	-	dah		
thåseråsyn secret son	thah	-	seer	-	rah	-	sin
theadoryn feels the truth	thee	-	a	-	door	-	ren
theadryn searches the past	thee	-	a	-	drinn		

The Book of Elf Names

theåndare star whisper	thee	-	ahn	-	dare	-	ree
theårynvål something snapped	thee	-	ah	-	ren	-	vahl
thedardre cooperates with nature	thee	-			dare	-	dree
thedaryn raindrop on a leaf	thee	-			dare	-	ren
thenėkssar spinning left	thee	-			nicks	-	sair
theoryndryl evoking elementals	thee	-	or	-	ren	-	drill
thorådyn young dragon	thor	-			rah	-	den
thorynda awaits the night	thor	-			ren	-	dah
thoryndor awaits his time	thor	-			ren	-	door
thorynsa lure of the unknown	thor	-			ren	-	sah
thynåla journeyed back	thin	-			nah	-	lah
thynieyl aspires to greatness	thin	-	nye	-	e	-	L
tiåfyna river wind	tie	-	ah	-	fin	-	nah
tialanda sways with the sea	tie	-	a	-	lane	-	dah
tialea sea foam	tie	-	a	-	lee	-	ah
tiålyndre speads happy thoughts	tie	-	ah	-	lynn	-	dree
tiåndare tree friend	tie	-	ahn	-	dare	-	ree

tiarathys   tie   -   air   -   a   -   thiss
covers the cities with plants

tiaryndåra   tie   -   air   -   ren   -   dar   -   rah
wide eyed magic

tidarea   tie   -   dare   -   ree   -   ah
often is the wiser of people their age

tidareyl   tie   -   dare   -   ree   -   L
sleeping under a star filled sky

tifäleån   tie   -   fah   -   lee   -   ahn
carries ones'elf with an elvish air

tifalyn   tie   -   fay   -   lynn
unlocking those abilities

tifela   tie   -   fee   -   lah
original form

tigarea   tie   -   fair   -   ree   -   ah
sleek fur

tilåndryn   tie   -   lahn   -   drinn
some deeper meaning that no one knows

tiländyr   tie   -   lan   -   der
the more I learn the more I become

tilaryn   tie   -   lair   -   ren
we've known each other for awhile

tilyldåle   tie   -   lil   -   dah   -   lee
wyardress of the wild things

tilyndra   tie   -   lynn   -   drah
finding my own

timareyl   tie   -   mare   -   ree   -   L
looks elsewhere

timereys   tie   -   mere   -   ree   -   iss
life of the mind

tirasys   tie   -   ray   -   sis
enchanted by Elfin

tiryndål   tie   -   ren   -   dahl
can't stop thinking how great it can be

The Book of Elf Names

tiryntås understands the ancient tongue	tie	-	ren	-	tahss		
tobyndryn loyal friend	toe	-	ben	-	drinn		
todabyn good father	toe	-	day	-	ben		
todobyn plays with sticks	toe	-	doe	-	ben		
tolajyn slowly stirring	toe	-	lay	-	gin		
toleådyn relieves worries	toe	-	lee	-	ah	-	den
toleåfyn elements come together	toe	-	lee	-	ah	-	fin
toleåla everything falls into place	toe	-	lee	-	ah	-	lah
toleålyn works elemental magics	toe	-	lee	-	ah	-	lynn
tolelyn poetic magic	toe	-	lee	-	lynn		
tolyndår to keep traveling forever	toe	-	lynn	-	dar		
tolyntar always have been	toe	-	lynn	-	tair		
tolyntåvor master archer	toe	-	lynn	-	tah	-	vour
tonadra devoted my life to doing so	toe	-	nay	-	drah		
tonådre nimble with magic	toe	-	nah	-	dree		
toparéli spinning fire	toe	-	pair	-	rell	-	lie
torander something amazing	toe	-	rain	-	deer		

298   The Silver Elves

| torarealdyn | toe | - | ray | - | ree | - | ale | - | den |
| rings the tree | | | | | | | | | |

| torazul | toe | - | ray | - | zule | (rhymes |
| protects the mountain | with rule) | | | | | |

| toreare | toe | - | ree | - | air | - | ree |
| gives life | | | | | | | |

| toreartre | toe | - | ree | - | air | - | tree |
| turns away from the world | | | | | | | |

| toreåvyn | toe | - | ree | - | ah | - | vin |
| makes faerie gifts | | | | | | | |

| toreylyn | toe | - | ree | - | L | - | lynn |
| days continue to get brighter | | | | | | | |

| toriador | toe | - | rye | - | a | - | door |
| tries to explain | | | | | | | |

| tormynda | tour | - | men | - | dah |
| steps lively | | | | | |

| torsardor | tour | - | sair | - | door |
| becoming better | | | | | |

| torvånådor | tour | - | vaughn | - | nah | - | door |
| has special powers | | | | | | | |

| torvardyn | tour | - | vair | - | den |
| sees from on high | | | | | |

| torvyndarėl | tour | - | vin | - | dare | - | rell |
| trice protected | | | | | | | |

| torynådor | tour | - | ren | - | nah | - | door |
| across the blue sea | | | | | | | |

| toryndår | tour | - | ren | - | dar |
| trice across | | | | | |

| toryndor | tour | - | ren | - | door |
| earth ways | | | | | |

| torynler | tour | - | ren | - | leer |
| passion rises | | | | | |

| torynsår | tour | - | ren | - | sar |
| defends the small | | | | | |

The Book of Elf Names

toryntali head in the clouds	tour	-	ren	-	tay	-	lie
toryntåryl carries the sacred flame	tour	-	ren	-	tah	-	rill
torynvådar watches from the hill	tour	-	ren	-	vah	-	dare
torynvadrys I just decided	tour	-	ren	-	vay	-	driss
torynvår my eyes truly opened	tour	-		ren	-		var
torynvidor hidden in the hills	tour	-	ren	-	vie	-	door
tosardryn sparkling radiantly	toe	-	sair	-			drinn
tosarlyn loves to share	toe	-	sair	-			lynn
toshåna begins to remember	toe	-	shah	-			nah
tovadryn sharing the magic	toe	-	vay	-			drinn
toyånta returning home	toe	-	yahn	-			tah
trålone what I know to be true	trah	-	low	-			knee
tranaryn appreciate their wisdom	tray	-	nair	-			ren
travåleon path maker	tray	-	vah	-	lee	-	ohn
tråvåndor aims true	trah	-	van	-			door
tråvyndae inner reality	trah	-	vin	-			dae
travynma soul calling	tray	-	vin	-			mah

The Silver Elves

treändra sister true	tree	-	ann	-	drah		
trearåvyn walks between the worlds	tree	-	air	-	rah	-	vin
treåvaryn enjoys traveling in the forest	tree	-	ah	-	vair	-	ren
treavyryl magic unfolding	tree	-	a	-	ver	-	rill
tredaryn in mountains dances	tree	-	dare	-	ren		
tregaryn open to the spirits	tree	-	gair	-	ren		
tregarys honored one	tree	-	gair	-	riss		
trenådan keeper of the hearth	tree	-	nah	-	dane		
trevälryn deep compassion	tree	-	val	-	ren		

trevålyn   tree - vah - lynn
that is the most beautiful song that I've ever heard

trevanåre soul of the clouds	tree	-	vain	-	nah	-	ree
trevåndryn love among the faeries	tree	-	vaughn	-	drinn		
trevaråve not too long past	tree	-	vair	-	rah	-	vee
trevareyl soothing to the soul	tree	-	vair	-	ree	-	L
trevareyn feels kind of silly	tree	-	vair	-	ree	-	in
trevaryn so I can help others	tree	-	vair	-	ren		
trevyndra get to realize	tree	-	vin	-	drah		

trevyndre ealization dawns	tree	-	vin	-	dree	r	
triarvyn wild imaginings	try	-	air	-	vin		
triåvynor belongs to the sea	try	-	ah	-	vin	-	nor
tribor bridgeling	try	-	boar				
trifylea mysteriously attractive	try	-	fill	-	lee	-	ah
trilan night dawn	try	-	lane				
trilea graceful beauty	try	-	lee	-	ah		
trodiarys lead by the hand	trow	-	dye	-	air	-	riss
trodoryn one love certain	trow	-	door	-	ren		
trofälyn forest seacher	trow	-	fowl	-	lynn		
trofälys frees the spirit	trow	-	fowl	-	liss		
trolyndar close to the sea	trow	-	lynn	-	dare		
truarådyn near at hand	true	-	air	-	rah	-	den
trudadryn different then I was before	true	-	day	-	drinn		
trudadyn call of the soul	true	-	day	-	den		
trudåla most importantly	true	-	dah	-	lah		
trudåndea learned much from them	true	-	don	-	dee	-	ah

trueldoryn joined in one body	true	-	eel	-	door	-	ren
trunåfådor striving for flight	true	-	nah	-	fah	-	door
trunåfyn honorable calling	true	-	nah	-	fin
truvålonyn one who tames the wind	true	-	vah	-	lone	-	nin
truvånåde late comer	true	-	vaughn	-	nah	-	dee
truvanavyn touched by the wild	true	-	vay	-	nay	-	vin
truvifara touched by faery	true	-	vie	-	fair	-	rah
tryndånadėl charm maker	trin	-	don	-	nay	-	dell
trysälyn reads the thoughts of animals	triss	-	sal	-	lynn
tudorea finally gave up trying to fit in	two	-	door	-	ree	-	ah
tuleåla maybe this is enough	two	-	lee	-	ah	-	lah
tuleålyn deep in thought	two	-	lee	-	ah	-	lynn
tulela need their help	two	-	lee	-	lah
tulile everytime something goes wrong I cry	two	-	lie	-	lee
tuloryn never suffers any great illness	two	-	lore	-	ren
tunåndåvyl more beautiful with age	two	-	non	-	dah	-	ville
tylådea otherworldly grace	till	-	lah	-	dee	-	ah

tyladre caring for all creatures	till	-	lay	-	dree		
tyladreyl trying to connect	till	-	lay	-	dree	-	L
tylådreyn choosing the path	till	-	lah	-	dree	-	in
tyladreys connects with those on the path	till	-	lay	-	dree	-	iss
tyladryn ensual beauty	till	-	lay	-	drinn		s
tyladrys take me as I am	till	-	lay	-	driss		
tylådyre know somehow	till	-	lah	-	der	-	ree
tylafyn so here I am today	till	-	lay	-	fin		
tyländar walks with dignity	till	-	lan	-	dare		
tylåndareyn air of dignity	till	-	lahn	-	dare	-	ree	-	in
tylåndra certain knowledge	till	-	lahn	-	drah		
tylåndrays whispers of ancient ways	till	-	lahn	-	drayce		
tyländre can't resist it	till	-	lan	-	dree		
tylandrea drastic point in life	till	-	lane	-	dree	-	ah
tylåndreyn step up and proclaim	till	-	lahn	-	dree	-	in
tylansår led away	till	-	lane	-	sar		
tylaryn sound of the breeze	till	-	lair	-	ren		

304

tylasyn spiritual warrior	till	-	lay	-	sin	
tylatheyl wild heart	till	-	lay	-	thee	-	L
tyldåladyn on the healing path	till	-	dah	-	lay	-	den
tyleåfyn how I want to be	till	-	lee	-	ah	-	fin
tyledyn happiest in those environments	till	-	lee	-	den	
tylevyn draws energy from the sun	till	-	lee	-	vin	
tylordyn allows others to shine	till	-	lore	-	den	
tyloreyn peaceful life	till	-	lore	-	ree	-	in
tylyndea hears their voices in the wee morning hours	till	-	lynn	-	dee	-	ah
tyndårklyn emotional certainty	tin	-	dark	-	lynn	
tyndårko rises suddenly	tin	-	dar	-	co	
tyndaryn in the darkness we find ours'elves	tin	-	dare	-	ren	
tyndéla wears a duster	tin	-	dell	-lah	
tyndeora shifting leaves	tin	-	dee	-	oh	-	rah
tyndora opposite reaction	tin	-	door	-	rah	
tyndyniyl wandering way	tin	-	den	-	nigh	-	L
tyntåla hour before dawn	tin	-	tah	-	lah	

The Book of Elf Names

tyntålådyn elf kind	tin	-	tah	-	lah	-	den
tyntålava always original	tin	-tah	-	lay	-	vah	
tyntålea finds their own way	tin	-	tah	-	lee	-	ah
typareyl unseen in the leaves	tip	-	pair	-	ree	-	L
tyråndor sparing with swords	ter	-	ron	-	door		
tyryntåva moves the tree	ter	-	ren	-	tah	-	vah

UNLIKE MOST MAGICAL AND ESOTERIC GROUPS, THE ELVES DO NOT MAKE A GREAT DEAL ABOUT THE SECRETS TO WHICH THEY ARE PRIVY. WHATEVER SECRETS THEY HAVE ARE OPEN SECRETS AND AVAILABLE TO ANYONE CAPABLE OF UNDERSTANDING THEM. IF SOMEONE ASKS THE ELVES IF THEY HAVE SECRETS, THEY WILL REPLY, "NONE TO SPEAK OF."

—OLD ELVEN KNOWLEDGE

U

Elven Name and Meaning   Pronunciation

Elven Name and Meaning	Pronunciation					
uarådyn have always had the desire	you	-	air	-	rah	-	den
ubarlyn y elf lover	ou	-	bare	-	lynn
ubordryl only this	you	-	boar	-	drill
ucaryn unicorn eyes	you	-	car	-	ren
udåndåfor understands the langauge of numbers	you	-	don	-	dah	-	for
udåndåryl the right to join in	you	-	don	-	dah	-	rill
udåndor drawn to sorcery	you	-	don	-	door
udändre broke free	you	-	dan	-	dree
udändryn for sometime now	you	-	dan	-	drinn
udåndryryn now I want to share this feeling	you	-	don	-	dryer	-	ren
udånfora the spirit that helps us grow	you	-	don	-	for	-	ah
udånthådor strength of a dragon	you	-	don	-	thah	-	door
udånthys free moments	you	-	don-	thiss
udarsha clearly mystical in origin	you	-	dare	-	shah

udarshe true calling	you	-	dare	-	she	
udarshyn senses the beyond	you	-	dare	-	shin	
udartheyl adore it immensely	you	-	dare	-	thee	-	L
udartheyn healing admiration	you	-	dare	-	thee	-	in
udarthys good with a long bow	you	-	dare	-	thiss	
udaryn new found personality	you	-	dare	-	ren	
udashyn so darned cool	you	-	day	-	shin	
udåsyna can always find the way	you	-	dah	-	sin	-	nah
udåsynar in exactly the right place	you	-	dah	-	sin	-	nair
udendre relieves the suffering	you	-	dean	-	dree	
uderadyn statuesque beauty	you	-	deer	-	ray	-	den
udere born from a flower	you	-	deer	-	ree	
udersha found a way to do it	you	-	deer	-	shah	
uderyn reads the stars	you	-	deer	-	ren	
udiadre looks after the people	you	-	dye	-	a	-	dree
udilyn strange affinities for the arts	you	-	dye	-	lynn	
udilys secrets of the spirit	you	-	dye	-	liss	

udorea the wings of a butterfly soothe me	you	-	door	-	ree	-	ah
udoryn sees eye to eye	you	-	door	-	ren		
udure trying to find out about myself	you	-	dur	-	ree		
udyndara fond of honey	you	-	den	-	dare	-	rah
uerdyn sees the shadows of the past	you	-	ear	-	den		
ueryth prepare for what is to come	you	-	ear	-	rith		
ufåndyryn laughing fits	you	-	fahn	-	der	-	ren
ufaryn rushes back	you	-	fair	-	ren		
uforeyl enters a different dimension	you	-	for	-	ree	-	L
uhatokyn awaits the decision	you	-	hay	-	toe	-	ken
ularea till the pages were worn	you	-	lair	-	ree	-	ah
ularfyn grass underfoot	you	-	lair	-	fin		
ularsyn faerie of fashion	you	-	lair	-	sin		
ularyn remembers the day when	you	-	lair	-	ren		
uldoryn strange ballad	yule	-	door	-	ren		
uleta moon shimmer	you	-	lee	-	tah		
ullorvyn mysterious light	yule	-	lore	-	vin		

The Book of Elf Names

ulodyn mighty one	you	-	low	-	den		
ultaryn call of the night	yule	-	tair	-	ren		
ůltoreon taking off	ul (as in ulterior)	-	tour ree	-	ohn	-	
ulyardyn not so wee one	yule	-	yair	-	den		
ulyndra searching for where I truly belong	you	-	lynn	-	drah		
umara as best I can	you	-	mare	-	rah		
umaråde affinity with all magical creatures	you	-	mare	-	rah	-	dee
umarådre cool moist air	you	-	mare	-	rah	-	dree
umarådyn more than just different	you	-	mare	-	rah	-	den
umardyn can't stop singing	you	-	mare	-	den		
umare sacred grove	you	-	mare	-	ree		
umareyl tree star	you	-	mare	-	ree	-	L
umarvyn hasn't lost the knack	you	-	mare	-	vin		
umåsådryn lover of nature	you	-	mah	-	sah	-	drinn
umåsyndra great talent for languages	you	-	mah	-	sin	-	drah
umera from the realm	you	-	mere	-	rah		
umerdyn call too strong to deny	you	-	mere	-	den		

The Silver Elves

umerfyn	you - mere - fin	wonder of small things
umerthyn	you - mere - thin	when I truly need something it comes to me
umerys	you - mere - riss	best friend
umire	you - mire - ree	that would be nice
umorfyn	you - more - fin	sees music
umorvår	you - more - var	blinded by the light
umureyn	you - muir - ree - in	path of learning
umuryn	you - muir - ren	believes in many things
unånduryn	you - non - dur - ren	as if something were missing
ündaltareyn	un - dale - tair - ree - in	makes the connection
undåndoryn	yune (rhymes with june) don - door - ren -	kin of the flowers
ündarsa	un - dare - sah	not that that is a bad thing
ündarse	un - dare - see	path of sharing
ündarso	un - dare - so	sword dancer
ündinyn	un - dye - nin	stares at the moon
undorea	yune - door - ree - ah	voice in the dark
unider	you - nigh - deer	told for a reason

untara listens to the sea's song	yune	-	tair	-	rah		
unvändyryn cheeky and cheerful	yune	-	van	-	der	-	ren
ůnvareyl fox spirit	un	-	vair	-	ree	-	L
uoryn can't tell dreams from reality	you	-	or	-	ren		
upånådån likes the elves	you	-	pahn	-	nah	-	don
urände world of sensual exploration	you	-	ran	-	dee		
uråndor listening to life stories	you	-	ron	-	door		
urändys changes like the wind	you	-	ran	-	diss		
uräntar cannot live without it	you	-	ran	-	tair		
urånthea walked a different path	you	-	ron	-	thee	-	ah
uratha wanders by the sea	you	-	ray	-	thah		
urathea pretty cool	you	-	ray	-	thee	-	ah
urdafa gift of flowers	your	-	day	-	fah		
urdånådėl inner beauty	your	-	don	-	nah	-	dell
urdanåthsys returns to her true form	your	-	day	-	nahth	-	sis
urdånåthyn wyzard in the flux	your	-	don	-	nah	-	thin
urdåndåfål be my guest	your	-	don	-	dah	-	fall

The Silver Elves

urdåndåle impatient to learn	your	-	don	-	dah	-	lee
urdåndålys lover of the arts	your	-	don	-	dah	-	liss
urdändålys perfectly unique	your	-	dan	-	dah	-	liss
urdandre never seen	your	-	dane		-		dree
urdändreyn into the unseen	your	-	dan	-	dree	-	in
urdanfa through the mist	your	-	dane		-		fah
urdarshyn love them dearly	your	-	dare		-		shin
urdaryn difficultly in the beginning	your	-	dare		-		ren
urdathos carries the rod	your	-	day		-		thoss
urdynathwae poem singer	your	-	den	-nayth		-	way
urearla not long ago	you	-	ree	-	air	-	lah
ureyla knows the truth	you	-	ree	-	L	-	lah
uriåda unserving desire	you	-	rye	-	ah	-	dah
uriadre on instincts relies	you	-	rye	-	a	-	dree

uridryn ever since then I've had the powerful drive to heal and help others whenever I can	you	-	rye	-	drinn
urondor gradual understanding of who I am	you	-	roan	-	door

urredyn touched by music	your	-	ree	-	den
ursäla breathless beauty	your	-	sal	-	lah
urthandas moves with the wind	your	-	thane	-	dayce
urthosi born for the green	your	-	tho	-	sigh
urvändor shadow wyzard	your	-	van	-	door
urynda one of the beautiful race	you	-	ren	-	dah
uryndål altered fantasies	you	-	ren	-	dahl
uryndel seer, sayer, magic maker	you	-	ren	-	deal
uryndre want to contribute in any way possible	you	-	ren	-	dree
urynrator joins the circle	your	-	ren	-	ray	-	tour
uryntėlar high among the trees	your	-	ren	-	tell	-	lair
urysdol scouts the forest edge	you	-	riss	-	dole
userea born to be	you	-	see	-	ree	-	ah
useryn I think I may have been one in a past life	you	-	see	-	ren
usyrna that is my home	you	-	sir	-	nah
utarloryn up to something	you	-	tair	-	lore	-	ren
uthena poker face	you	-	thee	-	nah

uvadra soft fire	you	-	vay	-	drah		
uvadre know exactly how they look	you	-	vay	-	dree		
uvadreyn speaks with the animals	you	-	vay	-	dree	-	in
uvadryn would love to be with people who are like me	you	-	vay	-	drinn		
uvåldor could be better	you	-	vahl	-	door		
uvaleyn just realized that that is me	you	-	vay	-	lee	-	in
uvålys out there, somewhere	you	-	vah	-	liss		
uvändåre work in progress	you	-	van	-	dah	-	ree
uvandaror all day in the woods	you	-	vane	-	dare	-	roar
uvändor eeks new paths	you	-	van	-	door	s	
uvändre mood shifter	you	-	van	-	dree		
uvandros mission of peace	you	-	vane	-	dross		
uvåndryn all of nature is sacred	you	-	vaughn	-	drinn		
uvaråde flare of the sensual	you	-	vair	-	rah	-	dee
uvare dragon caller	you	-	vair	-	ree		
uvaryndås eases the way	you	-	vair	-	ren	-	dahss
uvarys endures to the end	you	-	vair	-	riss		

uvernaryn	you	-	veer	-	nay	-	ren
in tune with all that is around							

uveryn	you	-	veer	-	ren
new ways to express ones'elf artistically					

uviader	you	-	vie	-	a	-	deer
watches her back							

uvidra	you	-	vie	-	drah
brought it back to life					

uvidre	you	-	vie	-	dree
fleet wing					

uvidryn	you	-	vie	-	drinn
everything from sunsets to praying mantis					

uvilyn	you	-	vie	-	lynn
with people one feels completely comfortable with					

uvorådås	you	-	vour	-	rah	-	dahss
amidst the wildlife							

uvordra	you	-	vour	-	drah
not quite known how					

uvure	you	-	view	-	ree
whispered on the winds					

uvuru	you	-	view	-	rue
power to heal and do go					

uvuryn	you	-	view	-	ren
soothes with the voice					

uvyndara	you	-	vin	-	dare	-	rah
eternally romantic							

uvyndarys	you	-	vin	-	dare	-	riss
lives among us							

uvynde	you	-	vin	-	dee
fun loving					

uvyndor	you	-	vin	-	door
can feel it all the time					

uvyndra	you	-	vin	-	drah
sees the mind					

uvyndre reflecting on the past	you	-	vin	-	dree		
uvyndrys powerful feelings	you	-	vin	-	driss		
uvynsa gift of hope	you	-	vin	-	sah		
uvysyryl shielding out the pain	you	-	viss	-	ser	-	rill
uymeryn walks in the sun dappled greenery	you	-	M	-	mere	-	ren
uyndåryn firey red leaf	you	-	in	-	dar	-	ren
uyndra underlying heartbeat	you	-	in	-	drah		
uzåle when I was very young	you	-	zah	-	lee		
uzalys so enchanting	you	-	zale	-	liss		
uzura at peace sitting on the mesa	you	-	zoo	-	rah		

AN ELF NAME OPENS A DOOR AND ALLOWS MAGIC
INTO ONE'S LIFE.

ν

Elven Name and Meaning   Pronunciation

Elven Name and Meaning						
vadådersa soft dancer	vay	-	dah	-	deer	- sah
vådalys gentle passion	vah	-	day	-	liss	
vadåndre dream shift	vay	-	don	-	dree	
vådaryn homey aura	vah	-	dare	-	ren	
vådor really important	vah		-		door	
vadornåfa bluer than blue	vay	-	door	-	nah	- fah
vådoryn yearns to be whole	vah	-	door	-	ren	
vadra silent watcher	vay		-		drah	
vadreån well, here we go	vay	-	dree	-	ahn	
vadryn glides through the woods	vay		-		drinn	
valaådryn soul washer	vay	-	lay	-	ah	- drinn

vålådahår vah -lah - day - har watches from the hillside

valaden walking on the beach barefoot	vay	-	lay	- den
väladra sister to the wolves	val	-	lay	- drah

vålådrafyn now I no longer fear	vah	-lah	-	dray	-	fin	
väladrea matters of the heart	val	-	lay	-	dree	-	ah
väladryn heals with music	val	-	lay	-	drinn		
vålådrynåda grew up with elves	vah	-	lah	-	drinn	-	ah - dah
vålale alternative thinking	vah	-	lay	-	lee		
valålodyn family and friends are first priority	vay	-	lah	-	low	-	den
vålansa born of elf magic	vah	-	lane	-	sah		
vålåråndor warrior of the spirits	vah	-	lah	-	ron	-	door
vålaryn radiant flower	vah	-	lair	-	ren		
vålårynsa shining lotus jewel	vah	-	lah	-	ren	-	sah
vålåsår mystery unfolds	vah	-	lah	-	sar		
vålealyn walks in the high trees	vah	-	lee	-	a	-	lynn
valesyna flutter of joy	vay	-	lee	-	sin	-	nah
våleyndra aspects of the inner s'elf that cannot be explained verbally	vah	-	lee	-	in	-	drah
våleyntara shine of the stars	vah	-	lee	-	in	-	tair - rah
vålodare loves to discover new things	vah	-	low	-	dare	-	ree
vålodråshyn hint of the blood	vah	-	low	-	drah	-	shin

The Book of Elf Names

valothyn just getting started	vay	-	low	-	thin	
valrynduryl greets the sunrise	vale	-	ren	-	dur	-	rill
vålyndas colors the trees	vah	-	lynn	-	dayce	
vålyndre tree whisperer	vah	-	lynn	-	dree	
vålyndresyn whispering in my thoughts	vah	-	lynn	-	dree	-	sin
vanådre beyond hate and anger	vay	-	nah	-	dree	
vånålyn loves to help	vah	-	nah	-	lynn	
vändåla much more out there	van	-	dah	-	lah	
vandaloryn sees the great possibilities	vane	-	day	-	lore	-	ren
våndånådèl preserves the good	vaughn	-	dah	-nah	-	dell	
vandara moon glow	vane	-	dare	-	rah	
våndarea flashes of light	vaughn	-	dare	-	ree	-	ah
våndareyn longing for the deep woods	vaughn	-	dare	-	ree	-	in
vändaryn sun warrior	van	-	dare	-	ren	
våndarys it has always been there	vaughn	-	dare	-	riss	
våndåvaryn attracts good things	vaughn	-	dah	-	vair	-	ren
våndèlwe searches for lost meaning	vaughn	-	dell	-	wee	

vändoreyn	van	-	door	-	ree	-	in
lots of people come and stay with us						
vändoryc	van	-	door	-	rick		
temper of the race						
våndrea	vaughn	-	dree	-	ah		
knew this to be true						
vandrealyn	vane	-	dree	-	a	-	lynn
stands in shifting sands						
vandreyl	vane	-	dree	-	L		
napping on patches of moss						
vandro	vane	–	dro			
magic of will						
vändryn	van	-	drinn	very		
different kind of person						
våradea	vah	-	ray	-	dee	-	ah
world between						
varådrefyn	vair	-	rah	-	dree	-	fin
bound by duty						
varåfena	vair	-	rah	-	fee	-	nah
moon's aura						
varåfyn	vair	-	rah	-	fin		
touched by starlight						
varaleyl	vair	-	ray	-	lee	-	L
truth to be known						
varåndre	vair	-	ron	-	dree		
calling up the wind						
vårändrys	vah	-	ran	-	driss		
are we ever really sure of anything						
varånea	vair	-	rah	-	knee	-	ah
explores the way						
våränve	vah	-	ran	-	vee		
magic unleashed						
varårea	vay	-	rah	-	ree	-	ah
splashes water						

vårdaryn passes the pipe	var	-	dare	-	ren		
vardorlulon speaks with dragons	vair	-	door	-	lou	-	lone
varhana humble power	vair	-	hay	-	nah		
variyna beginning to moult	vair	-	rye	-	in	-	nah
varnåthyn it was then that I knew I belonged	vair	-	nah	-	thin		
vartadalyn protector in the dark	vair	-	tay	-	day	-	lynn
varynalu like a panther	vair	-	ren	-	nay	-	lou
varyndor dreaming reality	vair	-	ren	-	door		
varyndre craving to accomplish	vair	-	ren	-	dree		
varynea not as it appears	vair	-	ren	-	knee	-	ah
varynetha living freely	vair	-	ren	-	knee	-	thah
varynve beyond imagining	vair	-	ren	-	vee		
väshe touched by the breeze	vass	-	shee				
våvåndre natural youth	vah	-	vaughn	-	dree		
våvardor in manifest form	vah	-	vair	-	door		
våvardorn strange connection	vah	-	vair	-	dorn		
vaylyn kindness returned	vay	-	L	-	lynn		

| våzyndåros renews the forest | vah | - | zen | - | dah | - | rowce |

vazyndrasos
cloud shadow — vay - zen - dray - sose (rhymes with dose)

veädyryn
aware of another presence — vee - add - der - ren

veåmoryn
feathered wings — vee - ah - more - ren

vearåla
peeks beyond the veil — vee - air - rah - lah

vearsa
extreme grace — vee - air - sah

vearsåla
glimpses the true — vee - air - sah - lah

veasorél
skimming the surface of the sea — vee - ace - so - rell

veävare
shows the world — vee - av (as in average) vair - ree -

vedarthyn
my companion has shown me the way — vee - dare - thin

vedaryn
call of the ancient lands — vee - dare - ren

veévåle
more beautiful than they know — vee - ev (as in ever) - vah lee -

velånsa
find it strange if you will, but it is the truth — vee - lahn - sah

vélånthas
sensitive to other kinds — vell - lah - thayce

vélazyn
feeling that has been growing — vell - lay - zen

véldånådor
compelled to learn about new things — vell - dah - nah - door

vélea
not sure how to explain it — vell - lee - ah

veleda frolicing barefoot	vee	-	lee	-	dah	
veledryn yet to realize	vell	-	lee	-	drinn	
veliålyn faery in glowing light	vell	-	lie	-	ah	-	lynn
velidra so people tell me	vell	-	lie	-	drah	
veltynsa spirit caller	vell	-	tin	-	sah	
venafari twirling gold dust	vee	-	nay	-	fair	-	rye
venaryn never realized it until now	vee	-	nair	-	ren	
venasa golden glow	vee	-	nay	-	sah	
veneryn inner child	vee	-	near	-	ren	
veråthånor elfin sword master	vee	-	rah	-	than	-	nor
verfaryn alone on the mountain	vee	-	fair	-	ren	
vericgår mastering rage	vee	-	rike	-	gar	
verondålor first, last and always an artist	veer	-	roan	-	dah	-	lore
veronel brings laughter to people's eyes	veer	-	roan	-	nell	
vervålyn taking charge	veer	-	vah	-	lynn	
vervaru shadow light	veer	-	vay	-	rue	
veryndae heals freely	veer	-	ren	-	day	

veryndro words of fire	veer	-	ren	-	dro		
vevonvåryn magical integrity	vee	-	vone	-	vah	-	ren
vezåla very mysterious	vee	-	zah	-	lah		
viådarshyn sparkling sea	vie	-	ah	-	dare	-	shin
viadrea awakened by the touch	vie	-	a	-	dree	-	ah
viådynar out of place	vie	-	ah	-	den	-	nair
viåndre loves love	vie	-	ahn	-	dree		
viaradyn sees beyond the normal	vie	-	air	-	ray	-	den
viareatha filled with grace	vie	-air	-	ree	-	a	- thah
viarla ready to fly	vie	-	air	-	lah		
viarlor floating by	vie	-	air	-	lore		
viåsådel slips into Faerie	vie	-	ah	-	sah	-	deal
viåvyna plays music with the elves	vie	-	ah	-	vin	-	nah
viåvynar turns anger into creativity	vie	-ah	-	vin	-	nair	
vidaryn it all made sense	vie	-	dare	-	ren		
vidråsůn in tune with the trees	vie	-	drah	-	soon		
vidrasys traveled far and wide	vie	-	dray	-	sis		

vimareyl master in training	vie	-	mare	-	ree	-	L
vimeråle good to the elves	vie	-	mere	-	rah	-	lee
vimere wonders galore	vie	-		mere	-	ree	
vimerfyn worth waiting for	vie	-		mere	-	fin	
virana looking for others	vie	-		ray	-	nah	
vireålyn healing touch	vie	-	ree	-	ah	-	lynn
vireda the beauty within	vie	-		ree	-	dah	
vivåndåle feel they can hear me	vie	-	vaughn	-	dah	-	lee
vivändrys shadow spirits	vie	-		van	-	driss	
vivynde dreams of returning	vie	-		vin	-	dee	
vivyndor passion for our people	vie	-		vin	-	door	
vivyndre glitter wings	vie	-		vin	-	dree	
viyndale governed by the love in her heart	vie	-	in	-	day	-	lee

vladdåvoryn   vlaid   -   dah   -   vour   -   ren
one who is deft at dealing with miscreants having been one at one time

vodålor more to life	voe	-	dah	-	lore
vodareyn mermaid charm	voe	-	dare	-	ree	-	in
vodarfyn waiting for something that will never come	voe	-	dare	-	fin

vodėleyn nothing can take it away from me	voe	-	dell	-	lee	-	in
vodrafor special child	voe	-	dray	-	for		
vodrasa wide variety of interests	voe	-	dray	-	sah		
voladaryn back to nature	voe	-	lay	-	dare	-	ren
volådyn awaits the call	voe	-	lah	-	den		
volålupi runs with wolves	voe	-	lah	-	lou	-	pie
volåndre great listener	voe	-	lahn	-	dree		
voleafyn moonlight on water	voe	-	lee	-	a	-	fin
voledryn hot to the touch	voe	-	lee	-	drinn		
volela I was curious	voe	-	lee	-	lah		
volelyn who better than you	voe	-	lee	-	lynn		
volynar special friend and healer	voe	-	lynn	-	nair		
volyniyn can't stop thinking about it	voe	-	lynn	-	nigh	-	in
volynsa rumors of the sacred tome	voe	-	lynn	-	sah		
vondåreyl free dreamer	vone (rhymes with phone) dah - ree - L						
vondeerys first to come	vone	-	dee	-	ear	-	riss
vondraėl sparkles like snow	vone	-	dray	-	L		

voradajyn	voe	-	ray	-	day	-	gin
speaks to the people							
vorasa	voe	-		ray	-		sah
pulls mind and soul to a better place							
voråsyl	voe	-		rah	-		sill
me all over							
vorasyn	voe	-		ray	-		sin
I've always been this way							
vordåjynår	vour	-	dah	-	gin	-	nar
learns of wisdom							
vordånådyl	vour	-	dah	-	nah	-	dill
keeps the faith							
vordånde	vour	-		don	-		dee
look into the mirror							
vordangar	vour	-		dane	-		gair
mighty swing							
vordånle	vor	-		dahn	-		lee
sounds the call							

vordarys   vor (rhymes with oar) dare - riss
on his way

vordathyn	vor	-		day	-		thin
rainbow green							
vordeana	vour	-	dee	-	a	-	nah
brings justice							

vordrea   vour   -   dree   -   ah
magical knowledge growing

vordyniėl	vour	-	den	-	nigh	-	L
follows the river							
voreåda	vour	-	ree	-	ah	-	dah
made me think of elves							
voreardyn	vour	-	ree	-	air	-	den
I liked them very much							
voredarna	vour	-	ree	-	dare	-	nah
brief overview							

vorékjyn wanderer of the sky	vour	-	reek	-			gin
vorendor something special	vour	-	reen	-			door
vorgéndor mighty roar	vour	-	gain	(as	in	again)	door
vorialyn edge of flight	vour	-	rye	-	a	-	lynn
voridre everything I plant grows	vour	-	rye	-			dree
voridyn rising unseen	vour	-	rye	-			den
vorisa of ancient days	vour	-	rye	-			sah
vorlasa becomes hers'elf	vour	-	lay	-			sah
vorondir song of remembering	vour	-	roan	-			dire
vorshadyn never lost touch	vour	-	shay	-			den
voryleyn feels what nature is feeling	vour	-	rill	-	lee	-	in
voryndél embraces them all	vour	-	ren	-			dell
voryndrasås strong within	vour	-	ren	-	dray	-	sahss
voryndre brings fantasy to life	vour	-	ren	-			dree
voryndyl tea partying	vour	-	ren	-			dill
voryndyn strength of s'elf	vour	-	ren	-			den
vorynthel taking it as it comes	vour	-	ren	-			theal

The Book of Elf Names

329

vorynve eagerly helps	vour	-	ren	-			vee
vryndaryn faerie's help	vrinn	-	dare	-			ren
vuarvyn full of love	view	-	air	-			vin
vudantha gift of empathy	view-		dane	-			thah
vudyndre signs at birth	view	-	den	-			dree
vuleathe very much	view	-	lee	-	a	-	thee
vuleryn I dream I walk around in beauty	view	-	lee	-			ren
vurera talented with words	view	-	ree	-			rah
vuvarys mostly in hiding	view	-	vair	-			riss
vydarys though I don't know why	vid	-	are	-			riss
vylådryn feels faerie all around	ville	-	lah	-			drinn
vylådyna born of a willow tree	ville	-	lah	-	den	-	nah
vyländor a deep feeling	ville	-	lan	-			door
vylånsa home at last	ville	-	lahn	-			sah
vylåvoryn a blessed and magical life	ville	-	lah	-	vour	-	ren
vylynåla scribbling away	ville	-	lynn	-	nah	-	lah
vynaca sneaks under	vin	-	nay	-			cah

vynåda singing bowl	vin	-	nah	-	dah			
vynalys full of life	vin	-	nay	-	liss			
vynaryn grew up in nature	vin	-	nair	-	ren			
vyndagaryn elf shadow	vin	-	day	-	gair	-	ren	
vyndåla natural magical abilities	vin	-	dah	-	lah			
vyndålåle enchanted by the thought of them	vin	-	dah	-	lah	-	lee	
vyndåle inspired to connect	vin	-	dah	-	lee			
vyndaloseyn be still my heart	vin	-	day	-	low	-	see	- in
vyndåndålor speaker of tones	vin	-	don	-	dah	-	lore	
vyndänder came to realize	vin	-	dan	-	deer			
vyndånle it found me	vin	-	don	-	lee			
vyndarlyn mirror in the window	vin	-	dare	-	lynn			
vyndarlys making magic manifest	vin	-	dare	-	liss			
vyndaryk lines of elegance	vin-		dare	-	rick			
vyndaryn awaken courage	vin	-	dare	-	ren			
vyndavae tells the tale	vin	-	day	-	vay			
vyndåve elf faerie blood	vin	-	dah	-	vee			

The Book of Elf Names

vyngareyn soothes the vines	vin-	gair	-	ree	-	in	
vynråseyn jewels on cheek	vin	-	rah	-	see	-	in
vynresa gypsy nature	vin	-	ree	-	sah		
vynvaråsyn glides over the sea	vin	-	vair	-	rah	-	sin
vynvardor harmonic nature	vin	-	vair	-	door		
vynvare heals with sound	vin	-	vair	-	ree		
vynvial blessed with the skill	vin	-	vie	-	ale		
vyråndyryl elf wise	ver	-	rahn	-	der	-	rill
vyryndra brooding silent	ver	-	ren	-	drah		
vyrynzara amorphous power	ver	-	ren	-	zair	-	rah
vyvåsea tangled in vines	viv	-	vah	-	see	-	ah

IF YOU ASK THE ELVES WHERE THEY'VE
BEEN, THEY MAY VERY WELL SAY, "HERE".
IF YOU ASK THEM WHERE THEY ARE GOING,
THEY MAY ALSO SAY "HERE". TO SOME THIS
MAY SEEM EVASIVE, BUT TO THE ELVES, IT IS
A MOST EVIDENT AND LITERAL TRUTH.

W

Elven Name and Meaning	Pronunciation						
waarynėl cried with joy that it might be true	way	-	air	-	ren	-	nell
wadålyn it came to me in a dream	way	-	dah	-	lynn		
wådåndor guards the sacred texts	wah	-	don	-	door		
wadaryn wants to come out	way	-	dare	-	ren		
wadiålyn paper bark birch	way	-	dye	-	ah	-	lynn
wakasa walks in forests	way	-	kay	-	sah		
wakensa magic sparkling	way	-	keen	-	sah		
wåmareyl dances in green	wah	-	mare	-	ree	-	L
wånarys gives of s'elf in meaningful ways	wah	-	nair	-	riss		
wanavra fondly remember	way	-	nav (as in navy)		rah		
wanavryn nature's way	way	-	nav	-	ren		
wandåleyl not among them	wayne	-	dah	-	lee	-	L
warånådål graced by Elfin	ware	-	ron	-	nah	-	dahl
waråthyn ways of the ancestors are awake within	ware	-	rah	-	thin		

warearyn	ware	-	ree	-	air	-	ren
when I came across this idea							
waronthori	ware	-	roan	-	thor	-	rye
cheeks that glow							
waryndåna	ware	-	ren	-	dah	-	nah
the one they talk to							
waryndèl	ware	-			ren	-	dell
belongs outside							
wasynta	way	-			sin	-	tah
honey keeper							
wasyntha	way	-			sin	-	thah
called up the wind							
wavondre	way	-			vone	-	dree
singing over the ocean at dawn							
wåvore	wah	-			vour	-	ree
quiet understanding							
wavoryn	way	-			vour	-	ren
truth settled in my soul							
wavorys	way	-			vour	-	riss
sharp of fang							
weådyna	wee	-	ah	-	den	-	nah
speaks the trees names							
weåndoryn	wee	-	ahn	-	door	-	ren
high magic powers							
wearådyn	wee	-	air	-	rah	-	den
seems like a goddess							
wearfyryn	wee	-	air	-	fur	-	ren
skips through her arms							
wearvyn	wee	-			air	-	vin
core of the soul							
weåsålyn	wee	-	ah	-	sah	-	lynn
elfin walk							
weborådyn	wee	-	boar	-	rah	-	den
words erupting from my fingers							

wedånsa everything is great	wee	-	don	-		sah
wedoryn making me wish I could do something	wee	-	door	-		ren
weduryn one that cannot be broken	wee	-	dur	-		ren
wedyndra it's a toss up	wee	-	den	-		drah
wefarjyna water jewel	wee	-	fair	-gin	-	nah
welåndara truly beautiful	well	-	lahn	-	dare	rah
welesar living the dream	well	-	lee	-		sair
welole recently learned	well	-	low	-		lee
welolynver sweet love	well	-	low	-	lynn	veer
welordyn people need each other	well	-	lore	-		den
welorvyn star on forehead	well	-	lore	-		vin
welotaryn moon howler	well	-	low	-	tair	ren
welyndra all of nature speaks to me	well	-	lynn	-		drah
welyndryn since I was really little	well	-	lynn	-		drinn
welynsa always wondered	well	-	lynn	-		sah
wemertha stands steady in the storm	wee	-	mere	-		thah
wemerthyn talent for healing	wee	-	mere	-		thin

The Book of Elf Names

335

wenadrån in my youth	wee	-	nay	-	dron
wenånda on the bluff	wee	-	non	-	dah
werdånla unlocking the memories	weir	-	don	-	lah
werdånlyn protective spirit	weir	-	don	-	lynn
werethayn sees the resemblence	weir	-	ree	-	thay	-	in
werondia blends with the heather	weir	-	roan	-	dye	-	ah
wervånåden sings haunting tunes	weir	-	vaughn	-	nah	-	dean
werwyndalas visualizes Elfin	weir	-	win	-	day	-	lace
weryndryn knowing we are one	weir	-	ren	-	drinn
werynvor swift and sure	weir	-	ren	-	vour
weshonli linked to the past	wee	-	shone	-	lie
wethynwa little kin	wee	-	thin	-	wah
wevadryn the essence of it fits	wee	-	vay	-	drinn
wevånre changing eyes	wee	-	vahn	-	ree
wevaråde not sure how it happened	wee	-	vair	-	rah	-	dee
wevora tying the threads	wee	-	vour	-	rah
wevynre unseen guardian	wee	-	vin	-	ree

The Silver Elves

wewyndåra soothes the soul	wee	-	win	-	dah	-	rah
wiåmar called to the life	why	-	ah	-	mare
wiandyryl protector of gnomes	why	-	ane	-	der	-	rill
wiaratyn jumps with glee	why	-	air	-	ray	-	tin
wiardre message carrier	why	-	air	-	dree
wiardryn feel the need to travel	why	-	air	-	drinn
wiboryn because I wanted to	why	-	boar	-	ren
widalyn called to faerie	why	-	day	-	lynn
widalynsa the spirit within	why	-	day	-	lynn	-	sah
widåndra despise those who torture the earth	why	-	don	-	drah
widarthyn signs of great power	why	-	dare	-	thin
widasu eager to return	why	-	day	-	sue
wideryn more beautiful than anyone can imagine	why	-	deer	-	ren
widorea weirdiest in a lot of ways	why	-	door	-	ree	-	ah
wieryn from the rocky coast	why	-	ear	-	ren
wiforyn my whole life long	why	-	for	-	ren
wimara never in my life felt so strongly	why	-	mare	-	rah

wimaryn songs of the heart	why	-	mare	-			ren
wimera grows stronger with age	why	-	mere	-			rah
wimerys spent a lot of time there	why	-	mere	-			riss
winälys healed by the mountains	why	-	nawl (rhymes with owl)	-			liss
winarvyn wind whispers	why	-	nair	-			vin
wisaryn peeks out from the shadows	why	-	say	-			ren
wishona close to hand	why	-	shone	-			nah
wivadra true friends who understand	why	-	vay	-			drah
wivadryn of the things I never knew	why	-	vay	-			drinn
wivadrys learning patience	why	-	vay	-			driss
wivåndaryn feeling of belonging	why	-	von	-	dare	-	ren
wivynre started to believe even more	why	-	vin	-			ree
wodåndor became a better person	woe	-	don	-			door
wodåndoryn using that attunement to heal mys'elf and others	woe	-	don	-	door	-	ren
wodyndor it was simply true	woe	-	den	-			door
wolåndre take it slowly and enjoy what life brings	woe	-	lahn	-			dree
worådyn obscured by the bushes	woe	-	rah	-			den

wŏriålor	wore	-	rye	-	ah	-	lore
eager to learn patience							

wovoryn	woe	-	vour	-	ren
glides through problems					

wudåndor	woo	-	don	-	door
have never forgotten					

wudåndre	woo	-	don	-	dree
powers returned					

wudare	woo	-	dare	-	ree
learns easily					

wuladra	woo	-	lay	-	drah
revealed over many years					

wulelyn	woo	-	lee	-	lynn
without them knowing who I am					

wulesardre	woo	-	lee	-	sair	-	dree
which made me realize							

wycasa	wick	-	cah	-	sah
plays with fire					

wydynda	wid	-	den	-	dah
hint of romance					

wyladea	will	-	lay	-	dee	-	ah
dreams uncertain							

wyladyna	will	-	lay	-	den	-	nah
yearns to return							

wylandeyn	will	-	lane	-	dee	-	in
wood dweller							

wylånter	will	-	lahn	-	tier
beyond classification					

wylasa	will	-	lay	-	sah
herbal shaman					

wylnasa	will	-	nay	-	sah
tired of the madness					

wylnåvyn	will	-	nah	-	vin
insightful dreams					

The Book of Elf Names

| wylynisa
watched over | will | - | lynn | - | nigh | - | sah |

wylynisa
watched over | will - lynn - nigh - sah

wylynsea
wouldn't it be surprised at all | will - lynn - see - ah

wynåver
bond that runs deep | win - nah - veer

wyndåldor
moves among them unseen | win - dahl - door

wyndålea
finding many adventures on the way | win - dah - lee - ah

wyndåleon
welcome connection | win - dah - lee - ohn

wyndålor
senses the ley lines | win - dah - lore

wyndålys
helps others come to appreciate | win - dah - liss

wyndånådryn
watches the layers of the world peel away | win - dah - nar - drinn

wyndånåfyr
wandering ranger | win - dah - nah - fur

wyndånåre
so much older than I look | win - dah - nar - ree

wyndånåthe
it's all I can relate to | win - dah - nah - thee (rhymes with fee)

wyndånedėl
friend forever | win - dah - knee - dell

wyndanyryn
finds the truth within | win - day - ner - ren

wyndar
wind on my face | win - dare

wyndaraden
remembers the life | win - dare - ray - den

wyndårėl
listens to unicorns | win - dah - rell

The Silver Elves

| wyndarfyn | win | - | dare | - | fin |
| called by nature | | | | | |

| wyndarva | win | - | dare | - | vah |
| mirror to another world | | | | | |

| wyndåthe | win | - | dah | - | thee |
| still discovering | | | | | |

| wyndava | win | - | day | - | vah |
| helps to mold the future of others | | | | | |

| wynddraden | wind | - | dray | - | den |
| finds her way home | | | | | |

| wynderådyn | win | - | deer | - | rah | - | den |
| in touch with the earth and the wind and the stars | | | | | | | |

| wyndoryn | win- | door | - | ren |
| this is what I'm truly meant to be | | | | |

| wyndreyl | win | - | dree | - | L |
| among the wee ones | | | | | |

| wynjamor | win | - | jay | - | more |
| glides unseen | | | | | |

| wynsa | win | - | sah |
| nature's child running free | | | |

| wynsalea | win | - | say | - | lee | - | ah |
| crème de la crème | | | | | | | |

| wynsiela | win | - | sigh | - | e | - | lah |
| deep in magic | | | | | | | |

| wynwedyn | win | - | wee | - | den |
| winged way | | | | | |

| wyrdånådyn | were | - | dah | - | nah | - | den |
| feeds the fae | | | | | | | |

| wyreynal | were | - | ree | - | N | - | nail |
| great night vision | | | | | | | |

| wyrona | were | - | roan | - | nah |
| wounded healer | | | | | |

| wyryndar | were | - | ren | - | dare |
| keeps his youth | | | | | |

The Book of Elf Names

wyrynor	were	-	ren	-		nor
passion for life						
wysareyn	wiss	-	sair	-	ree	-	in
born among them						
wyseleyl	wiss	-	see	-	lee	-	L
where the earth and water meet						
wysnoreyl	wis	-	nor	-	ree	-	L
bends with the trees in the wind						
wysonre	wis	-	sown	-		ree
sudden warmth						
wysoryn	wis	-	soar	-		ren
shedding magic						
wytreta	wit	-	tree	-		tah
guided into another stage of initiation						

ϒ

Elven Name and Meaning	Pronunciation					
yåbareyl woodsy green	yah	-	bare	-	ree	- L
yådåndryn rushes to the fore	yah	-	dahn	-	drinn	
yadarfyn honors the ancestors	yeah	-	dare	-	fin	
yådarlyn treading water	yah	-	dare	–	lynn	
yådarnathyn all life carries with it its own magic	yah	-	dare	- nay	-	thin
yådarvyn drawn to the night	yah	-	dare	-	vin	
yafyladyn eyes of an elf	yeah	-	fill	- lay	-	den
yafyndrėl adored by elves	yeah	-	fin	-	drell	
yafyndyryn love is the most important thing	yeah	-	fin	- der	-	ren
yålåsor yet to be	yah	-	lah	-	soar	
yålyndaryn very sensitive to the elements	yah	- lynn	-	dare	-	ren
yålyndyn among the elementals	yah	-	lynn	-	den	
yåmara destined to heal	yah	-	mare	-	rah	
yåmardre all things elemental	yah	-	mare	-	dree	

yåmardrys	yah	-	mare	-	driss

began to understand

yåmareys	yah	-	mare	-	ree	-	S

faded glory renewed

yåmari	yah	-	mare	-	rye

the razor's edge

yåmaryth	yah	-	mare	-	rith

makes dreams come true

yåmuryn	yah	-	muir	-	ren

honors the land

yanådryn	yeah	-	nah	-	drinn

fish out of water

yånarys	yah	-	nair	-	riss

freedom to choose one's own path

yånaviyl	yah	-	nay	-	vie	-	L

beneath the palm trees

yåndålåfyn	yahn	-	dah	-	lah	-	fin

speaks the language in their own way

yåndålyn	yahn	-	dah	-	lynn

no one I know has ever seen stuff like that

yåndålys	yahn	-	dah	-	liss

that's the way I am

yåndarfyn	yah	-	dare	-	fin

burns to come into full existence

yåndarfyna	yah	-	dare	-	fin	-	nah

studies in the wood

yandèlåfån	yane	-	dell	-	lah	-	fahn

elven dragon

yandoryn	yane	-	door	-	ren

cloud archer

yåndre	yahn	-	dree

funny bone a mile long

yanlafyn	yane	-	lay	-	fin

searches the stars

The Silver Elves

yantarys ticklish wings	yane	-	tear	(as	in	rip)	-	riss
yardynvar looks out from the mountain	yair	-	den				-	vair
yavådren according to the lore	yeah	-	dah				-	dreen
yåvåndre in between	yah	-	vahn				-	dree
yavardyn awoke in a hurry	yeah	-	vair				–	den
ydlanda touched by the rain	D	-	lane				-	dah
ydrudeyn endlessly persistent	D	-	drew	-	dee		-	in
yeådoryn silent connection	yee	-	ah	-	door		-	ren
yebaryn never wishes to grow up	yee	-	bare				-	ren
yedareyn listening to the sounds of nature	yee	-	dare	-	ree		-	in
yedarthyn dark broodings	yee	-	dare				-	thin
yedåva very witty	yee	-	dah				-	vah
yedoryn pretending to be human to avoid detection	yee	-	door				-	ren
yeduryth nothing energizes me more	yee	-	dur				-	rith
yèluryn able to taste the air	yell	-	lure				-	ren
yèlynda gentle, kind and caring personality	yell	-	lynn				-	dah
yemåna I feel like one	yee	-	mahn				-	nah

The Book of Elf Names

yemuryn mother's despair	yee	-	muir	-	ren		
yenaleth there unseen	yee	-	nay	-	leth		
yėndåla full of craft	yin	-	dah	-	lah		
yėnfalyn gentle mane	yen	-	fay	-	lynn		
yeronåvon long time searching	yee	-	row	-	nah	-	vone
yevändar struggles in the shadows	yee	-	van	-	dare		
yevånder senses the grim	yee	-	vahn	-	deer		
yevonådon endures hardship	yee	-	voe	-	nah	-	doan
yfarea thinking of tricks	F	-	fair	-	ree	-	ah
yfnarfyn stone sitter	F	-	nair	-	fin		
yfynar loves the beasts	F	-	fin	-	nair		
yiardyn beautifully serene	yi	-	air	-	den		
yifarea where everyone was kind	yi	-	fair	-	ree	-	ah
yïnyåsa bathes in the sea	yin	-	yah	-	sah		
yitarys voice in the wind	yi	-	tear (as in rip)	-	riss		
yivaryn when I was a baby	yi	-	vair	-	ren		
yivuryn feels things others cannot	yi	-	view	-	ren		

346   The Silver Elves

yivyndyryn fascinated with them	yi	-	ven	-	der	-	ren
yladro find's one's own	L	-	lay	-	dro		
ylåndor moving from place to place	L	-	lahn	-	door		
ylavyndra hums in the kitchen	L	-	lay	-	vin	-	drah
ylesa climbing since I could walk	L	-	lee	-	sah		
yllasor follows the code	L	-	lace	-	soar		
ylliadyn does what counts	L	-	lie	-	ah	-	den
yllonda scent of the trees	L	-	lone	-	dah		
ylwyndarea mysterious eyes	L	-	win	-	dare	-	ree	-	ah
ymaradyn obsessed by the vision	m	-	mare	-ray	-	den
ymåryl feels the purpose	m	-	mar	-	rill		
ymaryn longs to run in the woods	m	-	mare	-	ren		
ymdale powers arising	m	-	day	-	lee		
ymėlor magic spell of victory	m	-	mell	-	lore		
ymėloryn never beaten	m	-	mell	-	lore	-	ren
ymladyn know for sure	m	-	lay	-	den		
ymledra flashes of brilliance	m	-	lee	-	drah		

The Book of Elf Names

ympartea	m	-	pair	-	tea	-	ah
issues forth							
ympasheon	m	-	pay	-	she	-	ohn
flower of passion							
ynalor	n	--	nay	-	lore		
of many abilities							
yndåfareyn	n	-	dah	-	fair	-	ree	-	in
peace bringer							
yndålea	n	-	dah	-	lee	-	ah
strong affinity							
yndålor	n	-	dah	-	lore		
dreams that affect reality							
yndåna	n	-	dah	-	nah		
anytime they wish							
yndaråfyn	n	-	dare	-	rah	-	fin
speaks with the wolves							
yndare	n	-	dare	-	ree		
childlike							
yndåre	n	-	dar	-	ree		
protects the little ones							
yndareyn	n	-	dare	-	ree	-	in
inner strength							
yndarva	n	-	dare	-	vah		
morning of the drow							
yndårvyn	n	-	dar	-	vin		
when you break it down							
yndaryn	n	-	dare	-	ren		
flys with faeries							
yndåsån	n	-	dah	-	sahn		
courageous healer							
yndasel	n	-	day	-	seal		
whispering leaves							
yndåvae	n	-	dah	-	vay		
led by intuitions							

yndåveda not fully human	n	-	dah	-	vee	-	dah
yndialyn returns to the way	n	-	die	-	a	-	lynn
yndonåfyl searching the circle	n	-	doan	-	nah	-	fill
yndoreyn moon deer	n	-	door	-	ree	-	in
yndrånåfèl open eyes	n	-	drah	-	nah	-	fell
yndrosal whispers of magic	n	-	dro	-	sail		
yndurel whisper of mystery	n	-	dur	-	real		
yndurfyn affinity with ravens	n	-	dur	-	fin		
ynmårdras of the wild	n	-	mar	-	drayce		
ynmareyl gift of the sight	n	-	mare	-	ree	-	L
ynnedryn that one is me	n	-	knee	-	drinn		
yntåweda whispering wisdom	n	-	tah	-	wee	-dah	
ynvådrys twin souled	n	-	vah	-	driss		
ynvidra felt closest to	n	-	vie	-	drah		
ynvithyn life giver	n	-	vie	-	thin		
ynyorhe ponders deeply	n	-	your	-	he		
ynzardyn on the forest floor	n	-	zair	-	den		

The Book of Elf Names

yodåndryn	yo	-	dahn	-	drinn		
decision made on intuition							
yodynėl	yo	-	den	-	nell		
want to feel like a child again							
yojålys	yo	-	lah	-	liss		
ever since that fateful day							
yolelyn	yo	-	lee	-	lynn		
want to know I lived my life							
yomålyn	yo	-	mah	-	lynn		
never felt more at home							
yondarys	yone	-	dare	-	riss		
peacefully accepts all life							
yoreåda	yo	-	ree	-	ah	-	dah
gate to a field of everlasting blossoms							
yovidre	yo	-	vie	-	dree		
uncanny ability to learn							
yrboreåna	r	-	bore	-	ree	-	ah	-	nah
born of the trees							
yrdåndryl	r	-	dahn	-	drill		
flame of the luna moth							
yrdarys	r	-	dare	-	riss		
concrete acts of compassion							
yrrutyn	r	-	rue	-	tin		
shades of brown							
yryndåreo	r	-	ren	-	dah	-	ree	-	oh
fund of wisdom							
yrynvår	r	-	ren	-	var		
of stars born							
yssaryn	is	-	sair	-	ren		
helps to heal							
yssoryn	is	-	soar	-	ren		
befriended by the animals							
yyndålåfyn	yin	-	dah	-	lah	-	fin
in tune with the elements							

yyndåledyn	yin	-	dah	-	lee	-	den
have been searching ever since							

DOES ONE NEED AN ELVEN NAME TO BE AN
ELF? NOT AT ALL. AN ELF IS AN ELF NO
MATTER WHAT WE CALL OURSELVES.
HOWEVER, IT IS A BIT OF STARLIGHT THAT
HELPS LIGHT THE WAY TO THE DEEPER
REACHES OF FAERIE.

ELVES, LIKE OUR COUSINS THE VAMPIRES,
ARE SOMEWHAT PRONE TO ENNUI. HOWEVER,
THEN WE ROUSE OUR SPIRITS AND REMIND
OURSELVES THAT IF WE ARE LOOKING FOR
THE WORLD TO BE DIFFERENT THAN IT IS, IT
IS WE WHO MUST CREATE THAT CHANGE.

Z

Elven Name and Meaning	**Pronunciation**						
zådåle sunshine on dewy leave	zah	-	dah	-	lee		
zådålea a little more than what meets the eye	zah	-	dah	-	lee	-	ah
zadalyn sounds like poetry	zay	-	day	-	lynn		
zådea wandering protector	zah	-	dee	-	ah		
zåfaryn wyzard modest	zah	-	fair	-	ren		
zalåderfyn mountain valley opening to the ocean	zay	-	lah	-	deer	-	fin
zaladreyn highly emotional at times	zay	-	lay	-	dree	-	in
zålåndor sheltered by the earth	zah	-	lahn	-	door		
zålåndrea people are drawn to tell me about their lives	zah	-	lahn	-	dree	-	ah
zålåneyn looks directly into the eyes	zah	-	lah	-	knee	-	in
zålarea deep respect and understanding	zah	-	lay	-	ree	-	ah
zalasa on the right page	zay	-	lay	-	sah		
zaliadyn harnessing the silence	zay	-	lie	-	a	-	den
zålozor deep in the caves	zah	-	low	-	zoar		

The Silver Elves

zalvorlyn quiet storm	zale	-			vour	-		lynn
zålynve raindrop therapist	zahn	-			lynn	-		vee
zånådreara feels the sorrow	zahn	-	nah	-	dree	-	air	- rah
zåndåfarys ponders the ancient scripts	zahn	-	dah	-	fair	-		riss
zandålånedan talent for writing	zain	-	dah	-	lah	-	knee	dane
zåndåle spells of poetry	zahn	-			dah	-		lee
zändårea always will be	zan	-	dar	-	ree			ah
zåndorlyn the life I once had returns	zahn	-			door	-		lynn
zändreyl awakens from the illusion	zan	-			dree	-		L
zarådåntha visited by gnomes	zair	-	rah	-	dahn	-		thah
zarasyn healing warrior	zair	-			ray	-		sin
zaresa quick eyes	zair	-			ree	-		sah
zaresla sees the future in a new way	zair	-			reese	-		lah
zareyl doll maker	zair	-			ree	-		L
zareylsa have been all my life	zair	-	ree	-	L	-		sah
zarlorthyn seeks to remember the dreams	zair	-			lore	-		thin
zarvän brother mine	zair				-			vahn

The Book of Elf Names

zarvashadryn part of the puzzle	zair	-	vay	-	shay	-	drinn
zaryndåfål dust on wings	zay	-	ren	-	dah	-	fahl
zåväla mystical and sweet	zah	-		val		-	lah
zavaloar related to the earth	zay	-	vay	-	low	-	air
zavarasha wanders the forest	zay	-	vair	-	rah	-	shah
zåvarea speaks to the moon	zah	-	vair	-	ree	-	ah
zåvåroda wind upon the skin	zah	-	vah	-	row	-	dah
zavoryn unblinking stare	zay	-		vour		-	ren
zavorys walks nimbly	zay	-		vour		-	riss

zavyntara among the worthy	zay - vin - tear (as in rip) rah

zåzareyl ma and me	zah	-	zair	-	ree	-	L
zazyndi loves the beautiful	zay	-		zen		-	die
zearjyn begins to climb	zee	-		air		-	jen
zedånda yearn to go home	zee	-		dahn		-	dah
zedånsa path of the moon healer	zee	-		dahn		-	sah
zedåntha dreams come true	zee	-		dahn		-	thah
zedarthyn beneath the falling snow	zee	-		dare		-	thin

The Silver Elves

zelan reaching out	zell		-				lane
zélaryn feels some connection	zell	-	lair	-			ren
zeliåda mystical guidance	zell	-	lie	-	ah	-	dah
zélida interesting bits of nature	zell	-	lie	-			dah
zélidyn to show it to others	zell	-	lie	-			den
zélmyra guards the faery fort	zell		-mer	-			rah
zélyndor of the stars	zell	-	lynn	-			door
zemareyl care free spirit	zee	-	mare	-	ree	-	L
zemyryn it seems as though they are trying to talk to me	zee	-	mer	-			ren
zenarys certain purpose	zee	-	nair	-			riss
zenåtha wants to know more	zee	-	nah	-			thah
zeradea light as a feather	zee	-	ray	-	dee		ah
zerandea do you know more about this?	zee	-	rain	-	dee	-	ah
zevalei lost among humans	zee	-	vay	-	lee	-	eye
zevåndra still wants proof	zee	-	vahn	-			drah
zidålea abilities that single me out	zie	-	dah	-	lee	-	ah
zidårlys special connection with wolves	zie	-	dar	-			liss

The Book of Elf Names

zilea bird song	zie	-	lee	-	ah			
zileta art of healing herbs	zie	-	lee	-	tah			
zilydeyn it only makes sense	zie	-	lid	-	dee	-	in	
zinadůrlu sits among foxes	zie	-nay	-	dur	-	lou		
zinara knew the song before first hearing it	zie	-	nair	-	rah			
zodarfyn what a wonderful place	zo	-	dare	-	fin			
zoladyn realized that I was	zo	-	lay	-	den			
zolåndåfa faery friendly house	zo	-	lahn	-dah	-	fah		
zolåndar discovering my new s'elf	zo	-	lahn	-	dare			
zolånder likes unusual things	zo	-	lahn	-	deer			
zolandor spell caster	zo	-	lane	-	door			
zolealyn enjoys life as much as possible	zo	-	lee	-	a	-	lynn	
zoleynda ever dancing	zo	-	lee	-	yn	-	dah	
zolovynre willow moon	zo	-	low	-	vyn	-	re	
zolyndås ever since I was little	zo	-	lyn	-	dahs			
zolyndys practicing and developing my powers	zo	-	lynn	-	dis			
zoråbaryn feels the winds blow hard though the leaves	zo	-	rah	-	bare	-	ren	

zoradeyn a part of my life	zo	-	ray	-	dee	- in
zoråfan surrounded by elementals	zo	-	rah	-		fain
zoråndare listens to the music of the breeze	zo	-	rahn	-	dare	- ree
zoryndasa time of shadow	zo	-	ren	-	day	- sah
zorynėl natural magic	zo	-	ren	-		L
zovyndav their own truth	zo	-	vin	-		dave
zudila something inside tells me	zoo	-	dye	-		lah
zulyndae for which I take a lot of teasing	zoo	-	lynn	-		day
zunålyn put two and two together	zoo	-	nah	-		lynn
zurådor protect each other	zoo	-	rah	-		door
zurca touched something deep inside	zoor	-				cah
zurena secret one	zoo	-	re	-		nah
zuryndåth panther's fury	zoo	-	ryn	-		dahth
zylandros sits and observes	zill	-	lane	-		droos
zylansor feels the hum of the land	zill	-	lane	-		soar
zylasa marked by fate	zill	-	lay	-		sah
zylaveyn wild dreams	zill	-	lay	-	vee	- in

The Book of Elf Names

zylela my love for the culture	zill	-	lee	-	lah		
zylodor nature's healing power	zill	-	low	-	door		
zylvashyn searching for an answer	zill	-	vay	-	shin		
zyndåmar awaits the moment	zen	-	dah	-	mare		
zyndarfor wyzard's puzzle	zen	-	dare	-	for		
zyndartae courageous warrior	zen	-	dare	-	tay		
zyndåryn stirring wonder	zen	-	dah	-	ren		
zyndoryn wyzard's smile	zen	-	door	-	ren		
zyndranys dances with gnomes	zen	-	dray	-	niss		
zynfynlas feels like home	zen	-	fin	-	lace		
zynrea emerges from the mist	zen	-	re	-	ah		
zynsyndre star mage	zen	-	sin	-	dree		
zynzåle healer's apprentice	zen	-	zah	-	lee		
zynzarea charms the littles	zen	-	zair	-	re	-	ah
zynzartheyn shadows are not your best friends	zen - zayr (rhymes with fair) – thee - in						
zyryndåtha rides on horseback by the sea	zer	-	ren	-dah	-	thah	

ABOUT THE AUTHORS

The Silver Elves are a family of elves who have been living and sharing the Elven Way since 1975. They are the authors of *The Book of Elven Runes: A Passage Into Faerie; The Magical Elven Love Letters, volume 1, 2, and 3; An Elfin Book of Spirits: Evoking the Beneficent Powers of Faerie; Caressed by an Elfin Breeze: The Poems of Zardoa Silverstar; Eldafaryn: True Tales of Magic from the Lives of the Silver Elves; Arvyndase (Silverspeech): A Short Course in the Magical Language of the Silver Elves; The Elven Book of Dreams: A Magical Oracle of Faerie; The Book of Elven Magick: The Philosophy and Enchantments of the Seelie Elves, Volume 1 & 2; What An Elf Would Do: A Magical Guide to the Manners and Etiquette of the Faerie Folk; The Elven Tree of Life Eternal: A Magical Quest for One's True S'Elf; Magic Talks: On Being a Correspondence Between the Silver Elves and the Elf Queen's Daughters; Sorcerers' Dialogues: A Further Correspondence Between the Silver Elves and the Founders of the Elf Queen's Daughters; Discourses on High Sorcery: More Correspondence Between the Silver Elves and the Founders of the Elf Queen's Daughters; Ruminations on Necromancy: Continuing Correspondence Between the Silver Elves and the Founders of the Elf Queen's Daughter; and The Elven Way: The Magical Path of the Shining Ones..*

The Silver Elves have had various articles published in *Circle Network News Magazine* and have given out over 5,000 elven names to interested individuals in the Arvyndase language, with each elf name having a unique meaning specifically for that person. They are also mentioned numerous times in *Not In Kansas Anymore* by Christine Wicker (Harper San Francisco, 2005), and *A Field Guide to Otherkin* by Lupa (Megalithica Books, 2007). An interview with the Silver Elves is also included in Emily Carding's recent book *Faery Craft.*

The Silver Elves understand the world as a magical or miraculous phenomena, and that all beings, by pursuing their own true path, will become whomever they truly desire to be.

You are welcome to visit their website at http://silverelves@live.com and join them on Facebook with name as the "Silver Elves".

Printed in Great Britain
by Amazon

14950039R10206